St Thérèse of Lisieux

"I Choose All"

St Thérèse of Lisieux

"I CHOOSE ALL"

Sister Teresa Margaret, D.C.

GRACEWING

First published 1964, reprinted 2009

Gracewing
2 Southern Avenue
Leominster
Herefordshire HR6 0QF

Cover photograph of St Thérèse of Lisieux
© Office Centrale de Lisieux

Nihil Obstat: Ricardus Roche, S.T.D.,
              census deputatus

Imprimatur: + Francis
              Archiepiscopus Birmingamiensis

datam Birmingamiae, 3a Aprilis, 1964

The *Nihil Obstat* and *Imprimatur* are a declaration that a book or
pamphlet is considered to be free from doctrinal or moral error.
It is not implied that those who have granted the *Nihil Obstat* and
Imprimatur agree with the contents, opinions or statements
expressed

ISBN 978 0 85244 452 8

CONTENTS

Page

PREFACE (by the Very Rev. Fr. Gabriel, O.D.C.) . 9

PROLOGUE 11

CHAPTER 1. *CARMELITE AND
           CONTEMPLATIVE*

(*i*) The Work of Love 13
(*ii*) To suffer darkness is the way to great light . . 19
(*iii*) In solitude, God speaks to the soul . . . 24
(*iv*) The Silence of God 28
(*v*) Contemplation and the Apostolate . . . 31
(*vi*) Love is my Vocation 36
(*vii*) The Contemplative-Missionary Vocation . . 39

CHAPTER 2. *DISCOVERING A MISSION*

(*i*) Thérèse, living word of God (Pius XI) . . 44
(*ii*) God, our Father 48
(*iii*) Peace of Soul 52
(*iv*) Holiness and Wholeness 55
(*v*) The Letter and the Spirit 59
(*vi*) The Testing of Ideals 65
(*vii*) The Active Life of a Contemplative . . . 71

CHAPTER 3. *THE OTHER FACE*

(*i*) *Mon historien* 77
(*ii*) Improving the Image 86
(*iii*) Fact or Fancy? 91
(*iv*) Beauty and the Beast 95
(*v*) "Little Mother" 105
(*vi*) The Executrix 109

CHAPTER 4. *THE BLESSEDNESS OF BEING LITTLE*

(*i*) Concept of a "little" soul 116
(*ii*) A Theory of Littleness 122
(*iii*) Little and Humble in the Hands of God . . 133
(*iv*) Seed of Glory 140

CHAPTER 5. *ALL GOD'S CHILDREN*

(*i*) The Pathfinder 147
(*ii*) Taking up the Cross 155
(*iii*) I am thy reward exceeding great . . . 166
(*iv*) We shall never have finished with charity . . 171

CHAPTER 6. *FATHER AND DAUGHTER*

(*i*) The Life of Faith 176
(*ii*) Family Likenesses 182
(*iii*) Christ, the Way 187
(*iv*) All things are mine 192

CHAPTER 7. *THE GIFT OF SELF*

(*i*) Thérèse, living victim, united to the Victim perpetually offered (Pius XII) 198
(*ii*) Thy measure shall be My measure . . . 206
(*iii*) Salt and Fire 211
(*iv*) The Travail 218

CHAPTER 8. *UNTIL TIME IS NO MORE*

(*i*) Da mihi animas 226
(*ii*) Infinite Desires 232
(*iii*) Universal Apostle 235
(*iv*) The Flood will bear me far 240

NOTES 250

ABBREVIATIONS USED IN FOOTNOTE
REFERENCES ARE AS FOLLOWS:

A. (Autobiography)—*Saint Thérèse of Lisieux, the Little Flower of Jesus*: A revised translation of the definitive Carmelite edition of her Autobiography by the Very Rev. Canon T. N. Taylor. (Burns, Oates & Washbourne Ltd., London) 1947 ed.

A.S.—*Autobiography of a Saint.* Thérèse of Lisieux: The complete and authorized text of *L'Histoire d'une âme* newly translated by Ronald Knox. (The Harvill Press, London) 1958.

C.L.—*Collected Letters of Saint Thérèse of Lisieux,* edited by the Abbé Combes, translated by F. J. Sheed (Sheed & Ward, London), 1949.

N.V.—*Novissima Verba.* The last conversations of St. Thérèse of the Child Jesus, May–September, 1897. (Burns, Oates & Washbourne Ltd., London), 1929.

C. & R.—*Counsels and Reminiscences of St. Thérèse* (an appendix to Autobiography "A" above, pp. 293–330).

M. & D.—*Martyrdom and Death.* (Epilogue to Autobiography "A" above, pp. 211–242).

The Complete Works of St. John of the Cross, translated from the critical edition of P. Silverio de Santa Teresa, O.C.D., and edited by E. Allison Peers (Burns Oates, London) 1943.

Asc. Ascent of Mount Carmel D.N. Dark Night of the Soul	Volume I.
Sp.C. Spiritual Canticle	Volume II.

L.F.	Living Flame of Love	
	Cautions	
	Maxims	Volume III.
	Points of Love.	
	Spiritual Sayings.	

The Complete Works of Saint Teresa of Jesus, translated and edited by E. Allison Peers from the critical edition of P. Silverio de Santa Teresa, O.C.D., (Sheed & Ward Ltd., London) 1946.

	Life	Volume I.
W.P.	Way of Perfection	Volume II.
I.C.	Interior Castle.	
F.	Book of the Foundations	Volume III.

All quotations from Scripture are from the Knox version, with the exception of those included in other quotations, such as papal pronouncements, quotations from the writings of St. Thérèse, etc.

J.T. † J.M.

PREFACE

The aim of this book is to present St. Thérèse of Lisieux to the public in a threefold way: firstly, in the light of the Gospels; secondly, in the light of the various papal documents concerning her virtues and her universal mission; thirdly, against a background of genuine Carmelite tradition and the teaching of St. John of the Cross. The author, Sister Teresa Margaret, D.C., belongs to the Carmelite Community of Bridell, Wales, and her devoted research into the spirituality of the Saint of Lisieux has equipped her well for writing this sketch. She has disengaged the essential doctrine of St. Thérèse from the accretions both of sentimental piety and misplaced erudition, and presents her conclusions in a very readable form.

I CHOOSE ALL will be welcomed most gratefully, not only by members of the Carmelite Order, but by all who meditate on the Gospels in order to grow in the love of Jesus and Mary. The principal interest of the book lies in the fact that it shows how a modern saint achieved so perfect a likeness to Christ in her own life. It shows how the unchanging standards of our Saviour may yet be adapted in every way to the needs and problems of this present age; and in this there is encouragement for us all. It is unlikely, however, that the book will appeal to those who are wise in their own conceits; the deeper truths of the interior life can only be understood in the light of supernatural faith, and "truth flies from the soul that it does not find humble". (St. Gregory the Great.)

A great deal of study has gone into this work, but it wears its learning easily, and provides admirable spiritual reading for the type of Catholic who wants solid doctrine but who fights shy of books that are too technical. Sister Teresa Margaret dwells particularly on those points of St. Thérèse's doctrine which are most often misrepresented or made to look ridiculous, and the outcome is a true vade-mecum of solid spirituality, one of the best to appear in recent years.

Fr. Gabriel, O.D.C.

PROLOGUE

I Choose All

Léonie Martin, having decided that she had outgrown her dolls and childish toys, took them to where her small sisters Céline and the four-year-old Thérèse were playing, and offered them the choice of whatever they would like to take from her basket. Céline considered, and chose a woollen ball. Thérèse thought for a moment and then, seizing the doll and basket, stated: "I choose the whole lot", and thereupon carried off the basket, doll and all.

No doubt the child is father to the man. Commenting upon this twenty years later, Thérèse stated that the childish incident summed up the whole of her life, although it was not until long afterwards that she thought of putting a spiritual interpretation to the words. Certainly nobody ever had a greater capacity for making capital out of faults and imperfections than did Thérèse. The incident which she says gives the key to her whole life might, if left at that, have been no more than the action of a spoilt little girl. But Thérèse, realizing this, began forthwith to divert the tendency into more fruitful channels.

"Later on, when the idea of religious perfection came within my horizon, I realized at once that there was no reaching sanctity unless you were prepared to suffer a great deal, to be always on the look-out for something higher still, and to forget yourself. There were plenty of degrees in spiritual advancement, and every soul was free to answer our Lord's invitation by doing a little for Him, or by doing a lot for Him; in fact, He gave it a *choice* between various kinds of self-sacrifice He wanted it to offer. And then, as in babyhood, I found myself crying out: "My God, I choose the whole lot. No point in becoming a saint by halves. I'm not afraid of suffering for your sake; the only thing I'm afraid of is clinging to my own will. Take it, I want the whole lot, everything whatsoever that is your will for me'."[1]

[1] A.S. pp. 51-2.

CHAPTER ONE

CARMELITE AND CONTEMPLATIVE

The senses have their pleasures, shall the spirit be deprived
of its own? Give me one who loves and he will understand what
I am saying. Give me one devoured with desiring, and hunger-
ing and thirsting for the living waters of his eternal fatherland.
Give me such a one and he will understand what I am saying.

(St. Augustine)

(i) *The Work of Love*

It has been suggested in various ways that Thérèse's vocation
to Carmel was a matter of chance, and that she was attracted
there not so much by the ideal it proposed, or by a definite call
to that particular way of life, as by the fact that her beloved
Pauline had chosen Carmel, and Thérèse was determined to
do the same. That is to say, had Pauline followed her original
attraction to the Visitation Order, Thérèse also would have
become a Visitandine.

I do not underestimate in any way the influence of Mother
Agnes of Jesus on the great spiritual life of her young sister.
That Thérèse is today a great saint is without doubt due to the
action of the Holy Spirit, and after that to Mother Agnes. Her
affection for Pauline, her desire to be like her,[1] the influence
of Pauline upon her from her babyhood—all these factors,
great as they are, still do not add up to a blind following of
Pauline, a passive imitation, becoming a Carmelite just because Pauline, now Sister Agnes of Jesus, was one.

There are few vocations more misunderstood than that of
the Carmelite, and it is common to find highly articulate men
and women assuring us that had they lived in our generation,
neither St. Teresa of Avila nor St. Thérèse of Lisieux would

---

[1] "You were always my ideal, Mother, and I wanted to be exactly like you."
(A.S. p. 212).

have been religious at all, but energetic and enthusiastic lay apostles.

But they were not born in our day. God prepares His saints in a wonderful fashion, and according to the mission He entrusts to them, He also endows them with the necessary qualifications for their task; nor is it by chance that they are born into the world at one particular point of its history rather than another. It is futile to speculate what St. Teresa would have done in the twentieth century. We know what she did in the sixteenth, and we also know that God did not merely have to make do with the material conditions prevailing then; for they, no less than the qualities of mind and heart necessary to cope with them, were part of His eternal design.

Thérèse tells us that one of her earliest recollections is of hearing people say that Pauline would one day be a nun. Then without knowing what it really entailed, she would say to herself, "I'll be a nun, too." She was then two years old, and she adds that she had never since wavered in her resolution.

This precocious decision, of course, was not the result of reflection, or of any conviction of what was the more perfect life, which would have been impossible in a baby, but it does give us a glimpse of what her instincts were, even before reaching the use of reason, and an understanding of what she means when she says that, seeing nothing but good example around her, she wished to follow it.

However Thérèse was only nine years of age when she received what she considered a clear call to Carmel, and after that she never hesitated. In October, 1882, Pauline entered the Carmel at Lisieux, but beforehand she explained to her young sister the nature of the religious life which she would henceforth lead. Thérèse felt that Carmel was the desert to which she and Pauline had planned to retire, with a certainty that left no shadow of doubt in her mind. It was not merely the passing fancy of an impressionable child, but, she says, the decisiveness of a divine vocation. "I didn't want to go into Carmel for Pauline's sake, but for our Lord's sake and for no other reason." From then onwards, Thérèse's one aim in life was to remove the obstacles which lay between her and the desired "desert"; and this has often been regarded as proof of her innate stubbornness. But this is not how Thérèse viewed her conduct during the months of persistent endeavour to leave no stone unturned in her appeals to be allowed to enter Carmel at the age of fifteen. She firmly believed that she had received an imperative and unmistakable call from God; but she understood, no less, that it was her obvious duty to take the necessary steps to fulfil her vocation, as everyone is obliged to do. The Holy Spirit guides us all, and we are expected to follow the promptings of grace, acting upon them when we have the approval of those responsible for our welfare.

"I can see that Uncle is waiting for a miracle," she told Sister Agnes, referring to M. Guérin's original objection to her entering Carmel so young. "But of course God won't work a miracle for me. They say it's extraordinary to enter Carmel at fifteen. It's most unfortunate that it should be extraordinary; but it seems to me that the good God never asks the impossible, and He is asking this of *me*."[1] Thérèse felt she had to do everything in her power to follow this clear call, and what she considered to be required of her was far more than most of us would think necessary. Only when she had tried every avenue of appeal did she abandon the result to God, not in despair or defiance, but humbly: having done all she could, she then asked our Lord to set her free; and, she said, "He did set me free, although not in the way I had expected."

At the suggestion of Pauline, Thérèse had for some months been playing a game with the Child Jesus, offering herself as a toy for Him to use as He pleased. She liked to fancy herself as a ball which He could throw about, kick it from Him, make a hole in it, leave it lying unnoticed in a corner, or press it to His heart if He felt that way inclined. Thus she expressed her desire for our Lord to do exactly what He liked with her, and after her apparent refusal by the Holy Father, she felt that He had indeed taken her at her word.

Thérèse was never stubborn in her persistence. Always, she said, she was seeking God's will. The stubborn person is most often seeking her own. "If it pleases Him to break His toy, He

[1] C.L. p. 24. n.1.

is free to do so; truly I want only what He wants." There is no doubt that it was Thérèse's conduct during the pilgrimage to Rome that finally convinced the Abbé Révérony of her real sincerity; and his favourable recommendations to the Bishop produced, within a few weeks, permission for her to enter Carmel. Had she not taken this last step she might not have obtained that permission.

When she was fourteen Thérèse explained to her sister Céline why she had elected to enter Carmel, in spite of a real longing for active missionary life, and a strong inclination to join a foreign missions society. "It was," she said, "in order that I should suffer more and thereby gain more souls for Jesus." The work of conquering herself, she realized, would be the most arduous and toilsome task to which she could set her hand.

Hidden in her bare, comfortless cell, she set herself to accomplish this self-conquest, knowing that every insignificant act and suffering, by which she broke her self-will, was for the salvation of souls and the benefit of the missionary apostolate.

Such is the necessary programme for every soul desirous of becoming a true contemplative, and often it has to be carried out in pure faith, amidst aridity and plaguing distractions. As St. Thérèse writes: "Our Lord chooses to leave in the desert the sheep that have not gone astray . . . He is *sure of them*, they cannot go astray now, for they are love's captives; so Jesus robs them of His visible presence to bring His consolations to sinners; or even if He does meet them upon Mount Thabor, it is only for a few moments, the valleys are more often the place of His repose."[1]

That Thérèse was a contemplative cannot be doubted by anyone who understands the essential meaning of the term. Phenomena such as visions, locutions, ecstasies, raptures, and the like, are no more than passing experiences which may or may not have been caused by God. Prayer, moreover, does not necessarily require kneeling in choir, any more than silence means merely an absence of external noise. To hear God, the soul must be silent, in an atmosphere that is itself prayer. Only

[1] To Céline. C.L. p. 167.

in this true silence of the soul can we understand the love of God, and learn how we are to return it, for it is born of our union with God, and it grows in proportion as we learn how to pass over all that is not God or His will for us. The ideal is to adhere to God by work in the time of work, and by prayer in its proper season.

In the following description of her own interior attitude, the contemplative spirit of St. Thérèse is easy to discern: "I think of myself as a chick not yet fledged, and no eagle in any case; only somehow, feeble as I am, the eyes of my heart have caught the eagle's trick of staring at the sun, the sun of divine love. The poor fledgling can't hope to imitate those eagles, the great souls who make straight for the throne of the Blessed Trinity; it can only flap its wings in a pathetic attempt to fly. Nothing left for it, you'd think, but to die of disappointment when it finds itself so handicapped. But no, I don't even worry about that; by a bold act of self-committal, I stay where I am, keeping my eyes fixed on the sun, deterred by no obstacle; storm and rain and cloud-wrack may conceal its heavenly radiance, but I don't shift my view—I know that it is there all the time behind the clouds, its brightness never dimmed. Sometimes, to be sure, the storm thunders at my heart; I find it difficult to believe in the existence of anything except the clouds which limit my horizon. It's only then that I realize the possibilities of my weakness; find consolation in staying at my post, and directing my gaze towards one invisible light which communicates itself, now, only to the eye of faith."[1]

The activity of the contemplative soul is born of her contemplation, which is a combination of the habitual union of her will with God and of her actual submission in pure faith to the varying wishes of her divine spouse, Jesus Christ. Every act, everything she does outside of her prayer should reflect the peace and order that is in her interior life, her "house being now at rest".

Thus the contemplative life does not belong to one age more than to another. It is centred on God who does not change, and from this focal point it contributes to the Church today what it

[1] A.S. p. 239.

has given at all times, and will continue to contribute to the end of time. If we had greater faith, our prayer and our lives would of their own accord flower in contemplation. St. John of the Cross says that it is not God's will that contemplative souls should be few, but that few respond to His calls with sufficient generosity, and so many do not reach the heights for which He had destined them. Contemplation does not demand any special qualifications other than those powers received at baptism. Every soul possessing the sevenfold gifts of the Holy Spirit can, if she will co-operate, be led by God to supernatural contemplation and even to its flowering in mystical experience. Love is at the centre of the spiritual life, and contemplation is nothing but a simple gaze on truth, under the influence of love. To gaze upon God—He who Is—to be with Him, to love Him, is the supreme activity and the highest work of man.

True contemplation is the work of love which God performs in the soul, causing it to leave behind all sensible pleasure in order to rest in that pure faith, which appears as darkness to the human mind. Such a work of love is not confined to one's routine hours of prayer. It fills and colours one's whole life, and spills out over the trivial incidents of the day, transforming all one's actions, even the most indifferent, into acts of love. "It is a great delusion," declares the Carmelite lay-brother Lawrence of the Resurrection in his little treatise *The Practice of the Presence of God*, "to think that the times of prayer ought to differ from other times; we are as strictly obliged to adhere to God by action in the time of action as by prayer in its season." Recollection is essential at all times, and the daily life of all contemplative orders is planned and regulated with a view to guarding this for their members as far as possible. Sometimes, however, one discovers the deeper significance of prayer at a moment when one's heart feels as heavy as a stone, and this is how St. Thérèse herself describes the experience:

"Jesus took me by the hand and brought me into a subterranean way, where it is neither hot nor cold, where the sun does not shine, and rain and wind do not come; a tunnel where I see nothing but a brightness half-veiled, the glow from the downcast eyes in the face of my spouse. My spouse says nothing to me, nor do I say anything to Him either, save that *I love Him* more than *myself*, and in the depth of my heart I feel that this is true, for I am more His than my own! ... I do not see that we are advancing towards the mountain that is our goal, because our journey is under the earth; yet I have a feeling that we are approaching it, without knowing why. The road I follow is one of no consolation for me, yet it brings me all consolation, because it is Jesus who has chosen it, and I desire to console Him only."[1]

(ii) "To suffer darkness is the way to great light".

It need cause us no surprise, still less should we be shocked, that one of St. Thérèse's few descriptions of her prayer was "distractions and drowsiness". But, significantly, she adds that instead of distressing herself because of the inadequate welcome she has given her sacramental Lord, she resolved to make amends by turning the rest of the day into a thanksgiving after Communion. And her whole day, every conscious moment of it, was a continuation of that thanksgiving, a perpetual act of love.

She knew, too, that the will is the most important part in this exercise, and that to will to pray is to pray. She never sat back on her heels and went to sleep, taking the opportunity of the quiet and dim choir to make up for all that she had missed during the night. If sleep overcame her, she fell asleep loving God, her will firmly fixed in His, and awoke in the same dispositions. Having desired to know and love Him, she was content not to be able to think beautiful thoughts about Him, and she knew in her heart that this confused and wandering imagination did not detract from the prayer value of her immense desires.

"*In terra deserta* ... O God, thou art my God; how eager my quest for thee, body athirst and soul longing for thee, like some parched wilderness, where stream is none!" (Psalm 62). This desert land, without way or water, this trackless wilderness, is the ordinary way of contemplation stripped of its glamour. It

---

[1] To Sister Agnes, written during Thérèse's retreat prior to her profession. C.L. p. 121.

was the way Thérèse entered from the outset of her religious
life, and which she described as a "tunnel" during her retreat
before profession.

It is true that our cloisters are not filled with souls who have
attained already to the heights or depths of perfection, but
certainly they contain many generous souls who genuinely
tend and strive towards perfection with a constant and often
heroic effort. And those who are as yet unable to appropriate
to themselves the prerogatives of a bride may, with St. Thérèse,
claim the favour of a child, knowing that all its father's goods
belong to it.

The prospect and actuality of this barren desert (or subterranean tunnel) is something that appals us, and St. John of the
Cross says that many return to the sunshine of sensible consolations, unable to believe that anything but annihilation is
to be found in this stark wilderness. These are typified by the
disciples who exclaimed: "This is a hard saying, and who can
bear it?" and walked with our Lord no more. If the contemplative does not become disheartened and fall from her first
high ideals, she gives to God the one thing He asks of her, an
empty vessel to be filled, a devouring thirst which He alone can
quench. The filling is His part. God and the soul form a part-
nership, but the success of the enterprise depends solely on the
work of God; and this success is ensured if the soul co-operates,
for the only way in which it can be frustrated, wholly or in
part, is by the infidelity of the soul.

Thérèse never had any misgivings on that score. Never once
did she doubt that what was happening to her was God's working in her soul, that Jesus ever led her by the hand, and the
more He took from her all feeling and sense of pleasure in His
service, the more she prepared herself to give.

Here I think we might tidy up some rather loose thinking on
her use of the words "joy" and "happiness". Many times she
tells us that she was, in the midst of her sufferings, the happiest
of mortals; and that although it was always dark and arid night
in her soul, yet she was at peace, and even knew joy in suffering. Thérèse saw everything through other-worldly eyes. "I
have found joy and happiness on earth," she said two months

before her death, "but solely in suffering, because I have suffered much down here . . . Since my first communion, when I asked Jesus to change into bitterness all the consolations of earth, I have had a ceaseless desire to suffer. I did not at first think of making it my joy. That was a grace that was accorded me later on."[1]

We are tempted to wonder sometimes whether Thérèse does not exaggerate in statements like this. Were her sufferings as acute as she believed them to have been, or was the peace she felt herself to enjoy merely a delusion? She herself seems to have sensed the paradox and anticipated possible misunderstanding of it, for she has explained her feelings on the subject in a letter to Céline: "Let us suffer in *peace*! I admit that the word peace struck me as rather strong, but the other day, thinking over it, I hit upon the secret of suffering in peace. The word *peace* does not mean *joy*, at least not *felt joy*: to suffer in peace, it is enough to will whatever Jesus wills."[2]

St. Thérèse certainly was not the first to discover this secret source of strength in suffering. When Blessed Margaret Clitherow was informed that she would die in two days' time (and she already knew the horrible form her death was to take), she admitted that she knew fear—cold, physical terror in the face of death. But she steadfastly claimed that, despite this acknowledged fear, she was not unhappy; that while her body trembled with fear, her spirit was full of joy. And as she was led away from the prison to her martyrdom, she was smiling and serene. "It is," she said, "as short a way to heaven as any other."

Thérèse had learned the lessons taught in the *Imitation of Christ*, which she knew by heart: "If thou wilt have me to be in darkness, be thou blessed; and if thou wilt have me to be in light, be thou again blessed; if thou vouchsafest to comfort me, be thou blessed; and if it be thy will that I should be afflicted, be thou always equally blessed." (Bk. III, Ch. 17.)

No one can escape suffering—this life is full of pain of every kind. But suffering and pain, which are contrary to pleasure,

---

[1] N.V. 31st July, 1897.
[2] C.L. p. 85. Written when Thérèse was sixteen years of age.

can reside in the soul together with happiness and joy. Suffering is not necessarily opposed to joy for, as Thérèse found, suffering accepted as it was meant by God to be accepted, produced pure joy in the depths of her soul, in proportion to the costliness of her self-giving. When we attempt to gauge happiness by the amount or degree of pleasure we derive from a thing, we are trying to equate two factors that have not necessarily any common denominator. Pleasure is selfish, and suffers when deprived of anything it wants or desires, whereas joy is unselfish; it ignores suffering or even goes out to embrace it, knowing it to be the source of ultimate good, by purifying the soul of its greatest obstacle, which is self-love. But above unselfishness, there is still a higher plane, on which is found selflessness, where one does not see things in the light of the advantage or disadvantage, or even of the joy or sorrow that they may mean for oneself. To be designated unselfish usually implies that we have the capacity for seeing what would be to our own taste or advantage, and deliberately sacrificing it for other people or to follow God's call. But the selfless person takes the personal element out of the situation; instead of rising above her own point of view, she simply and immediately sees God's point of view without thinking much about the consequences, either of happiness or suffering, for herself, except as the expression of the will of God.

We can only know true joy in willing what we were made to will; that is, what God wills. Therefore not only does suffering not kill joy, it can even strengthen it, provided our sufferings are God-sent, and accepted from His hand, and not self-inflicted recoils from our own passions and perversions. This joy is the conquest of suffering by perfect love, and this joy pain cannot touch. If suffering were an evil in itself, if happiness could not reside under the same roof with it, how could we explain the happiness which religious life engenders? For although by our religious profession we lay ourselves open to suffering to a degree which would not have been our portion, perhaps, in another sphere, although our lives are in a sense dedicated to suffering, yet the joy and gaiety of the Carmelites and Poor Clares is proverbial. Our Lord warned us that we must lose our life in order to gain it, and for this reason the seal that identifies all His followers is the sign of the cross.

"Let us not fancy we can love without suffering, without suffering deeply. Our *poor nature* is there, and it is not there for nothing! It is our wealth, our livelihood! It is so precious that Jesus came on earth on purpose to make it His own. Let us suffer bitterly, that is without courage! ... Jesus suffered with *sorrow*: could the soul be suffering if there were no sorrow?"[1]

The cross is no mere symbol of suffering. We must become identified in our sufferings with the sufferings of Christ, filling up in our own flesh what is wanting to them. Our own particular cross must never be allowed to become a solitary load, a personal burden unrelated to the crucified Christ. "This is my supreme philosophy," declared St. Bernard, "to know Jesus and Him crucified. Do ye also gather so delectable a burden ... yet heave it not up on your shoulders behind you, but bear it before you, lest it be nought but a burden to weigh you down, and its savour be not able to refresh you; for in keeping ever before your eyes who He is that you bear, the vision of our Lord's pains will aid you to bear your own lightly."

Embracing the cross, Thérèse could claim that she knew only one joy on earth, to suffer for Jesus; "but this *unfelt* joy is above every joy." Almost instinctively, suffering or pain drew her gaze to the cross and to Him who hung upon it, so that suffering became a "treasure" for her, as more and more she understood its power to unite her with Christ, and experienced the joys of accepting suffering for His love. But in desiring to be attracted or to *feel* joy in suffering, she told her sister Marie, one merely seeks for consolation, since when we love a thing, the pain evaporates.

St. Thérèse's spirit was not beaten down, or even unduly upset, by her helplessness in this arid state, for peace of soul is not incompatible with spiritual dryness or emotional turmoil. It is the peace of God which is not merely beyond the reach of the senses, but is on an entirely different plane, so that tranquillity can and often does dwell in the soul together with dryness and even distaste in prayer. For most of us, aridity is an

[1] To Céline. C.L. p. 88.

experience that must be lived through, and its duration is more or less protracted according to our response. For Thérèse it was a cross that accompanied her throughout the whole of her religious life. Even up to the moment of her death there was no light or sign of sensible consolation. Rather, in the last eighteen months of her life, the darkness increased until it seemed to be an impenetrable wall, reaching up to heaven and blotting out even the light of the stars. For her it was night, always darkest night. She loved with her indomitable will, and allowing herself to be led by God through the wilderness by the path He knew best suited her, desiring no other guide than that of His unseen hand, no other support than her own faith and loving trust in God alone, she was eventually and very rapidly led to a state of unchanging peace, wherein her understanding and memory were also made perfectly one with God.

This is her "little way"—the way of complete abandonment to God—but to be lived in its fullness as St. Thérèse conceived and lived it, it presupposes heroic faith, hope and love. He who does not fear to abandon his spiritual progress (or apparent lack of progress) into the hands of God, who firmly believes that God is directing it and has not abandoned him even when he feels most abandoned, will be led very quickly, as was St. Thérèse, to the peace of union with Him.

(iii) *"In solitude, God speaks to the soul".*

St. John of the Cross has said: "The soul that attains to this state (of contemplation) has no longer any ways or methods, still less is it attached to such things . . . it has within itself all ways, after the way of one that possesses nothing, yet possesses all things."[1]

Many commentators have gone to considerable trouble in attempting to classify, from her own written evidence, a method of prayer as practised by St. Thérèse; but no sooner do they manage, through one of her admissions, to place her in one category, than her next utterance contradicts their theory.

Thérèse is not to be pinned down to any particular method

[1] *Asc.*, Bk. II, Ch. IV, para 5.

of prayer on the lines of the standardized stages of spiritual growth, for at the outset, she takes up the life of prayer at a level where "methods of prayer" as they are commonly understood are no longer necessary, and would be either a hindrance or an impossibility to the soul, who "will frequently find itself in this loving and peaceful state of waiting upon God without in any way exercising its faculties with respect to particular acts, and without working actively at all, but only receiving. In order to reach this state, it will frequently need to make use of meditation, quietly and in moderation; but when once the soul is brought into this other state, it acts not at all with its faculties . . . We say that the soul works not at all, not because it understands not, but because it understands things not discovered by its own industry and receives only that which is given to it, as comes to pass in the enlightenment or inspirations of God."[1]

What Thérèse has to say on the subject is in close agreement with this, although expressed in vastly different words:

"You know, I always have the feeling that our Lord doesn't supply me with provisions for my journey—He gives me food unexpectedly when and as I need it; I find it there without knowing how it got there. It simply comes to this, that our Lord dwells unseen in the depths of my miserable soul, and so works upon me by grace that I can always find out what He wants me to do at this particular moment."[2] This she wrote in describing her profession, at which time we know from her letters that her spiritual life was a blind groping in the dark, under the earth as it were. Then again: "For myself, I never heard the sound of His voice, but I know that He dwells within me all the time, guiding me and inspiring me whenever I do or say anything. A light, of which I'd caught no glimmer before, comes to me at the very moment when it's needed; and this doesn't generally happen in the course of my prayer, however devout it may be, but more often in the middle of my daily work: "[3] St. John of the Cross gives us a more methodical classification, but not a clearer picture of the workings of God in the

[1] *Asc.*, Bk. II, Ch. XV, para. 2.
[2] A.S. pp. 198-9.
[3] A.S. p. 219.

soul that are known as "infused contemplation" (cf. *Asc.* Bk. II, Chapters XIII-XV). By following Christ, walking in faith, coming to the knowledge and love of God through the remote means of meditation, the soul prepares itself to enter this higher state of prayer or superior exercise of loving faith which is contemplation in its essential form.

As a child, Thérèse had endeavoured to "make mental prayer" in the formal manner, and had requested to be instructed in the rules of discursive meditation, but at a very early age she found herself immersed in this confused and loving knowledge, which begins sooner than many people imagine. In the case of those who are called to this type of prayer, the active mental prayer should be no more than a preliminary which will be rapidly outgrown, for apart from St. John of the Cross' famous indications as to when this has occurred, one's own inability to concentrate on points and particulars make the method impracticable. "Lift up thine heart unto God with a meek stirring of love," advises the author of the *Cloud of Unknowing*, "and mean Himself and none of His goods . . . so that naught work in thy mind, nor in thy will, but only Himself."

Thérèse did not possess the gifts of her Carmelite mother and father in analysing and classifying her soul's progress, but where those two doctors have left detailed accounts of what takes place in the soul during this period, Thérèse has merely told us: "Hidden lights break in . . . I find the food I need without knowing how it got there"; and she says that for her, prayer consists of lifting up her heart towards God, turning her gaze quite simply to heaven with grateful love, whether it be a time of joy or of suffering. "It's a vast supernatural force which opens out my heart and binds me close to Jesus." But she is unable to explain or define it any more clearly, and if we wish to do so, we have only to take her words, and with them in mind, study the treatises of St. John of the Cross, for her spiritual life is a practical version of his own exposition, and in the *Living Flame of Love* one can read a comprehensive description of what her prayer was really like.

When her spiritual life was fully developed, Thérèse required no other help or nourishment for her soul than the gospels. In her reading, she apparently opened the New Testament at random, and a few verses sufficed to rekindle the spirit of prayer already present in her soul. Her confession that she often fell asleep during prayer need not surprise us. As has been said, the disposition of her heart never changed, and if the worn-out child fell asleep in the arms of her heavenly father, she awoke still held in His arms, and continued where she had left off, unperturbed, undismayed, never discouraged. When she came from her prayer, dry and comfortless enough though it usually was, she was refreshed and reinvigorated, not because of the clever reflections or the uplifting resolutions she had made, but because of the love which pervaded her heart and soul. How can we doubt that her prayer was contemplative?

Distractions do not spoil our prayer, although they may be a nuisance and a source of acute suffering to us. Speaking of her retreat before making her vows, Thérèse says: "Once more, our Lord was asleep on the boat; how few souls there are that let Him have His sleep out! He can't be always doing all the work, responding to all the calls made upon Him; so for my own part I am content to leave Him undisturbed. I dare say He won't make His presence felt till I start out on the great retreat of eternity; I don't complain of that, I want it to happen." And later: "What excuse have I, after seven years in religion, for going through all my prayers and my thanksgivings as mechanically as if I, too, were asleep?" But she thought of little children, and the way they lie relaxed in slumber under the loving eyes of their parents, taking comfort in the knowledge that, as the psalmist says, the Lord knows the stuff of which we are made, and remembers that we are only dust. "If Jesus chooses to sleep, what reason have I to complain?" was Thérèse's attitude, as it is that of all who have learned to subordinate to God's will their own interest and pleasure. She found consolation in the fact that He did not bother standing on ceremony or "making conversation" with her, for by thus exercising the prerogative of familiarity, "He shows me that I am no stranger to Him."

Thérèse, in her prayer, was thinking solely of God; when we are disturbed unduly by our involuntary distractions, we are often thinking principally, if not solely, of ourselves and the pleasure we are missing, upset because, as we say, it spoils *my* prayer. Prayer is not an exercise of the human mind, but of faith, hope and charity under the direction of the Holy Spirit of Love; therefore only voluntary distractions or deliberate failure in the practice of recollection will constitute a hindrance to progress. God could, if He wished, banish all distractions and fill our minds to overflowing with elevating and prayerful thoughts. Usually He does no such thing, and Thérèse was content with His choice, well aware that, as she said, "Papa knows best."

Most important of all, she refused to allow herself to be disturbed by this difficulty in recollection, but still tranquil, resumed once more her task of love. And whenever she caught herself wandering away into distraction, she offered a prayer for the one who was absorbing her attention and threatening to withdraw it from God.

Either we must pray all day long, during our work and because we are always one with Jesus through sanctifying grace, or else we shall find prayer difficult even during the hours set aside for that exercise. In the old monastic régime, the monks had no set hour of prayer. Daily work, choir offices, manual labour, all was prayer offered to God in the spirit of the theological virtues. Certainly our remote preparation for prayer should never cease; if we are recollected, if we are constantly in the presence of God during our working hours, we shall need no other preparation, proximate or otherwise, nor points for meditation to put us in a state of prayer when we kneel before God and turn our minds consciously to Him in formal prayer. As Père Plus, S.J., says, "Not to forget God does not mean to be always thinking of Him, but not to leave Him out of any detail of our life. One cannot always be in the act of prayer. One ought always to remain in the state of prayer."

(iv) *The Silence of God*

For some reason many people associate a type of glamour

with the name contemplative. In hard fact, essential contemplation is in no way dramatic, least of all in those who attain in this life to its perfection. There is nothing spectacular about it, nothing out of the ordinary. Like Jesus and Mary in Nazareth, the true contemplative seeks only to do the Father's will.

This mortification of one's own will and judgment, in little things especially, is by far the most searching test for an interior soul. Mortification of one's body is as nothing by comparison. All the masters of the spiritual life are agreed on this point, but usually it is learned only after a period of trial and error in regard to the practices of asceticism. St. Thérèse, on the other hand, was quick to notice the dangers of self-deception. Shrewdly she observed that the nuns most given to penitential practices (apart from those legislated) were not always the holiest or the most charitable, and thenceforward she concentrated upon the task she had set herself during the three months of waiting for the time of her postponed entry into Carmel— that is, from her fifteenth birthday—of checking her self-will.

Thérèse tells us much about her sufferings, but adds that they were unknown to others, and that her sisters in religion regarded her as having been pampered by the prioress. Thérèse's desire for suffering was genuine, and prompted solely by love. When at last she crossed the threshold of Carmel, she was treated with severity by her prioress, and a certain antipathy between herself and the novice mistress made it virtually impossible for Thérèse to confide in her and benefit from the instructions and guidance she might reasonably have counted upon. Added to this failure of spiritual comfort and assistance from the two persons from whom the neophyte might justly have expected help, and much harder to bear, was the continual dryness in prayer.

"He who has heard the word of God," said St. Ignatius Loyola, "can bear His silences and wait for understanding." The silence of God! How much evidence there is of it in the letters of Thérèse. After three months of religious life, she writes to Céline: "Yes, life *costs*, it is *hard* beginning a day's work . . . If only one felt Jesus close at hand! Oh! one would do all for Him . . . but no, He seems a thousand leagues away, we are alone with ourselves; oh! how wearisome is company when Jesus is not there." Six months later, during the retreat which preceded her taking the habit, she says to Sister Agnes: "Nothing from Jesus. Dryness! . . . Sleep!"[1]

Thérèse never allowed herself to become discouraged, and her love did not shrivel up and perish as it would have done had it been merely sweet and superficial sentiment. This is the stage at which the postulant who is not made of the right stuff packs up and returns home, quite happy that the religious life is not for her. Thérèse's love, on the contrary, grew stronger and more heroic the further she was removed from any feeling or sense of it. "Let us love Him enough to suffer for Him whatever He chooses, even griefs of soul, aridities, anguish, seeming frigidities. Ah! that is indeed a great love, to love Jesus without feeling the sweetness of that love, there you have martyrdom . . . there you have love pushed even to heroism."[2]

There can be little doubt that one of her greatest sufferings was the continued dryness and aridity in spiritual things, especially coming as it did after the months of fervour and spiritual exaltation that had preceded her entry into Carmel. There is nothing unusual in this, and in many cases the "drying up" of the affections in prayer is probably no more than a psychological reaction, more common today perhaps when a large number of postulants have been subjected to the severe emotional strain of parental opposition right up to the time of their entry. But this is a very different thing from the dryness which is a fruit of God's action on the soul in the night of sense. St. John of the Cross gives three well-known signs by which the soul must judge whether this aridity in prayer is authentically contemplative. If it is, she has the obligation of respecting God's action and completing it with her co-operation; but if these signs are not present, St. John of the Cross bids the soul to return to meditation and activity of the faculties.

The theological virtue of faith is "the only proportionate and proximate means for attaining God", and it is faith which elevates the intellect that submits to it, and in the truly con-

[1] C.L. pp. 48, 71.
[2] C.L. pp. 97-8.

templative dryness, faith penetrates into its divine object and is there perfected in its exercise by the action of God through the gifts of the Holy Spirit. It thus becomes a faith increasingly animated by charity, and begets such deep peace in the human mind that the soul rests tranquilly in its divine object.

St. Thérèse discovered in the writings of St. John of the Cross the description of the darkness in which she found herself. He "explained her to herself", and confirmed for her what she had already divined by intuition, that under the cover of this emptiness, God was acting silently but very efficaciously, and that she could rely confidently on the fulfilment of her immense desires for love. Souls who are absorbed in their own devotions, determined to lose nothing of the sweetness they experience, understand very little of the road to the attainment of union, for as St. Teresa of Avila was continually pointing out, what the Lord desires is works. Commenting on this, Père Marie-Eugene of the Child Jesus, O.C.D., remarked that it is not only in the extraordinary graces of prayer and contemplation that God infuses the love that purifies and transforms; "works and sufferings merit inflowings of love and are even necessary for spiritual ascent in these high regions".

(v) Contemplation and the Apostolate

The first task of the contemplative is to sanctify herself. But the renouncing of her own will, the acceptance of the hardships of common life, of poverty, and all the hourly mortification that that imposes, are not merely for her own sanctification. True contemplation is apostolic, and this is especially true of a Carmelite—"a daughter of the seraphic St. Teresa, who would have given a thousand lives to save a single soul"—for whom zeal for souls must be a distinguishing feature.

But how can a beggar distribute alms? Fundamentally all of us, as members of Christ's Mystical Body, assist each other on the path of holiness, and none knows in this life to whom she owes the graces she has received. That, St. Thérèse anticipated, would be one of the great joys of heaven. By a consistent effort to raise the level of her own spiritual life she does very much more than enrich her own soul—she becomes

a channel through which graces can pass to those who are not
in a good position for obtaining them for themselves. The soul
may be likened to a vessel placed near a fountain. First it must
itself be filled to the brim before, in overflowing, it can convey
water to the ground around it. This is the apostolic aim of the
contemplative: to place herself close to the source of all graces
so that, receiving them in full measure, she can pass on the
"overflow" to others. But even in the saintliest of people, perfection in this life is a relative matter; and if anyone imagines
that he or she has no further room for improvement in the
question of virtue, that person is in no way led by the Spirit of
God. In fact, the higher the genuine saint is led, and the greater
the favours she receives, the more does she become aware of
the immeasurable gulf that separates her, while still in this
life, from God. And it is no mere pious hyperbole that causes
the saintly to be forever bewailing their own sinfulness and
unworthiness. But saints, such as Teresa of Avila and John of
the Cross, who have arrived in this life at the stage of transforming union, will normally obtain much more from God
(for themselves and for others) by one action or aspiration,
than could a whole community of imperfect souls by long
prayers.

Such a work is its own recompense, and the recompense is
always greater than the labour. Souls truly given to God do
not "work with one eye on the clock" as it were; and even
though they know it will gain them immense and everlasting
profit, that is still not their main concern.

When contemplation is highest and purest, it overflows into
activity. Thus we have what is called the "mixed life", which
is defined by St. Thomas Aquinas as the highest state—that is,
contemplation flowering into action, or sharing one's contemplation with others and bringing one's fellow-men to the knowledge of God that is given to those who love Him perfectly;
and St. Thomas himself was the perfect examplar of his own
definition.

"The Rule," says St. John of the Cross, "aims at making
persons observe the mixed and compounded life so that they
may embrace and include within themselves two lives, the

active and the contemplative, in one. This mixed life the Lord chose for Himself because it is the most perfect. And the state and method of the religious who embraces it is the most perfect of its kind."[1]

Often contemplation is regarded as being opposed to the active life. St. Thomas says that we should first devote ourselves to contemplation, and then share with others its fruit. Obviously it is better to pass on what has been gained in contemplation than to stop at contemplation, making it an end in itself; for to do this is to appropriate for oneself that which has been gratuitously given for the purpose of sharing with others, not solely for one's own personal enjoyment here, or even for individual beatitude hereafter.

Contradictory as it may seem at first sight, St. Thérèse is a remarkable and outstanding example of this. She was first of all and conspicuously a contemplative, and she was apostolic to a degree. She could not be considered as having lived the "mixed life" in that she was not called upon to impart her gifts to others by teaching and preaching in this life. But as her short span of years drew to its close she became increasingly aware that she had received a vocation to teach, which could not conceivably be fulfilled in this life. Then gradually dawned the consciousness, growing stronger and more certain as her life ebbed away, that her mission would be fulfilled not in time, but in eternity.

Is this to say that all enclosed contemplatives (with the exception of St. Thérèse, who had the unique privilege of completing the second half of her "mixed" vocation in heaven) fail to realize their calling? There is another way of sharing one's spiritual riches, which is open to all, regardless of sex or state, and here again St. Thérèse has set us the example. That is not to say that she was the first to arrive at it, but as usual she has given a strikingly original twist to an already known and formulated doctrine. There was no act of Thérèse's, however trivial, however indifferent, down to every breath she drew, which was not offered to God for the needs of the Church, for the suffering, for sinners. Not until time had ceased to be

---

[1] Sixth Spiritual Saying.

will we know the number of souls saved by the apostolic ardour of this "little" soul, because not until time is at an end will the activity of this truly great contemplative have drawn into the loving arms of God her last sinner.

"Yes, I shall spend my heaven in doing good upon earth. That is not impossible, since from the midst of the beatific vision itself the angels watch over us. No, I shall not be able to take any rest until the end of the world, so long as there are souls to be saved. But when the angel shall declare that *Time shall be no more,* then I shall take my rest; then I shall be able to rejoice, because the number of the elect will be complete, and all shall have entered into their joy and their repose."[1]

Indeed St. Thérèse chose the contemplative life deliberately, not because she feared the hardships of ordinary work in the world, but because she realized that sanctification is more important. Like Mary of Bethany, she chose the better part—and then she set about serving her neighbours too.

It is possible that many elect to enter a teaching or nursing congregation simply because it seems the obvious and natural thing to do. They have been trained to such tasks, and feel that there they will use their talents to the greatest advantage. They know they will also serve their neighbours, which gives added incentive. But the decisive factor in many cases has been their own aptitudes and attractions, the knowledge that they are making a tangible contribution to the relief of sickness, suffering, ignorance and want; and it is on our exercise of these practical works of mercy that we are to be judged. "When you did it to one of the least of my brethren here, you did it to me." (Matt. 25: 40.) Sometimes, however, there is the temptation to regard one who has deliberately laid aside the exercise of her gifts in these fields to serve God alone in the silence of the cloister, as having deserted the battlefield selfishly to seek her own repose.

Pope Pius XI, whose leaning towards the propagation of the faith and the expansion of the active apostolate cannot be questioned, has long since declared the mind of the Church in this matter, by his Apostolic Constitution *Umbratilem*: *"If*

---

[1] N.V. 17th July, 1897.

ever it was needful that there should be anchorites . . . in the Church of God, it is most specially expedient nowadays . . . There are perhaps some who still deem that the virtues which are misnamed passive have long grown obsolete, and that the broader and more liberal exercise of the active virtues should be substituted for the ancient discipline of the cloister . . . No one can fail to see how harmful and baneful that opinion is to Christian perfection as it is taught and practised by the Church."

It may seem that the desire to die to self in order to live for God and love Him alone is a selfish search for peace or even a neglect of the apostolate. But to live for God only is certainly not to live for oneself; it might entail withdrawing from one's neighbours in physical presence, but they may not be excluded from one's love and prayer.

The more closely a soul is held captive by love, the more she is identified with all humanity, for charity causes her to enter into all suffering, all sin, wherever there are souls to be saved. There is no alternative for one united with Christ than of being also consolidated with His members. In finding her place in the Church, Thérèse progressively discovered the whole Christ, the Church, His Mystical Body. Having entered into the heart of the Church (where she would be "love"), she found there the niche and the mission that God's immemorial design had assigned for her in time and eternity.

Minds unable to see past the exercise of natural virtue look at most problems with the wisdom of this world, and in that light they can never understand the tremendous force and efficacy of the contemplative life in the Church. The most powerful and undoubtedly the most popular saint of this century of speed and hyperactivity is not, as one might have expected, a missionary teacher or nurse, an apostle or preacher, but a Carmelite nun who for the whole span of her brief religious life (just under a decade) did absolutely nothing to benefit humanity, except to pray, suffer and obey, and offer it for mankind. In the material order she accomplished no works of any sort, but in the spiritual world she moved mountains. Today we see her exercising throughout the world, amid every

class and race, a moral influence almost without parallel. It is
no exaggeration to say that, after our Blessed Lady, no saint is
more often and more universally invoked by the faithful than
St. Thérèse of the Child Jesus.

In the last year of her life she wrote to the Abbé Bellière, one
of her missionary "brothers", that her sole desire was the will
of God, and that if she could no longer work for His glory in
heaven, she would prefer to remain an exile on earth than be
taken to the heaven that had been the goal of all her striving.
These are not just pious aspirations of a sentimental little nun,
and what God has achieved through her in the past sixty years
is clear vindication of the supernatural instinct which dictated
her words. In this generation her glory and visible power are
astonishing. She has been held up to the world by five succes-
sive pontiffs as the model for the faithful of every class and
condition, the guiding star of Pope Pius XI and the beacon of
hope for all Christians. Today, with no enclosure to confine
her zealous ardour, she fills the whole earth, and her influence
is felt in every country and class and condition of man. She is,
in the words of Pope Pius XI, "the child loved by all the
world", and our century, hall-marked by cynicism and sophis·
tication and atheistic communism, is witness to a spectacle for
which it can offer no explanation, the wholesale infatuation
which she herself predicted on her deathbed: *"All the world
will love me."*

Such universal homage is not the result of merely temporal
favours, even at the rate at which they are dispensed by such a
miracle-worker as Thérèse has proved to be. Lavish as she is to
her petitioners, it is the gift of divine grace which accompanies
her gift that is the real secret of her attraction and of her power
with souls.

(vi) Love is my Vocation

To believe that the contemplative religious is selfish in her
motive for retiring from the world, or escapist in her attitude
to the cares of family life is to miss the point entirely. Some
may lack generosity in fulfilling their vocation, but that is
another matter. By the vows of religion, the monk and nun

draw down upon themselves a degree of suffering which would not have been their portion in the world. The cloister, it is true, is not indispensable for individual salvation or perfection (except God so wills it), but the existence in the Church of this communal form of praise and sacrifice to God is without parallel in winning souls for Christ. The contemplative religious does not seek to evade responsibilities, but to make herself available to shoulder the burdens of others, perhaps too weak to face the task alone. She seeks to become the mother of countless souls, for whose spiritual welfare their natural parents know not how to provide, and the cost of such efforts would be overwhelming if our Lord Himself did not support her. It is He who gives her peace, but not the peace understood by the world, a peace won and held at the point of the sword. Freed from the material cares of the world, contemplatives are especially dedicated to earning the spiritual livelihood of all, and if their way of life gives more exterior aids to attaining their own sanctification, it is so that all their fellow-Christians may be enriched by their holiness.

The communion of saints forms a fund of merit, to which each contributes according to his means, or draws upon to meet his needs, and there is no one, even one who is not in the state of grace, who may not hope for pardon because of some gratuitous grace won for him by the sacrifices and penances and prayers of one very close to God, of whom he has never heard and never will in this life. "Often without knowing it," said Thérèse, "the graces and lights which we receive are due to some hidden soul, because God wills that the saints communicate His grace from one to another by prayer, so that in heaven they may love one another with greater love, a love that will exceed that of a family, even of the most ideal family upon earth. How many times have I not thought that perhaps all the graces that I have received are due to the prayers of some little soul who has obtained them for me from God, and whom I shall never know till I get to heaven . . . what will it be like, then, up in heaven, when souls shall know those who have been the means of their salvation?"[1]

[1] N.V. 15th July, 23rd August.

In the mystical body, as in the human body, no member can
be sufficient unto himself, or work solely for his own salvation.
Whether he likes it or not, the way he has lived his life will
affect countless other lives. As St. Paul points out, the eye cannot perform the function of the hand, and therefore is unable
to dispense with its services. The defection of one cell causes
deterioration in the whole organism, more or less serious
according to the importance of the function of the particular
cell. This law, which is as inflexible in the spiritual as in the
natural order, is found to apply even to those contemplatives
who are considered most aloof from the fray, as St. John of the
Cross points out.

The contemplative who seems to have turned her back on
her fellow-men in order to keep her gaze fixed on God alone
and to live only for Him, has not deserted them, but now,
loving them in and through God, her love is purer and more
efficacious for their assistance. The greatest contemplatives,
when obedience required it of them, showed themselves ex-
ceedingly capable as active workers. St. Teresa of Avila is a
notable example. St. John of the Cross could handle affairs and
responsibilities efficiently when called upon to do so, although
essentially he was a man of God and preferred not to engage
in exterior activities, while the amazingly versatile St. Teresa
appeared equally at home in one situation or another.

It is not surprising that the prayers of contemplatives have
such power with God for they live in close union with Him
who holds all things in His hand. They draw God by their
prayer, and because they are surrendered and conformed to
His will, merely by abandoning themselves to His action they
lay the world open to Him.

St. Thérèse copied out the following extract from Tauler's
*Sermon for the Fifth Sunday after the Feast of the Blessed
Trinity*, which appealed greatly to her: "If I love the good
which is in my neighbour more than he himself loves it, this
good is more mine than his. If I love in St. Paul all the favours
that God has bestowed on him, all, by the same title, belong to
me. By this communion I can be enriched by all the good that
is in heaven and upon earth, in the angels and saints, and in

all who love God."[1] Thérèse re-discovered this law of love. She understood that the contemplative, placed at the heart of the Church, is from there able to animate and elevate all works done with little or lukewarm love, or even from insufficiently disinterested motives. She realized that it was this love which enabled the other members of the Church to act, and that should it cease to function the apostles would neglect to preach the gospel, the martyrs would refuse to shed their blood. Love, in short, is the vocation which includes all else: "It's a universe of its own, comprising all time and space—it's eternal!"

Then Thérèse, having placed herself in the heart of the Church, saw clearly that without leaving her cell, she could perform all the missionary actions of all the apostles from the beginning of time, for it was her prerogative to contribute the love that alone could vivify and supernaturalize their labours.

"Jesus, my love! I've found my vocation, and my vocation is love." She had discovered her place in the Church, the niche that God had appointed for her from all eternity: to be nothing else than love in the heart of Mother Church. Thus she would be everything at once, and in being all things to all men, would help to make all labours fruitful and satisfy the longings of her own heart.

(vii) The Contemplative-Missionary Vocation

In stressing the importance of the contemplative life—an importance endorsed time and again by the popes in their allocutions and apostolic writings—it is not to be thought that the value of the work done for the Church by other religious and by devoted seculars, least of all by the clergy, is in any way underestimated. Their enormous labours of preaching, catechizing, nursing, and relieving every kind of corporal and spiritual need of our human misery are one of the glories of the Church. But when there is so much crying out to be done, schools, parishes and hospitals to be staffed, mission stations calling for help and supplies, sufferings of the poor and neglected to be alleviated, we can be lured into a feverish

[1] *The Spirit of St. Thérèse*, p. 87.

exterior activity that cannot be really fruitful unless it has its
roots deep in a life of prayer and union with God, and fall into
what Pope Pius XII aptly termed "the heresy of good works".
No amount of learning, nor the most arduous labour, can convert a single soul without the grace of God, and that generally
is obtained by prayer and suffering.

Many a young priest, setting eagerly out upon his long-
anticipated apostolate, brings a great zeal and earnestness to
his quest for souls, and sometimes fails to grasp why results do
not appear commensurate with his strenuous efforts. He might
think it is merely that his approach is at fault, and try a new
technique, only to fail again in securing the conversions his
energy and persistent efforts seem to merit. It is usually only
through the wisdom of experience and the graces received in
prayer that he eventually comes to realize that nobody can ever
"convert" a soul. That is accomplished by love alone, the unseen leaven of grace working slowly and effectively in silence
and hiddenness. Souls are won not by the preacher's eloquence
or his up-to-date methods in the apostolate, but by the love of
God that radiates from the Sacred Heart through the hands
and the mouth of one who is truly Christ-centred.

St. Bernard's advice to missionaries "to be cisterns and not
aqueducts" is well known. The metaphor is obvious. An aque-
duct conveys water which passes through, leaving it empty.
For a cistern to supply water, on the other hand, it must itself
be filled first, and then without emptying or exhausting its
contents, it pours out from its reservoir what is needed else-
where. "The Church today," concluded St. Bernard, "has
many aqueducts, but very few cisterns."

St. Thérèse said: "When I began to learn the history of
France, the story of Joan of Arc's exploits entranced me; I felt
in my heart the desire and the courage to imitate her; it seemed
to me that our Lord meant me for great things too. I was not
mistaken, but in places of voices from heaven calling me to war,
I heard in the depths of my soul a voice sweeter, more powerful
still, the voice of the spouse of virgins calling me to other exploits, conquests still more glorious, and in the solitude of
Carmel I realized that my mission was not to get a mortal king

crowned, but to get the King of Heaven loved, to bring the realm of hearts under His sway."[1]

Thérèse had no illusions about the life she would lead in Carmel. She never imagined that in the silence and solitude of the cloister she would find a place of rest and exemption from all initiative. She would doubtless have endorsed Cardinal Newman's statement that solitude is to be sought not because of the relief from those who are not there, but for His sake who is. "I found the religious life exactly what I'd expected it to be. The sacrifices I had to make never for a moment took me by surprise—and yet, as you know, Mother, those first footsteps of mine brought me up against more thorns than roses."[2] On the contrary, she envisaged it as the one place where she could labour most efficaciously for souls.

It is an error to imagine that when we are working at top pressure we are necessarily giving our utmost. The merit of our actions is not their greatness or difficulty, but the love which inspires them. Likewise our lives are pleasing to God not because of the amount we do, nor even the trouble it costs us to do it, but by and in proportion to our sanctity and union with Him. If we fail to curb an impatient word, to mortify our curiosity, if we neglect prayer and are incapable of withdrawing into ourselves, we may be certain that despite all the apparent success we may achieve we are not exercising any real influence on souls. Indeed, as St. John of the Cross says, we are doing nothing at all, or perhaps even harm. A single soul such as St. Thérèse, sanctifying herself unnoticed even by those around her and attaining a high degree of perfection, will do more good throughout the word for all time by one seemingly trivial action than an imperfect and unmortified soul will do by many years of feverish activity—as is witnessed by the works she has achieved and continues to perform for souls. God would do all that she willed in heaven, was her confident prediction, for the simple reason that she had never done her own will upon earth.

Her whole religious life was a perpetual putting into prac-

[1] C.L. p. 287.
[2] A.S. p. 184.

2*

tice of the teaching of her father St. John of the Cross, and it
was from him that she learned to set the value of love above
the value of works. (cf. *Sp. C.*, Annotation for Stanza XXIX,
2nd Red.)

The Church, following the teaching of her divine master,
has always insisted that the life of prayer is superior to the life
of action. Jesus taught his disciples their obligation in the
matter. "And He told them a parable, shewing them that they
ought to pray continually, and never be discouraged." (Luke
18:1.) However, He did not send them into the desert to
become hermits in order to do so, but "like sheep among
wolves" out over the world to preach the gospel to the whole of
creation. Thérèse plainly expressed her belief that the power
of prayer has apostolic value superior to and farther reaching
than that of mere activity itself as normally exercised in the
external apostolate, where the solitary missionary is very often
exposed to all the hardships and distractions of worldly surroundings and contacts, with none of the safeguards and
consolations of community life. "Is not the apostolate of
prayer lifted higher, so to speak, than the apostolate of preaching? Our mission, as Carmelites, is to form those gospel
labourers, they will save millions of souls, whose mothers we
shall be ... our vocation ... is not to go harvesting in the fields
of ripe corn . . . our mission is still loftier. Here are Jesus'
words: 'Lift up your eyes and see . . .' See how in my heaven
there are places empty; it is for you to fill them . . . What have
priests that we need envy!"[1]

Here Thérèse puts her finger straight on the core of the
issue, aiming her apostolate at priests, knowing well that one
priest formed in the love of God is a potential parish converted. "She exercises her apostolate for priests," says Père
Matteo Crawley, the great apostle of devotion to the Sacred
Heart, "because they are *multipliers*." And Thérèse's words
are: "How can I cease to pray for all missionaries everywhere?
Not to mention those ordinary parish priests whose work is
sometimes quite as uphill work as preaching to the heathen."[2]

[1] C.L. p. 153.
[2] A.S. pp. 304-5.

It has been said that there are many workers for Christ, but few lovers of Christ. Thérèse's certainty of the apostolic value of love was the basis on which she built her spiritual life, and her message for priests is the completeness of a life of love. Appropriating to herself the words of St. John of the Cross she designed for herself a "mystical coat of arms" bearing the motto: *Love is repaid by love alone.*

"I have never given God anything but love," she told Mother Agnes, "and He will repay me with love." And her last recorded words to Céline, the day before her death, were "It is love *alone* that counts."

CHAPTER TWO

DISCOVERING A MISSION

*"The word of the Lord came to me, and his message was . . .
'I have a prophet's errand for thee among the nations.'*
*'Alas, alas, Lord God' (said I), 'I am but a child that has
never learned to speak.'*
*'A child, sayest thou?' the Lord answered. 'Nay, I have a
mission for thee to undertake, a message to entrust to thee.
Have no human fears; am I not at thy side, to protect thee
from harm? . . . Here and now I give thee authority over
nations and kingdoms everywhere'."*

(Jeremias, I: 4-10)

(*i*) *"Thérèse, living word of God"* (Pius XI)

St. Thérèse of the Child Jesus made some daring predictions
before her death. We are so familiar with them nowadays that
they do not startle us at all; but at the time it was not considered prudent to present some of them to the public.

It was surprising, to say the least of it, to hear that an unknown Carmelite nun on her deathbed had announced her
intention of spending her heaven in doing good upon earth.
According to reason, her chances of conducting any sort of
mission were at an end, yet confidently she declared that hers
was about to begin. It was the will of God that the accomplish
ment of this mission should be put off until eternity, just as
Jesus Himself had to die before His Church could be born,
yet this was too obvious for the world to see. Thérèse, however,
as her life ebbed away, became more and more certain of it.
God would not, she felt sure, inspire in her ambitions that
could not be attained. He would not have given her the desire
to do good upon earth after her death if He did not will to
realize it; rather He would have given her the desire for rest
instead.

The extraordinary thing about it all is that she has literally fulfilled every one of her predictions, however unlikely it may have seemed at the time. Sixty years of experience have proved that she has, since her death, done everything—indeed very much more—that she claimed she would do.

The burning desire to save souls for Jesus, to snatch the unregenerate back from eternal damnation, had pointed the way to her immolation as a Carmelite, but even so her missionary apostolate is expressed rather as the preparation of souls to receive the divine love in its fullness than as the salvation of souls, however dear to her heart that work may be. It was to be one of making souls love God, to love and to be loved, and *to return to earth and make Love loved.*

The salvation of souls will necessarily flow out of this as a logical result. With her direct approach to the crucial point, Thérèse saw that sanctifying priests was the sure way of reaching the maximum number of souls, and to make those souls love God as she loved Him would assure a fruitful apostolate.

Looking at a photograph of St. Joan of Arc in prison she said: "The saints encourage me also in my prison. They say to me: As long as you are in chains, you cannot fulfil your mission; but later on after your death, then shall come the time of your conquest."[1]

The speed with which St. Thérèse was canonized surely indicated some special mission entrusted to her by God for the salvation of souls. She herself became increasingly aware of the sense of mission towards the end of her life, although she did not seem at first to realize exactly what it was to be. Little by little she moved, hesitantly, almost timorously towards an intuition of her eternal vocation, until at last she announced with absolute conviction that her mission would be to make God loved and to teach her "little way" to souls. Since her death this mission has obviously been fulfilled abundantly, for she has carried out a world-wide apostolate, and quite apart from her countless miracles and temporal favours, has helped to raise the level of prayer and holiness in the lives of millions. "From one end of the world to the other, there are countless

[1] N.V. 10th August.

souls whose interior lives have been helped by St. Thérèse of Lisieux," said Pope Pius XII (then Cardinal Pacelli) at Lisieux in July, 1937.

St. Thérèse has been chosen to teach anew to a world which has forgotten them, the simplicity of the gospel maxims of the fatherhood of God, the necessity of a life of spiritual childhood, and the confidence of the one in the love and mercy of the other. We are always helpless children—nothing more; but what we often lack is the confidence and simplicity of little children. And it is to show us this that we have been given St. Thérèse, for "of such is the kingdom of heaven". The timelessness of her message and the timeliness of her mission become daily more evident when everywhere around us we see men and women falling into despair at the apparent futility of a life without the God in whom they profess not to believe. They realize all too clearly that we have here no abiding city, and do not see any prospect of finding one beyond the grave. Thérèse calls us back to a belief in the fatherhood of God—God not merely to be worshipped as our supreme Lord and Creator, but to be loved as a most tender father. And from the fatherhood of God we must by a logical process be led to the brotherhood of man, for unless we recognize our common parentage and behave like sons and daughters of our heavenly father, there is no hope for the world, no prospect of anything but ever-increasing fear and hatred and universal devastation. In 1922 the newly-elected Pope Pius XI, outlining his programme for Catholic Action in the encyclical *Ubi Arcano Dei*, made the following observation: "The habit of life which can be called really Christian has in great measure disappeared, so that human society does not seem to be progressing on the road to good, as is men's boast, but actually going back towards barbarism." Once we forget that God is our father, we very soon disregard the fact that our neighbour is our brother (unless we happen to feel a natural liking for him), and when the charity of Christ ceases to influence the dispositions of our heart, the step towards total unbelief is not far off. Today it is an increasingly urgent necessity for the individual soul and for Christendom in general to be "converted and become as

little children", forsaking the natural excellence of merely
human ideals, and placing all its hopes in Jesus crucified. The
more gifted we are according to the natural intellect, the
greater is the temptation to make God into a projection of our
own "self" instead of worshipping Him according to the Spirit
of Truth. Both Pope Pius XI and his predecessor Benedict XV
have pointed out repeatedly that St. Thérèse of the Child Jesus
has been given to us not merely as a model whose virtues are
to be admired, but also as a teacher who is to initiate us into
their practical imitation and application to our own lives.

In her own mind Thérèse never confused her individual
spiritual life, the sanctification of her own soul to be achieved
in this world, and the universal mission that was to be hers in
the next. She, Thérèse, who had striven only to remain little
and humble in the hands of God, would go to Him possessing
nothing but boundless confidence in His love and mercy. It
would be His task to perfect and shape the tool for the work
He had predestined, putting His treasure into the empty
hands of a child. Therefore, despite the gradually increasing
certainty of a future mission, her whole effort in preparation
was not to grow bigger, but to remain small, or if possible to
become even smaller. She was merely the instrument; the
work was God's.

Just before her death Thérèse told her sister that she felt her
mission was about to begin. And when asked what that mission
would be, she declared: "To make souls love God as I love
Him, to teach them my little way of confidence and total
abandon." It was not a mission to a privileged few living a life
of contemplation, isolated from the cares and anxieties of the
world; it was one that could be extended to every person,
irrespective of age or state in life, given the grace of God and
a sincere desire for perfection according to the spirit of the
gospels.

In a letter to the Carmel of Lisieux of 7th August, 1947,
Pope Pius XII said: "There are many who imagine that this
is a special way, reserved for the innocent souls of young
novices to guide them in their early steps, but that it is not
suited to people of mature years who need prudence on

account of their greater responsibilities. Such people forget
that it was our Lord Himself who recommended this way to
all God's children, even to those who, like the apostles whom
He was training, hold the highest responsibilities: that of the
care of souls. It is also too often forgotten that in order to see
clearly amid the complex questions that torture humanity
today, one requires, together with prudence, that outstanding
simplicity which wisdom brings and which St. Thérèse mani-
fests in so irresistible a manner that she thereby draws all
hearts towards her."

It is, then, applicable to all. No one is exempted from
practising the virtues of spiritual childhood, from imitating
the spirit of the Child Jesus Himself. However, it is wholly
incompatible with natural religion and the deification of man's
human achievements, so it is hardly surprising that its critics
should be so numerous. The power of St. Thérèse is not greater
than that of her crucified Master, Jesus Christ, and it was in
union with Him that she predicted: "I will spend my heaven
in doing good upon earth."

(ii) God, our Father

It is an interesting fact, as pointed out by the Abbé Combes
in his books *The Spirituality of St. Thérèse* and *St. Thérèse
and Her Mission*, that St. Thérèse herself never penned the
expression *spiritual childhood*. The first time it is placed on
her lips is in the pages of *Novissima Verba*, a small volume
which comprises the conversations of Thérèse during her last
months in the infirmary, recorded by her sister and "little
mother", Reverend Mother Agnes of Jesus.

"Mother," she said, when questioned about her little way,
"it is the way of *spiritual childhood*: the path of confidence
and total abandonment." But whenever she mentioned her
mission, it was not of teaching the spirit of childhood that
Thérèse spoke, but always without exception of her *little way*.
"I feel that my mission is about to begin: my mission of making souls love God as I love Him, *to teach my little way to
souls*."

What matters most is the actual love of Thérèse for God as

her father, her unshakeable confidence in His power and His providence in her regard. From this is derived *her mission* to make God loved as she loved Him, to recall to present-day Christians that He is not only the omnipotent God but also our most solicitous and loving father who always and everywhere surrounds us with love and protection and care in all the details, from the least to the greatest, of our lives. The great work of our Lord's public life, apart from laying the foundations of His Church, was to reveal the father in this light, and to teach us that under the new law, love was to be the activating motive of our lives, rather than the fear which until then had been the principal deterrent against offending a God so terrible and so powerful to avenge.

Perhaps the most distinctive characteristic of Thérèse's spirituality can be summed up in her recognition of God as her father—revealed however in the person of Jesus Christ. Jesus was her saviour and her spouse, but first and foremost He was her most loving father. God for her simply means the divine nature *as given to this world* through the Word incarnate. The greatest earthly love Thérèse had known had been for her own father; he had been her ideal, her "incomparable king". Thus she understood fully the tenderness of a father's love for a beloved youngest child, and she knew too the fullness of the love a child bears for its venerated father. "There is no father so much a father as God," said Tertullian; and indeed the intense love for her "king" was but a shadow of Thérèse's all-embracing love of God. In Him she saw a father whom she loved and by whom she knew herself to be loved; and she served Him and prayed to Him as a child to its father. Consequently she regarded herself as dependent on Him for everything, just as—during the difficult years following her mother's death—she had looked to her earthly father for everything. As we are by nature, so does God sanctify us; so there is nothing in this aspect of Thérèse's psychology that need surprise us.

So many of us seem to regard the spiritual life as something incredibly complicated: a narrow, dangerous road with a deep chasm on one side and a precipice on the other, where one dares not relax for a moment lest he fall and be dashed to his death. Despite the doctrinal instruction we have received about the fatherhood of God, many of us give to our heavenly father little of the love and confidence we show to our natural fathers. For all its effect on our daily lives, we might never have heard of any such teaching as the fatherhood of God, which is fundamental to the Christian message (as is evident from the gospels). And the repeating of it is the essential point of the message of St. Thérèse.

How comforting it is to know that God's justice does not require the dispassionate, impartial weighing of all evidence for and against us, as our human exercise of this virtue implies, or entering each credit against its corresponding debit in a kind of celestial journal, wherein is recorded every deed of our lives, all of which are to be aired and used in evidence against us at the particular judgment. Certain retreat-masters are devoted to variations on this theme, and we are told how the inexorable justice of God demands the payment of the "last farthing" in purgatory. This is perfectly true, of course, but it is not with the attitude of a strict gaoler that God detains souls in purgatory. They are as perfect in charity as they will ever be; but if in this life they have failed to make full satisfaction for sins committed, or to develop to the full their individual capacities for the beatific vision[1] then it follows that they will require further assistance from the church militant before becoming capable for the face-to-face vision of God.

There are many ways of looking at the justice of God, and that of Thérèse was to behold it in the resplendent mirror of His mercy, from which it is inseparable. All our life long He is our loving father and best friend, not an adjudicator at an eisteddfod who notes the tone, the pitch, the various technical faults and merits, and awards judgment on the whole performance. One act of perfect love can wipe out a thousand faults and sins that separate us from Him, and in the twinkling of an eye make us fit to come into His presence and throw ourselves into His arms, instead of flinging ourselves in horror from His sight. We hear the expression used in connection

---

[1] Not a moral issue as such, but one pertaining to the positive sanctifying in faith of the natural intelligence.

with the judgment of the soul: "The time for mercy has
passed; now is the time for justice"; as though God were incapable of entertaining two moods simultaneously. Certainly
the "righteous judge of retribution" of the *Dies iræ* tends to
support such a rendering; but weaving through the trumpet
blasts of dread and fear that seem to dominate this powerful
hymn, come the accents of confidence in the mercy of God
and appeal to the infinite merits of Christ's redemptive love.
God who is infinitely just does not suddenly cease to be infinitely merciful when we stand in His presence. "It will be a
great thing at the hour of our death," reflected St. Teresa of
Avila, "to realize that we shall be judged by one whom we
have loved above all things."[1]

It is the privilege of Christians to be called to live as adopted
sons of our heavenly father and on terms of intimacy with
Him, sharing, so to speak, His family life. One of St. Thérèse's
missionary "brothers" said that he could never attain to her
degree of familiarity with God. But Thérèse would regard as
unnatural a child who did not love his father, and still more
unnatural one who, loving Him, stood on ceremony with Him
or was cold and formal in his behaviour. She lived out in practice her message before giving it to the world. We cannot dis-
sociate her from the love of God. The word is on her lips and
in her heart as often as it was with St. John the Evangelist. The
love of God filled and penetrated every crevice of them both.
Indeed Thérèse felt that her heart was so entirely filled with
the will of God that when something approached from without, it could not penetrate, any more than oil poured on water
could mix with it. It was this "imperviousness" which gave
her the sense of always resting in a profound peace in the
depths of her soul, which nothing was able to disturb.

However, familiarity such as hers does not imply any lack
of reverence or respect; on the contrary it grows out of
reverence, just as the Gift of Piety is a development of the Gift
of Fear. Thus intimacy with God goes hand in hand with
reverential awe and self-knowledge. We are no longer God's
servants but His friends, members of His household, children

[1] W.P., Ch. 40, pp. 175-6.

of the father, through whose eyes we now look out upon the world and see that all things are good.

(iii) Peace of Soul

"My little way is all confidence and love," Thérèse wrote to Père Roulland in the last year of her life. This is certainly astonishing when one recalls that only ten years earlier she had suffered from scruples to such an acute degree. It has been suggested that her way of surrender to the love and mercy of God was the outcome of the scruples, giving her, as it did, a sense of peace and confidence in the midst of doubts and insecurity. But this is surely impossible, and anyone with experience of scrupulous souls will know that the one thing they cannot do is throw themselves on the mercy of God with unreserved confidence.

Whatever the nature of the scruples, and whatever their cause in the individual soul, such persons of themselves are powerless to combat the affliction. Only God can deliver them, but the way to such healing consists of faith in the Sacred Humanity (with or without expressed appeals to our Lady and the saints as well). By means of such faith in Jesus Christ, even a victim of "compulsive neurosis" (see Note 1) can establish an oasis of supernatural peace in his or her deeper soul (until such time as God wills to grant perfect freedom), but it is thus and thus only that the healing effects of divine charity are enabled to permeate the disordered senses and emotions of the patient.

"Little children are not damned," Thérèse declared, echoing St. Paul's statement that "no judgment stands against those who live in Christ Jesus", (Rom. 8: 1). This calm and confident assertion could never have been made by a sufferer from scruples; rather it is the statement of a child who knows quite well that her father will forgive her if she asks his pardon. "You must leave far behind the *sterile fear* of being unfaithful," she counselled one of her sisters, because such fear as that is incompatible with childhood.

Fear, doubt and discouragement can pollute the whole of our supernatural atmosphere, their poisonous, stultifying

fumes blighting everything we do and foredooming all to
failure. The confidence of childhood, far removed from sterile
fear, is dynamic and productive. It is not a superstructure
erected on or camouflaging a repressed fear or sense of guilt,
but the "perfect love that casts out fear". Thérèse's whole life
and her spiritual doctrine are a logical and concise exposition
of the fourth chapter of St. John's first Epistle, particularly
verses 17–21.

When one is firmly convinced of God's assistance in a personal way, emotional crises or the perplexities and burdens of
life become relatively unimportant. For with so clear and
realistic a conception of God, His plans for and claims upon
the soul, one has a firm foothold despite the difficulties, and
is able to control both thoughts and conduct—something that
is beyond the power of a victim of scruples without constant
direction and his minute obedience to instructions.

For a year and a half, Thérèse says, she suffered from
scruples, and her release was apparently a direct answer to
prayer. Unlike most scrupulous persons, however, she did not
withdraw from holy Communion, and this was doubtless on
the instructions of her sister Marie, in whom she confided her
doubts and miseries. Later when her cousin wrote for advice
in a similar difficulty, Thérèse stated without hesitation:
"When the devil has succeeded in keeping a soul away from
holy Communion, he has *gained all* . . . laugh at him, and go
without fear to receive the Jesus of peace and love! . . . *receive
Communion often*, very often . . . there you have the *sole*
remedy if you want to be cured."[1]

Many souls are so proud by nature, so consumed by their
own natural excellence, that it takes some disorder of the
nervous system to bring them to their knees and to teach them
the secret of supernatural dependence in faith and hope on the
Sacred Humanity of our Lord. From God's point of view, at
any rate, it is better that His children should suffer the distress
of scruples than that they should be the victims of spiritual or
intellectual pride.

There is not the slightest trace of scrupulosity in Thérèse's

[1] C.L. pp. 94-5 (written when Thérèse was sixteen years of age).

religious life. This showed a marked development indeed, but in quite the other direction. The whole spirit of the mature Thérèse, her humility, confidence, self-forgetfulness and immense charity, is utterly opposed to scrupulosity, and in the full bloom of her sanctity would have formed an infallible protection against even the temptation to such a malady. It is fairly certain that her scruples were not cured by her own reasoning, or by Marie's counsel, but solely as a response to her almost desperate prayer. Thérèse herself has told us where she found peace of soul and release from the anxieties that tormented her. Having lost her earthly confidante on Marie's entering Carmel, she turned to heaven for assistance, thinking particularly of the four brothers and sister who had died in infancy. Surely, she thought, never having lived to experience earth's troubles and fears, they would pity and help their sister, so sorely tried on earth? To them she addressed her prayers, and says that before long a delicious sense of peace flooded her soul. "I realized that there were people who loved me in heaven too."

Her little way came much later, long after she had been freed from this bondage, and it did not come clear-cut, as a revelation, but as a gradually developing thing that matured as she lived it; its development moreover would have been stunted at the outset by the presence of scruples.

I am not a professional psychologist, nor it seems are some of those who in recent years have undertaken so-called psychological studies of the saint. It must always be a cause for regret when one finds such persons refusing to take into consideration the action of divine grace, or allowing no play for it in their calculations or therapy, but treating all phenomena solely on the material plane. It is tragic when we find Catholic writers falling into the same error; still worse when the subject of the study is a saint, who can never be considered merely as an object of historical or psychical research, but primarily, if not exclusively, in the sphere of supernatural grace, which refines, perfects, guides and strengthens all that is purely natural in them unto God's greater service.

It was only after the retreat of 1891 that Thérèse was

"launched in full sail on the sea of confidence and love". The period of her scruples was between June 1885 and the date of her "complete conversion", December 1886. She did not, because of her scruples, throw herself in blind confidence on the love and mercy of God; on the contrary, because she was freed from her scruples, she was enabled to do so, and thus discover her method and her mission.

Thérèse herself clearly realized this. She explains St. Peter's denial of our Lord as a permitted fall, because, being destined for the mission of governing the Church, in which there are many sinners, it was God's will that he should experience in himself how. weak is human nature when it depends solely upon its own strength rather than looking for all things from God. And thus, through the recollection of his own sin, St. Peter knew all too well, and so could teach others, what man is without God.

Thérèse's own experience of her weakness was to have a similar effect, and this in large part explains her own growth and the development of her little way; as well as her mission to teach it to others in an era when more people than at any other period of history, perhaps, are dominated by fear and the sense of insecurity. "I will show them the little means that I have found so perfectly successful"—the path of confidence and total abandonment, far removed either from anxious doubts or a presumptuous self-reliance, casting all one's cares on Him who cares for us.

(iv) Holiness and Wholeness

For Thérèse, as has been seen, everything came to her direct from her most tender father, hand-picked by Him for His dearly-loved child. Therefore to her everything seemed a grace, as indeed it is, although few of us can see clearly enough to recognize it as anything but a nuisance when it comes knocking at our door. Everything is a grace because it is a gift of God; whether it be a joy or a sorrow, a cross or a crown, it is a grace which has been preordained from all eternity for the furthering of our sanctification as St. Paul explains so emphatically in the eighth chapter of the Epistle to the Romans (vv. 28–35).

Why so few of us respond to its promptings is that it usually comes in the guise of hard work. It is a humbling thought that the interruption in the middle of that precious five minutes which would have allowed us to finish an important letter was part of the divine plan for our supernatural perfection even before we were born; also that our reaction to it, our use or abuse of grace, will have incalculable repercussions on all the other ingredients of that plan. How right and clear-sighted was Thérèse. "All is well," she said, "when one seeks only the will of God." And therefore, even though she might be deprived of the last sacraments, of which there was a distinct possibility, that too—even that—she declared, would be a grace.

"Holiness does not consist in this or that practice; it consists in a *disposition of the heart,* which makes us always humble and little in the hands of God, well aware of our feebleness, but confident to audacity in the father's goodness."[1] This is surely a reassurance and comfort to all Christians, whatever the problem to be faced.

It does not imply, however, that the work of our sanctification is the sole affair of God, who will accomplish the task without any struggle or effort on our part. St. Thérèse has told us some of her struggles, but has added that many pages of her story will never be read on earth. She is humble enough to relate simply and frankly the small irritations and inconveniences which tried her at times almost to the limit of her endurance, and the trifles which often enough she was unable to overcome. Only God knows how much she struggled and suffered, and yet at the end of her life she placed all merit not in this or that practice, but in a disposition of the heart. Because everything is a grace, the action of God's love must come first. He looks for our good will, and once He finds it He puts into our hands the means to achieve our desire. From the top of the ladder, she says, He looks down lovingly. Presently, touched by our fruitless efforts, He will come down and carry us in His arms to His kingdom. We must desire effectively and not merely "wish for" sanctity, and God will not fail to put into the incidents that make up our day the means necessary

[1] N.V. 3rd August.

to attain it. All we have to do is to be faithful to His graces, accept and use those He sends, and be ever alert and watchful not to miss the little opportunities so liberally provided. And if we have this essential disposition of the heart we shall not be unwary.

The "confidence to the point of audacity" which is a characteristic of spiritual childhood is based on a realization of the infinite love our heavenly father bears towards His ungrateful and unworthy children. We must "bear with our imperfections without even becoming discouraged", not merely enduring them as something we can do nothing about, or accepting them in a way that would be presumptuous, but striving always to rise above them, yet never becoming disheartened by our failures to do so. Abandonment and self-surrender are heavily underlined in this way of spirituality, which is a constant struggle against self-will in the smallest as in the greatest things. And if we desire to follow St. Thérèse along her little way, it must be in the spirit of children that we do so, making our lives one continuous offering to God's merciful love, through the ordinary duties and tasks that present themselves to our hands day by day. If we make the mistake of regarding these trivialities as hindrances to our spiritual lives, and looking forward to the day when, emancipated from them, we can begin to live for God alone, we shall never take even the first step along this road.

Such a disposition of the heart is another essential or fundamental feature of the little way, for spiritual childhood is not a phase of growth like natural childhood, beyond which we pass in time as we come to maturity. It is a way of life, and it is marked by two characteristics which at first sight seem to oppose each other. On the one hand, there is the heart's knowledge of its own natural weakness and insufficiency; on the other hand its audacious supernatural confidence in the goodness and willingness of God to support this infirmity. These characteristics are in fact complementary.

To be convinced of one's own natural weakness or inability is doubtless to possess valuable self-knowledge; but that is not what is meant in speaking of St. Thérèse's consciousness of her "littleness and nothingness". This is not an acknowledgement of a natural disadvantage which can be exploited, but a supernatural effect of faith on the natural understanding; something that is infused gratuitously, and which we cannot produce sincerely by our own efforts. It is no part of the mission of St. Thérèse to force souls whom our Lord is leading by other paths into the "way of nothingness"; rather it is her purpose to give the necessary reassurance to those who already find themselves in this predicament. Compared with earlier times this twentieth century is an age far more of mental or nervous misery than any other form of purely physical suffering. Surely the grim paradox of our era is the vast spiritual darkness which exists in the midst of unparalleled scientific enlightenment. That is why the particular psychology of St. Thérèse is so powerfully instrumental in bringing such sufferers to our Lord's feet. Those who scoff at her and her little way either have no spirit of faith wherewith to "see", or else have no conception as yet of what it is to lack self-sufficiency.

The two apparent opposites, then, which St. Thérèse reconciled so effectively in her life and which she offers us for imitation, are the conviction of her own weakness and littleness and inability to achieve the desired end unaided, and the persevering action that will compel God to intervene and come to the aid of His child. "We must do all that in us lies, give without counting, *steadily renounce self*; in a word, prove our love by every good deed in our power. But in truth, as that is little enough, it is above all necessary to put our confidence in Him who alone sanctifies our works, and acknowledge ourselves 'unprofitable servants', hoping that the good God in His mercy will give all that we desire."[1]

On the night of Christmas, 1886, Thérèse ceased to be a child in the strict sense of the word. She describes this night as the occasion of her "complete conversion" when the new-born saviour turned her darkness into a flood of light; sharing her human weakness, she said, He brought her the strength and courage she lacked, arming her so well that she never afterwards looked back. "Our Lord meant to show me that I ought

[1] *The Spirit of St. Thérèse*, p. 17.

to be getting rid of my childish defects." Her tears dried up at their source, and she received the grace once for all to put away the things of childhood.

"This right about turn," comments Père Lucien-Marie of St. Joseph, O.C.D., "could be explained as a passive purification, wherein St. John of the Cross declares that grace triumphs above all, even certain psychological instabilities until then impossible to overcome." Up till this time, Thérèse had been in the habit of weeping at the slightest provocation, then "crying for having cried". Her touchiness, as she said, was unbearable. Arguments were unavailing. Nothing would cure her of this unpleasant habit. The ability to rise above it on this one occasion after which she never slipped back, she considers to have been an extraordinary grace, a "miracle on a small scale".

Like everything else in her little way, Thérèse's discovery that "nothing is beyond my powers thanks to the strength God gives me" was reached only through trial and error, and experience of apparent failure. Far from being discouraged by her weakness, she deliberately and consistently used such seeming handicaps in developing her conscious dependence on the strength of God. Not until she had plumbed the depths of humiliation, realized to the full how little she could do when God took His hand away, was she able to visualize the possibilities of making of her very helplessness and failures a "lift". Only after she had lived out in practice her way of littleness was she able to perceive its value for countless others in the same predicament, and to glimpse the wide horizons her gradually dawning "mission" was to open up.

(v) The Letter and the Spirit

Many people blame St. Thérèse's style for their own failure to study her writings in a prayerful spirit. The autobiography they regard as "sugary-sweet", while the valuable book of her collected letters is beneath their notice entirely. A certain type of piety which has grown up around her cult has served to estrange them further. I do not attempt to make any apology for the many statues and pictures of her that adorn our shrines

and repositories, but would venture to suggest that they are
certainly no worse than many other examples of ecclesiastical
"art". As Paul Claudel wrote: "I have heard good souls working themselves up because at Lisieux St. Thérèse has been
dressed in white satin and coloured velvet-pile in imitation
of the Carmelite serge. But the idea was no doubt to show as
far as could be the transfiguration of our workaday integument.
We had not the morning light at our command, but we had
that velvet-pile and satin, which seem almost as wonderful
to unstaled souls. I am not defending the art of Lisieux, but
often there, as in other holy places, beneath the imbecility of
the execution, you unearth a poetic intention. At Lisieux it
is the Holy Face above the altar that dominates everything,
whereas St. Thérèse below effaces herself, and fades into the
roses of childhood which she is scattering with both hands . . .
All that infantry of St. Sulpice, all those soldiers of Christ,
whom their mothers made with flesh and blood, whom grace
re-made with fire and the Rue Bonaparte with butter, all those
St. Josephs in coconut and those standardized St. Thérèses—
how many simple pieties have they not charmed? How many
solitudes have they not consoled? How many repentances and
sacrifices have they not occasioned and witnessed? Of how
many graces the instrument?"[1]

Like M. Claudel, I am not defending this kind of "reposi-
tory-art". But however much one may deplore it as art, one
cannot entirely banish the feeling that the serenely-smiling
Thérèse scattering unnatural-looking roses conveys something
to the mass of her devotees that the presentation of the actual
and untouched photographs of a haggard-looking nun, marked
with the signs of illness and great suffering, do not. And after
all that is the sole reason for their existence. Churches and
shrines are not art galleries, although one feels the effect to be
happier when real devotion can be inspired by the type of
embellishment that is not a source of embarrassment. But that
is not the final criterion, and as J. B. Morton pointed out, it is
extremely doubtful whether anyone really prays more fer-
vently in Chartres Cathedral than in his own ugly little parish

[1] *Ways and Crossways*, pp. 163 (n. 1), 162.

church at home. It is true that works of art may help to raise our mind and heart to God, but equally they may hinder the human spirit from rising above its natural appreciation of such beauty.

Obviously St. Thérèse was not endowed with a very distinguished aesthetic sense; neither was the Curé of Ars nor Julie Billiart—nor, for that matter, many another saint. We have become accustomed in the past half-century to hearing that the autobiography of St. Thérèse as we knew it had been rewritten by Mother Agnes, and that if we saw the original it would be a different story altogether, and would reveal a vastly altered Thérèse. It has now, through the generosity of the Carmel of Lisieux, been given to us in the original, and it is the same story and the same style, which was that of Thérèse as much as of Pauline and of their class and era.

"O divine Word, you are the adored Eagle, I love you and you *draw* me to you," wrote Thérèse in a letter to her sister Marie, giving us possibly one of the most beautiful passages of spiritual lyricism written in modern times. Yet this paragraph was immediately preceded by that pathetic allegory "the story of the little bird", which was omitted from *The Story of a Soul* "through the need to preserve the balance of Chapter XIII"—which is as much as to say that it was altogether too infantile, too much out of tone with the real heights, spiritual and literary, to which Thérèse rose in the same composition. Some of her letters to Céline are childish in the extreme, both in style and metaphor, but in their content almost every one of them is astoundingly mature, confident and wise, as are the letters to her two missionary "brothers"—so much so that one needs to remind oneself now and then how very young she was at the time of their writing.

Thérèse was a child, and apparently an extremely childish one, up to the night of Christmas 1886, the occasion of her self-styled "conversion". Writing of it to Père Roulland ten years later, she recalls: "On that blest night, of which it is written that it *illumines God's own delights*, Jesus, who became a child for love of me, deigned to bring me forth from the swaddling-clothes and imperfections of infancy. He transformed me so utterly that I no longer recognized myself. But for this change, I should have had to remain many years longer in the world . . . St. Teresa would have been unwilling to acknowledge me as her child, if the Lord had not clad me in His divine strength, if He had not armed me for war."[1]

She was, without question, endowed with an intelligence beyond the average, and in relating the story of her infant years she said candidly that God had permitted her mind to develop early. There is abundant evidence in the letters written by her mother that Thérèse was exceptionally quick and bright as a baby. At school she outstripped classmates older than herself, thus incurring the jealousy and ill-will of some, which proved to be one of the greatest trials of her schooldays. Although she found difficulty in memorizing set passages from text books, she nevertheless had a retentive mind and a remarkable instinct for selecting the best and most substantial from what she read. This she stored away, later enriching her interior life by drawing upon it as required. For instance she knew the entire *Imitation* by heart (no mean feat), the New Testament she could quote from memory in nearly every instance, and even during her last illness she could accurately recite long passages from St. John of the Cross' writings.

Mother Agnes of Jesus has related in an unpublished reminiscence: "On 12th September, 1897, when she was in the infirmary, Sister Thérèse asked me to read the gospel of the Sunday (the fourteenth after Pentecost). I did not have the book and simply said to her: 'It is the gospel where our Lord teaches us that we cannot serve two masters.' Then she recited the lesson word for word."

I cannot understand how anyone can label Thérèse puerile; it is a complete misnomer. Allowing for all the diminutives, the childish expressions and flowery figures of speech which were current coin at the time, one has always the sense of being in the presence of a soul utterly absorbed and penetrated by God. How could such a one be puerile? And whatever one may feel about her literary style, it is an undeniable fact that her words are a source of profound spirituality which is best

[1] C.L. p. 259.

tapped by prayer and meditation upon them. Theologians never seem to tire of drawing out commentaries on some of her expressions, and they have proved over and over again that beneath her simple and seemingly commonplace words there lies a mine of inexhaustible doctrinal instruction, throwing a new and clearer light on many a familiar truth.

She drew most of her nourishment from holy scripture—that is, after her entry into Carmel. Here again is a significant fact, indicating her selectiveness. Most of her readers have taken it for granted, because of the profusion of her quotations and her apparent familiarity with the texts, that she was continually using for her spiritual reading the books of the Old Testament. But the Carmel of Lisieux have assured me that, far from this being the case, it is most unlikely that St. Thérèse ever had a bible in her hands.

"We had asked our Mother Agnes of Jesus," they say, "if during the time of St. Thérèse of the Child Jesus there was a copy of the complete bible made available for the sisters in the ante-choir. Neither she nor Sister Geneviève were able to confirm this, but they remembered perfectly that the young sisters (see Note 2) did not have permission to use the copies of the Old Testament which were in the community. St. Thérèse therefore never opened one. Nevertheless there is no doubt that instead of the Old Testament in its entirety she consulted various translations of the psalms, the prophets, perhaps other books, and the New Testament. A study of the quotations from the Old and New Testament used by the saint in her writings (as well as those found in *Novissima Verba*) has proved beyond doubt that she drew the divine word from different sources. The quotations from Psalms, for example, were taken for the most part from the *Christian Manual*. From the copybook manuscript of Sister Geneviève of the Holy Face she took several quotations from the Old Testament, especially *Whoever is a little one, let him come to me* (Prov. 9: 4). The verse in the Canticle of Canticles *Draw me! We will run after thee to the odour of thy ointments* (Cant. 1: 3) was taken from a translation which she found in the Explanation of the *Spiritual Canticle* of St. John of the Cross (Stanza XXV, Red

2). The expression *Sun of Justice* (Mal. 3 : 20—4.2 in English versions) used to describe our Lord she borrowed from the *Liturgical Year* by Dom Gueranger. These various examples suffice to illustrate the fact that St. Thérèse of the Child Jesus carefully garnered the divine word wherever she found it."

And we may add, like her heavenly mother, she "treasured all these things and reflected on them in her heart".

The copybook manuscript referred to above by the Carmel of Lisieux was a collection of biblical texts compiled by Céline while still living with the Guérins and contained passages from the following books (in the order in which they were transcribed): Canticle of Canticles, Ecclesiasticus, Wisdom, Proverbs, Isaias, Tobias, Ecclesiastes, Ezechiel, Osee, Habacuc, Sophonias, Malachias, Joel, Amos, Micheas and Zacharias. As well as these, she had the writings of St. John of the Cross—which are a rich mine of quotations from the Old Testament—and of course the Psalter, the translation of the breviary lessons and, as mentioned above, the *Liturgical Year* and *Christian Manual*. All these divergent sources and varying translations yielded differing interpretations of the texts, which fact sometimes troubled Thérèse. She told Céline that, had she been a priest, she would have studied Greek and Hebrew "so as to read the word of God as He deigned to utter it in human speech".

Thérèse certainly possessed a genius for selection. Always, with an unerring instinct, she went straight for what was best, and it is all the more remarkable that she was able to apply so appositely some of these obscure passages.

"The books of holy scripture and particularly the gospels became her delight," Sister Mary of the Trinity (Thérèse's favourite novice) declared. "Their hidden meaning became illumined and she was able to interpret them perfectly. In her conversations with me and in my instructions from her, quotations invariably arose from the divine books confirming what she said, and she knew them by heart."

And, asks Mother Agnes: "Instructed and fortified as she was by these divine teachings, how can one believe that St. Thérèse of the Child Jesus had a childish and affected piety, that infantile roguishness that is sometimes attributed to her?"

However, it was the New Testament that was her constant companion, and she carried a copy of the gospels on her person, next to her heart. With reference to this, the Carmel of Lisieux have said: "She was the first person to ask such a permission, which was granted. As we did not possess a small enough edition of the New Testament, the saint detached the four gospels from her *Christian Manual* and asked her sister Céline, who was still in the world, to bind them for her. This edition was rather too large to be carried constantly but it guided her in making a smaller one."

And anyone inclined to dismiss Thérèse as a "milk-sop" whose devotion was based on pious twaddle, should refer to *Novissima Verba* where is recorded the remark of a sister that angels would come at the moment of her death and accompany her to our Lord, when she would see them all resplendent with light and beauty. To this, Thérèse, somewhat wearied, replied: "Oh, none of these fancies can do me any good. I can only nourish myself upon the truth."

Such is the reaction of every soul whose mind is illumined by the Gift of Understanding.

(vi) The Testing of Ideals

Thérèse's brief life was a voyage of discovery, or rather of re-discovery; for the little way of spiritual childhood is as old as Christianity itself, yet new when compared with some of the complicated and discouraging methods of spirituality. She describes this way as one of trust and absolute self-surrender, which she regarded as her mission to teach to mankind. There are many ways to God, but this is a way particularly vital to the world at this period of its existence, a period so characterized by pride, self-reliance and selfishness. It is the antidote which goes to the very roots of these evils, and to give us this salutary lesson, God chose not one of the great names of the world, but a humble and self-effacing nun who could truly say that she had lived entirely as a child of God. She had proved her theory: that there is only one thing to be done on earth, to "throw Jesus the flowers of little sacrifices and win Him by caresses". That was what she had done, and she felt that she was called to demonstrate to others these "little means" which she had found so potent in the life of love.

Since the beginning of the nineteenth century, materialism has been gaining ground steadily. More and more, those who would claim fellowship with the intellectuals have placed their faith in science as the only truth, looking upon it as the dawn of reason after a long night of superstitious error and the one solution to all the problems besetting man. We today have lived to see the wavering of that faith, the growth of the doubt that perhaps after all science did not have the last word to say with regard to the world and its direction. In a letter to the Carmel of Lisieux on the occasion of the great Thérèsian Congress in September 1947, Pope Pius XII said: "The present world, led astray by so many causes, but particularly by the pride of scientific discoveries and exclusive preoccupation with mundane matters and their conflicting interests, is in dire need of this message of humility, simplicity and supernatural inspiration."

The contributions of science to our civilization are certainly not to be scoffed at, but they must be kept in their proper perspective. Some of the greatest scientists have been men with a vision, who saw their work as a God-given task of bringing the riches of nature into the service of mankind, of utilizing for our benefit and happiness and comfort the enormous power that lies dormant in nature. Moreover, the scientist who faces this task of forwarding the frontiers of knowledge with humility and integrity, remains true to himself and sincere in his relationship with God. As Pope Paul VI said, the Church "looks towards men of culture and learning, scientists, artists; whom she esteems and from whom she desires to receive the fruit of their experiences. She desires to strengthen their intellectual life, defend their liberty, provide a space where their troubled spirits can expand joyously within the luminous sphere of the divine word and divine grace." We cannot discover more about the material world, nor yet about the spiritual universe, than God so wills; and at the end of it all, our knowledge is no more than "the quantity of a hazel nut" held in the palm of the hand, as shown to Julian of Norwich five hundred years ago as *All that is made.* "I marvelled how it might last," she said, "for methought it might fall suddenly to naught for littleness. And I was answered: *It lasteth, and ever shall last, because God loves it,* and so hath everything its being through the love of God."

We are like children building sand castles on the beach, enamoured of our creative and inventive genius, yet helpless to stop the inrush of the waves which can sweep away in an instant the result of our labours. God who is infinitely patient with our limited powers of perception, and who sees all things in one simple gaze, bears with paternal indulgence our childish displays of pride in the secrets which we have only partially wrested from nature after centuries of endeavour. He who "swung the earth between its poles" has designed this world with infinite care and perfection, down to the meticulous marking of the tiniest creature, the intricate venation of the smallest leaf. He is not impressed by our achievements in splitting the atom or the conquest of space. We could not release energy unless it was potentially there to be released, and it is a far lesser achievement than bringing into being the lowest amoeba which is endowed with life.

There is a lesson for us in the spiritual life here. Whether our way lies among great or humble duties, we can bring our best endeavour to them, and the least action done for love is, in the sight of God, as noble a deed as an heroic one.

Thérèse's small though courageous acts of self-control and self-denial often appeared to others as nothing more than the fruit of natural virtue, the pliability of a gentle and loving disposition; yet that did not detract from their supernatural value in the sight of God. On the contrary, the very hiddenness of these acts from the observation of her companions increased their value a hundredfold. So often one reads remarks to the effect that "she was unnoticed in her own community, who regarded her merely as a perfect religious, nothing more". Now this is truly extraordinary. In the first place, it is extremely rare to be considered "a perfect religious" by one's own community—that implies at least tacit admission of great virtue.

And secondly, what more could one desire? To be a perfect religious is in itself to have attained heroic (i.e. canonizable) virtue. "In her mode of life and action," said Pope Benedict XV, himself a religious, "she fulfilled with alacrity, generosity and perseverance, her special vocation. *Now this is what constitutes precisely heroic virtue, and is the sure evidence of its existence.*" (My italics.) And one of his predecessors is said to have stated that were he shown "a perfect religious", one who had faithfully and consistently fulfilled every prescription of rule and daily observance, he would, without the further witness of miracles, be prepared to canonize him.

It was certainly not her community as a whole who knew Thérèse to be a perfect religious, or who even guessed at her hidden life of sacrifice and her great progress in perfection, but only those few who had intimate knowledge of her interior life: her immediate superiors, Mother Agnes of Jesus and Mother Mary Gonzaga, who were entitled to know the state of her soul; and the novices under her guidance, who were permitted to see something of the virtue of her into whose hands the formation of their own souls had been entrusted. For the rest, the posthumous revelation of her sanctity was an eye-opener to most of the sisters, however much they had loved and esteemed her. Two months before her death one remarked: "I do not see why anyone should speak of Sister Thérèse of the Child Jesus as a saint. She has practised virtue perhaps, but not a virtue acquired through suffering and humiliation. Her life has been tranquil, free of great sufferings." There is again the oft-quoted (and as oft-misquoted) anecdote of the lay sister who stated: "Sister Thérèse will not live much longer, and really I wonder what our Mother will find to say of her when she dies. She will be puzzled, for although the little sister is very good, she has certainly never done anything worth speaking about." Another lay sister brought to the infirmary a meat beverage which she thought her dying sister would find strengthening. Thérèse at that time was unable to take any food without nausea and signed that she could not accept the broth. The lay sister was indignant, and stated roundly that there was nothing saintly about Sister Thérèse who, in her opinion, was not even a good religious. "How happy it makes me," remarked Thérèse on hearing of this, "to know that at the hour of my death I am considered to be imperfect."

On another occasion she declared that her devotion to the Holy Face, and in fact all her piety, had been based on the text from Isaias: *There was no beauty nor comeliness in Him; His face was as it were hidden and despised whereupon we esteemed Him not.* "I also desire to be without glory or beauty, 'to tread the winepress alone' unrecognized by any creature." This is a flat contradiction to those who consider her predilection for such titles as "the Child Jesus" and "little Flower" evidence of a "rose-water-piety".

"Her devotion to the Child Jesus was very tender," Mother Agnes said of her, "but the Holy Face was her real devotion." Thérèse's passionate attachment was to the cross, and to Him who hung on it. In spirit she had taken her stand beneath it at the age of fourteen, and from that day onwards her one desire was to be crucified herself. Directed into supernatural channels, the hypersensitiveness which was such a burden to herself and to others during her adolescent years became the means by which she was able to understand and appreciate the co-redemptive value of suffering, for herself and for others. "Our Lord let me see clearly that if I wanted to win souls, I'd got to do it by bearing a cross; so the more suffering came my way, the more strongly did suffering attract me."[1] She thus succeeded once more in turning to great advantage what might have proved an exasperating fault.

She was a child of God and a daughter of the Church; and despite her preference for the metaphors of childhood (such as the well-known ninepins, kaleidoscope, etc.) she was a stern realist and not, as is often supposed, incurably sentimental in her devotions. Even the nursery jargon so often employed was not always used to express her own dispositions, but as advice and assistance to some of the novices, couched in language and images readily intelligible and appealing to them. Sister Mary of the Trinity (the recipient of the "ninepins" letter, which has evoked much criticism because of its extreme, and

[1] A.S. pp. 184-5.

apparently deliberate childishness of expression) has said: "As I was rather childish in my ways, the Holy Child, in order to encourage me in the practice of virtue, inspired me with the idea of playing with Him, and *I chose the game of ninepins.*" (Italics mine.)

Sister Mary of the Trinity is almost as well known to the readers of Thérèse's memoirs and the *Counsels and Souvenirs* compiled after her death, as is Céline. She had a lively disposition, and while impetuous and eager to please others, was very immature and given to easy tears and dejection over her many shortcomings. Thérèse, by adapting her language to the needs of this novice, succeeded in laying the foundations of the most solid religious virtues. Later the sister, whose acceptance had been touch and go, was to become one of the leading exponents (next in importance only to Mother Agnes and Sister Geneviève) of the spirituality of St. Thérèse. Formed in the religious life from the commencement of her postulancy (16th June, 1894) by Thérèse, who initiated her into the way of spiritual childhood, she was one of the most telling witnesses at the process of beatification for her former novice mistress. It became her task until her own death, to aid the prioress and Thérèse's sisters in the publication of her writings. It is well to disentangle genuine spiritual childhood as envisaged and lived by St. Thérèse from any adaptations which, in her wisdom, she saw necessary to make for some of her companions still less advanced than herself in the practice of virtue. As a school teacher of my acquaintance was wont to say: "The doctor who prescribes a medicine which he knows his patient will not take is an ass."

To encourage another novice entrusted to her care, the lay sister Marthe of Jesus, Thérèse began counting her acts of virtue on a chaplet as she had done when a very small child. "I am even obliged to have a rosary of practices," she wrote to Céline. "I made it through charity for one of my companions. I shall tell you about it in detail, it is quite amusing . . . I am caught in nets *which please me not at all*, but which are very useful to me in the state of soul in which I am."[1]

---

[1] C.L. p. 171. (Italics mine.)

The disciple of St. Thérése must enter on the way of the cross; for the cross, as she told Abbé Bellière, had accompanied her from her cradle, and she had never desired anything else; rather she had come to love and to value it above every other gift. If she chose to disguise the harsh outlines with rose-petals, that was merely her characteristic manner of accepting it, concealing her suffering from the eyes of others and giving it back to God enhanced by her "flowers of little sacrifices".

Cross-bearing is one of her most important and valuable lessons, the one that is the hardest to learn and the point on which she is most often misunderstood and misinterpreted. This is hardly surprising, since few of us have taken in our Lord's teaching and example on this painful necessity. Thérèse will not succeed where Christ Himself does not succeed, and those who despise and misunderstand her teaching will equally fail to understand the spirit of the gospels. "A disciple is no better than his master."

(vii) The Active Life of a Contemplative

Where does the eternal mission of St. Thérèse lie? Is there such a thing?

She herself firmly believed in it, and defined it as making souls love God as she loved Him, and teaching them her little way—in other words, leading souls to God through the "little means" that had provided such a perfect method for her own wayfaring steps. She stated this quite clearly about six weeks before her death, at the same time predicting her further vocation of spending eternity in doing good upon earth; and such "good works" consist of the execution of the programme that she visualized as her "mission".

Like most of Thérèse's utterances, this appears transparently simple. Her mission, however, is extremely complex, all the more so because of a tendency to reduce it to one or another facet of her "doctrine", or to confuse it with her patronage of the mission-fields of the world.

In order to evaluate the mission of Thérèse and its significance in the Church, it is essential that her life and writings be considered as a whole. Here I have only provided indications from the written sources, in the hope that readers will examine them more fully in their context and setting. When certain incidents are isolated, particular devotions lopped off (either because they appeal or because they do the very reverse), one does not see the picture in focus as Thérèse viewed it. It is quite certain that many well-meaning Catholics—and religious are not lacking from their ranks—have embarked on a "little way" that would neither be recognized nor acknowledged by its foundress, either in fundamental principles or external expression of them. Convinced that they are enrolled under the Thérèsian banner, that they are practising evangelical childhood according to her teaching and example, and so are well on the way to perfection, they are, in fact, cluttering up their lives with valueless practices, reproducing selected traits copied from Thérèse to veneer over the lack of solid foundations; and the result is a mere caricature which has done more than anything else to draw derision on "the roses of Lisieux". All there is to it is to become a little child again. This sounds simple enough, and in practice it should create no difficulty for anyone, although in actual fact it has produced a plethora of distorted and truncated forms of spirituality which have become all too familiar in the past half century, every one of which is laid at Thérèse's door. It is these pious deformities that have largely hindered the action of St. Thérèse and prevented her from fulfilling her mission in such souls. For spiritual childhood is indeed simple, but with the simplicity that belongs to unity and perfection, "the simplicity which wisdom brings", as Pope Pius XII expressed it. It is concerned with the noblest and certainly the most mysterious relationship that can exist in our lives—that of the soul with God. Thérèse never had any illusions about this, and in defining her mission of teaching souls her way to God, she had no intention of reducing everything in the spiritual life to its least common denominator, as some of her self-styled followers have done. Simple faith is faith that has been simplified by the operation of the Holy Spirit; a supernatural effect won through prayer. It is very far removed from the sentimental ignorance and mock humility with which it is often equated.

St. Thérèse during her last days on earth knew with ever-increasing certainty that her mission was to begin after her death—her mission of love. In his homily at her canonization, Pope Pius XI expressed his most ardent desire that "all the faithful should study her in order to copy her", and continued: "She taught the way of spiritual childhood by word and example to the novices in her monastery. She set it forth clearly in her writings which have gone to the end of the world . . . We nurse the hope today of seeing springing up in the souls of the faithful of Christ a burning desire of leading a life of spiritual childhood."

Thérèse never forgot the lesson she had learned during her journey to Rome, when she moved among a wider circle of acquaintances than ever before. Up till this time, she says, she had not understood the need to pray for priests, and the realization was forced upon her that, despite their high status, even "good holy priests" are still human beings, and like other men not without their frailties and weaknesses.

"Oh, for priests, priests who are on fire!" St. Thérèse who had no liking for long, formal prayers, composed and recited this one daily, and of her Pope Benedict XV has said: "She has been given a mission to teach priests to love Jesus Christ."

"It is *always* the same thing I have to say to you: let us pray for priests." St. Thérèse returned time after time to this theme in her manuscript and in most of her letters to Céline. The apostolate of prayer seemed to her even higher than the apostolate of preaching. "Our mission is to form those gospel labourers. They will save millions of souls whose mothers we shall be."

This gradual realization of her universal mission seems to have first dawned upon her mind when she was writing the last pages of her autobiography for Mother Mary Gonzaga, some time between 3rd June and 2nd July, 1897. She had appropriated to herself the words of our Lord's discourse at the Last Supper (Jn. 17: 4–24), and then she added: "Those are the words I would like to repeat after you, dear Lord, before I take refuge in your arms. Am I being rash? I don't

think so; you've allowed me to take liberties with you this long
time past. You've said to me what the father said to the prodigal son in the parable: 'Everything that I have is already
thine', and as these are your words, dear Jesus, they belong to
me. So I'm at liberty to use them, in the hope of bringing down
on the souls that are linked with mine whatever blessings our
heavenly father has to give . . . dear Jesus, I can have no certainty about this, but I don't see how you could squander more
love on a human soul than you have on mine! That's why I
venture to ask that these souls you've entrusted to me may
experience your love as I have. One day, maybe, in heaven, I
shall find out that you love them better than me, and I shall
be glad of that, glad to think that these people earned your love
better than I ever did. But here on earth, I just don't find it
possible to imagine a greater wealth of love than the love
you've squandered on me without my doing anything to earn
it."[1]

This spiritual audacity on the part of Thérèse has been
criticised severely by certain commentators (so far removed is
their interior awareness from hers), but she herself anticipates
the objection, and adds the following disarming afterthought:
"Dear Mother, it is time I came back to you. I can't think how
I came to write what I've written above; I never meant to, but
there it is, so it had better stay there."

Another point is this: at the moment of writing these pages,
Thérèse apparently had in mind only her sisters and her two
missionary "brothers", those with whom she was immediately
and intimately connected upon earth. As she wrote, however,
it seems that a deeper realization of the import of our Lord's
parting words to His disciples dawned on her; she saw Him
giving them the promise of His abiding presence with them,
His assurance that He would send the Holy Spirit to strengthen
and comfort them; she understood the connection between
His departure and the beginning of His mission, since this
last depended for its realization on the pentecostal power of the
Holy Spirit. It is probable, then, that Thérèse was granted
some intuition of her own future mission whilst meditating on

[1] A.S. pp. 308, 309.

these words, and recognized the expediency of her own approaching death. It is unlikely, however, that she realized the full impact of what the Holy Spirit was guiding her to write, since the full grace of transformation according to the Gift of Understanding was not granted to her until three or four months later. Thérèse was neither the author nor the finisher of the mission entrusted to her from above; rather was she an instrument used by God for the fulfilment of His eternal redemptive plans. According as His will became clear to her mind, so did she receive and co-operate with these fragments of divine enlightenment, but not until the end was she given to see the full beauty of the design. During the last months of her life, then, we can observe how the thought of teaching, strengthening and comforting the souls entrusted to her continued to grow and take shape. Her verbal references to it reveal an ever deepening confidence and relative certainty, and when told by one of the sisters that she would look down upon them from heaven, she asserted emphatically: "I shall not look down, I shall come down!"

"When a gardener takes a great deal of trouble with some fruit he wants to ripen before its time, he doesn't mean to leave it hanging on the tree; it must be served up at a banquet. And it was on the same principle that our Lord lavished His graces on such a tender plant as I was."[1] Thérèse here acknowledges that her development has been precocious, and admits that she knows well the real cause for it, as she recognizes the spiritual treasure which placed her from the beginning above the learned of this world. The knowledge she possessed, she knew, surpassed all human wisdom or acquired science, and she felt certain that she was required to pass it on.

"Without the world-wide circulation of *The Story of a Soul*," said Pope Benedict XV, "it would not have been possible for the mission of Sister Thérèse to have been fulfilled."

As the "world-wide circulation" of Thérèse's writings has been the subject of some of the bitterest criticisms levelled at

[1] A.S. p. 136.

the saint herself and the Lisieux Carmel, before going on to speak of her doctrine of "littleness", it may be as well to examine briefly some of the more damaging charges that have been made.

CHAPTER THREE

THE OTHER FACE

*"We have behaved . . . with singleheartedness and sincerity
in God's sight, not using human wisdom, but the light of God's
grace. And we mean by our letters nothing else than what you
read in them, and understand us to mean. I hope that you will
come to understand us better."*

(II Cor. 1 : 12–13)

(i) Mon historien

It is the fashion nowadays to accuse Mother Agnes of Jesus
of all manner of deceptions, from re-touching the photographs
of her sister and re-writing the autobiography with ulterior
motives, even to engineering the whole process of canonization.
It seems to be taken for granted in many quarters that in distributing *L'Histoire d'une Ame* in 1898, the Carmelites of
Lisieux were launching an elaborately planned campaign to
promote Thérèse's beatification. This is not so. When two
thousand copies of the printed "circular" were ordered, most
of the nuns were highly critical, wondering how on earth they
were ever to dispose of them. One is tempted to ask whether
it is believed that Mother Agnes' organizing ability was so
efficient that she "arranged for" the avalanche of miracles as
well.

Ida Görres in *The Hidden Face* puts forward the quite unbelievable picture of a "vast propaganda apparatus" with
Mother Agnes and her assistants employing to the full all the
machinery of publicity and advertising media with the calcu-
lated intention of projecting the image as concocted by them
upon the world, and thus foisting off on the Church and the
faithful a composite "saint" of their own construction.

What did this "vast propaganda apparatus" consist of: high-
pressure advertising, advance publicity, flooding of bookstalls

with their publications, requests for favourable notices and reviews by magazines? No; merely the distribution of a few hundred copies of a young nun's memoirs to the cloistered convents of her own Order. The subsequent demands from the world for copies were in no way promoted or even anticipated at Lisieux.

In his book *Two Portraits of St. Thérèse*, Father Robo makes much of the matter of the difference between the so-called "authentic photographs" and those issued by the Carmel of Lisieux as being the more true likenesses, and he appears to have arrived at a hypothesis that, as they touched up the photographs so that they are no longer true likenesses, they must also have tampered with the manuscript, with similar results.

For many years there have been assurances that if ever we saw the autobiography as it came from Thérèse's pen it would be a vastly different Thérèse whom we should meet—a "sturdy oak" rather than a "little flower", despite the fact that this latter title was self-chosen. We have now the actual photostat reproductions of the original manuscript, with which we can easily compare *L'Histoire d'une Ame* as published by Mother Agnes, and thus see for ourselves to what extent her alterations could be regarded as forgeries. It is interesting to remember that the title "Autobiography" was the sub-title given by the late Monsignor (then Canon) Taylor to his English translation of *L'Histoire d'une Ame*, and that is the title by which the book is referred to most generally in this country. Monsignor Knox entitled his translation of the original manuscript *The Autobiography of a Saint*. The edition by Mother Agnes was (and in France still is) published under the title *The Story of a Soul*. Mother Agnes never at any time claimed to have presented Thérèse's words verbatim. Her volume was an uncritical biography. Undoubtedly she did entirely re-write the manuscript—there have been seven thousand alterations noted—but there is absolutely no ground for a charge of dishonesty, and her authority for any alterations or omissions, however sweeping, came from Thérèse herself, who referred to her sister as "my biographer".

"My little Mother," she said, "it will be well for you to revise all I have written. If you find it necessary to retrench some things, or to add something I have said *viva voce*, it will be the same as if I had done it myself. Remember that afterwards, and do not have any scruple in this matter."[1]

The very next entry in *Novissima Verba* is a record of an addition which Thérèse suggested might be inserted in the manuscript by Mother Agnes. She recalled that in her memoir she had said almost nothing on the subject of God's justice, but that she had expressed her thoughts about it in a letter written to Père Roulland two months earlier, on 9th May, 1897, and that Mother Agnes could, if she wished, incorporate the contents of this letter into the manuscript. Thérèse made no request. "Do so," she said, "*if you like.*" She could hardly have shown more clearly how complete was the authority she delegated to her "biographer".

Again on 11th July she specifically requested Mother Agnes to include the story related in the *Lives of the Desert Fathers* of the converted sinner who died of love, and which is now the last paragraph of Chapter XI entitled "The Apostle of Prayer". As he worked from the manuscript in which it does not appear, Mgr. Knox's book does not contain this.

However, it would seem that these additions made by Mother Agnes are not objected to so much as are her sweeping deletions.

Reviewing the translation by Mgr. Knox of the manuscript of St. Thérèse in *Doctrine and Life*, Mgr. Vernon Johnson wrote: "Mother Agnes has been severely criticised for cutting out as much as she did, and for introducing her personality so much into the changes that, at St. Thérèse's request, she made. Seven thousand changes sounds grave indeed; it is good propaganda, but gives a completely wrong impression. Of the thirty-five pages of cuts given in the introduction to the French edition, twenty-two pages come from the first manuscript, which deals almost entirely with her childhood and girlhood's days, and was written solely for her own sisters: its details would have held no interest for the general public." And it

[1] N.V. 16th July.

does seem, on checking through the omissions, that humility and modesty directed the suppression of some of the passages which were addressed to herself by Thérèse, who wrote quite as spontaneously and freely of persons and intimate family details as she would have done in a letter or conversation.

"Further," Mgr. Johnson continues, "it seems somewhat unreasonable to apply, as some have recently done, the standards of modern scientific criticism to an enclosed religious conditioned by the age in which she lived fifty years ago. We owe a great debt of gratitude to Mother Agnes; if it had not been for her tact and extraordinary courage, the manuscript might easily have been destroyed . . . But for Mother Agnes, the modern critics might have had no manuscript to criticise at all."

"It would certainly have been impossible to publish Thérèse's manuscript word for word at the time," says Père François, who edited the fascimile edition *Manuscrits Autobiographiques de Sainte Thérèse de l'Enfant Jesus.* "Nobody who has looked at the fascimiles can doubt this. In a period when so much importance was attached to perfect correctness of style and scrupulous respect for literary conventions, to publish the rough notes of a young and unknown nun would have meant making oneself ridiculous as well as betraying the author."[1]

This was the considered judgment given by Dom Godefroid Madelaine, to whom Mother Mary Gonzaga submitted a copy of the manuscript when its publication was first considered, asking for his advice on the matter. "For you," he said, "everything here is precious, but for the public, there are details so intimate, so much above the ordinary level, that I think it would be preferable to withhold them from print." It was Dom Godefroid who approached the Bishop for permission to publish the manuscript, and who suggested the singularly appropriate title *L'Histoire d'une Ame.*

There is no doubt that many of the erasures made on the manuscript were the work of Thérèse herself, and Mother

[1] A.S. p. 25.

Agnes certainly used with utmost liberality the authority
Thérèse had given her to alter or amplify the text. But it seems
equally certain that every one of her emendations was made
for the sole purpose of making the rather disjointed notes
read more smoothly, to tidy up some of the loose and ungram-
matical expressions, and never merely to superimpose her own
personality and style upon that of her sister. There is, in fact,
no essential difference between the manuscript as written by
Thérèse and *The Story of a Soul* as edited by Mother Agnes.
At the time of the original publication, of course, all the names
of nuns then living in the community were suppressed, but
these were later restored.

As Mgr. Johnson points out in the review referred to above,
there are deletions from the latter parts of the manuscript
totalling the equivalent of thirteen pages. This includes "the
story of the little bird" from the manuscript addressed to Sister
Mary of the Sacred Heart which has been commented on in
the previous chapter (p. 61), and the suppressed passages were
published with the collected letters of St. Thérèse as long ago
as 1949; further it includes the large amount of space devoted
by Thérèse to apologies for her disconnected thoughts, the
numerous interruptions causing such lack of continuity, and
her poor literary style. Considering the editorial freedom
given to Mother Agnes by Thérèse herself, no one reasonably
could complain at this treatment, particularly as Mother
Agnes had no professional knowledge or guidance as to the
canons of editorship, nor could she have foreseen that within
a quarter of a century her work would be scrutinized with
searchlights and microscopes by professional theologians and
students.

There are only very few sentences, owing to the destruction
of the paper, where the experts who worked on the original
pages penned by St. Thérèse have been unable to reconstitute
the actual words she wrote; and that this should be done was
the express wish of the Lisieux Carmel. But it is quite certain
that none of the alterations made by Mother Agnes have in any
way hindered souls from contacting the real Thérèse or of
grasping her message. Mother Agnes knew and understood

it too well to have adulterated it in any way. "The more I read of the original manuscript," wrote Mgr. Ronald Knox, "the more I feel you are right about there being NO essential difference between the old *Recit d'une Ame* and the new . . . I think that nearly all of Sœur Agnes' editing was designed to make things read more effortlessly and more continuously: the critics have found a mare's nest."[1]

The Story of a Soul and its English translation the "Auto-biography" carry a real grace, and had there been any intentional deceit or fraud in the editing, the work would not have been blessed so abundantly. On 18th June, 1956, the late Cardinal Piazza, then Secretary of the Congregation of Rites, wrote to the prioress of the Lisieux Carmel: "I am convinced that Mother Agnes was guided not merely by the directives authorized by the Sacred Congregation of Rites, but also by a clear inspiration from on high. If she had made a mistake there could not have been so many conversions brought about by the publication of *L'Histoire d'une Ame*. And this is the seal of God, always so wonderful in His providential designs. St. Thérèse and Mother Agnes of Jesus are so linked in the providential course of events and in the spirit of the Catholic world that no shadow and no attack by evil tongue can separate them."

"One passage (of the manuscript) concerning the saint's childhood has been tampered with. It is a quotation from a letter of Mme. Martin's in which, in Thérèse's own words, her faults 'shine forth with great clarity'. It describes the young Thérèse as a 'nervy child' (*une enfant bien nerveuse*), and it is immediately followed by the passage in which we have 'the poor little angel sitting quietly for two or three hours' during Céline's lessons. This passage concerning Thérèse's childhood bouts of nerves was toned down considerably. This is the only example of significant interference with the manuscript. It is unfortunate, yet strangely this very passage serves as a guarantee of Mother Agnes' good faith and accuracy in the matter of her sister's canonization. For the experts have succeeded in

---

[1] Letter to Mgr. Vernon Johnson, quoted in his review of *Autobiography of a Saint*: (*Doctrine and Life*, Dominican Publications, Dublin).

restoring the original of this passage, and the result agrees exactly with the text in the copies made by her from the manuscript for the ecclesiastical tribunal concerned with the canonization process.

"Did Mother Agnes give us a false portrait of Thérèse, making her out to be better than she was, more the conventional 'good, holy nun'? The answer is definitely 'No'. Those who really know the Thérèse of *The Story of a Soul* will not find the Thérèse of the manuscripts the least bit strange or new. The manuscript brings the saint nearer to us, but it is the same wonderful person that half the world has long known and loved. There is the same love of Jesus and Mary, the same childlike confidence in the good God, the same purity and delicacy and tenderness of affection, the same finesse and clarity of intelligence. There is the same strength, too, showing itself especially in that final heroism of racked body and darkened soul. In a word, it is the same personality as that presented by Mother Agnes in *The Story of a Soul*. Certain facets stand out more clearly, especially a keen wit and gentle irony, but it is the same personality.

"So far was Mother Agnes from presenting *another* doctrine that she was the first to recognize that the manuscript is a real treasure house and that her book by no means opened up every part of it. 'It all fits together', she wrote to Mgr. Tiel, 'and sometimes the smallest detail expresses a most profound reflection'."[1]

When the beatification process was in course, the original text was restored and submitted to Rome, and both it and the published version were then, and later during the canonization process, subjected to searching scrutiny, after which the Sacred Congregation not only declared itself satisfied with the results of its investigations, but gave high praise to Mother Agnes for what she had done, and counselled her not to change anything. As a result of this, even after the canonization the published version continued to be that edited by Mother Agnes. However, quite recently, to satisfy the requests of many for the original writings of St. Thérèse, facsimile copies of her

[1] Fr. Noel Dermot, O.C.D., *Spiritual Life*, March 1959.

manuscripts were prepared with great care and published.

The fact that the photostat copies were not made available until after the death of Mother Agnes does not, as has been thought, indicate any unwillingness on her part to publish them. In 1947 when one of the definitors general of the Order advised her to act on the permission of her Bishop to publish the original text, Mother Agnes was eighty-six years of age and ill, and she felt quite incapable of undertaking such a task. It was Rome that decreed that the project should be postponed, and out of consideration for her, suspended the publication during her lifetime. Mother Agnes died on 18th July, 1951, two months before her ninetieth birthday, and in September, 1952, the ban on publication was lifted. The Carmel of Lisieux then placed in the capable hands of Père François de Ste. Marie, O.C.D., the responsibility for producing the facsimile of the original manuscript.

The Autobiography is an appeal for love, it stirs in the souls of its readers the desire to love. A statement of the Congregation of Rites in 1921 says: "This reading moves the hearts of men, inclines their wills, amends their lives, kindles charity and produces other salutary results which absolutely transcend human power, and can find no adequate explanation except in the action of divine grace itself." Commentaries and exegeses by the score will doubtless continue to be written, but "in the opinion of competent authorities, the autobiography is and will continue to be Sœur Thérèse's chief means of influence. The book really possesses a mysterious grace which no other biography or study of the saint will ever have."[1]

As an appendix to *The Story of a Soul*, a collection of excerpts from Thérèse's letters was given. There were fifty-two letters, grouped together according to subject matter and they were, strictly speaking, an anthology of selected passages from the actual letters written by Thérèse. The mass of correspondence was merely drawn on for phrases expressing her ideas or instructions, and there was no intention of producing a critical edition of the letters of St. Thérèse. However, in

[1] H. Petitot, O.P., *St. Teresa of Liseux: A Spiritual Renascence*, p. xx.

1947, the complete letters (numbering in all 247) were collected, arranged in chronological order, and edited by the
Abbé André Combes, in a copiously annotated volume, which
was translated by F. J. Sheed and published in Great Britain
in 1949.

I have never heard of any suggestion that the letters in this
collection had been in any way "doctored", and yet some of
those who are most critical about the alterations to the autobiography do not even mention this extremely valuable
volume. It is an exhaustive and comprehensive collection of
almost everything Thérèse ever committed to paper in her
life; everything, that is, which has been preserved. And that is
much, for at that period it would appear that the mania for
cherishing old letters and notes was at its peak. From this
volume is missing one letter, the loss of which Thérèse herself
regretted. It was to her former spiritual director, Père Almire
Pichon, S.J., who, either because he travelled considerably, or
because on transferring to the new world he had shed the
European habit of hoarding, kept none of the letters which
Thérèse wrote from time to time. This last letter, written from
the infirmary, was long, and told of all that God had done for
her, all her thoughts on His love and mercy, her hopes and her
desire of spending eternity doing good upon earth. When
Thérèse heard that the letter had been despatched without a copy having been taken, she said: "My whole soul was
in it"; and she would like to have left it to her sisters as a
spiritual testament.

The Collected Letters of St. Thérèse begins with a "letter"
of one line written—with the assistance of the six-year-old
Céline—to her sister Marie when Thérèse was three years of
age, and includes even notes and scraps scribbled hurriedly
on cards for her sisters, up till the final entry three weeks before her death: an inscription on the back of a picture of Our
Lady of Victories, which is a superb cry of love. "Mary, if I
were the Queen of Heaven and you were Thérèse, I should
want to be Thérèse that you might be the Queen of Heaven."

This book is precious indeed to the student of St. Thérèse's
spirituality, not by any means because of its literary merits—

of which in fact it has few—but for the picture it gives us of the saint in the making. The points of view, the emotions recorded here, were the instinctive reactions of the moment, not a carefully thought out treatise on a virtue. It is particularly enlightening to find how often they are faithfully echoed by the maturer, considered judgment given in the autobiography where, as it were, we see the finished product. By the time Thérèse commenced writing the first pages, she was firmly established in her little way along which she was rapidly running to full sanctity. From this stage, she looks back on her life and sees the merciful love of God which has surrounded her from her earliest years, and in this radiant light tells us her story. But in the volume of letters, penned at the time when the waters of tribulation were lapping well up around her, swamping her at times, we see her in the midst of her struggles, battling with the trials of daily life, sometimes unable to rise above them but always steadily progressing along the course she had set for herself and from which she never deviated. The letters, when read in conjunction with her memoirs, give us a living image of her soul, far more precious and important than any portrait of the "envelope", and we are enabled to watch her daily growth in holiness, the development of the little way by which she sped to sanctity and along which she beckons us to follow her.

(ii) *Improving the Image*

What now can one say of the portraits of St. Thérèse, concerning which there has been so long and heated a controversy? The Carmel of Lisieux has been criticised severely, and not always justly, for what is commonly termed "beauty-parlour-treatment" of the saint, under which her features have become the insipid and characterless portrayals with which we are all too familiar.

It is improbable that anyone has ever been deceived in this matter, for it has always been common knowledge that the photographs had been touched up. Referring to the portrait of St. Thérèse that figures as the frontispiece to the English version of *The Story of a Soul*, Père Petitot says that impartial and sound judges who knew Thérèse personally "do not scruple to say that it is a far better likeness than all the other photographs said to be more exact. Everyone knows that photographs can never convey the expression of some very mobile and sensitive faces."

This is a matter on which almost everybody can put forward a different opinion. There is obviously some justification in the claim, however, when one remembers that the rather primitive photographic equipment of seventy years ago necessitated time exposures of some ten seconds, and that even in this short interval facial expression can change considerably, especially under the self-consciousness of "holding a pose".

The portrait in question is perhaps the most frequently reproduced of all the pictures of Thérèse. It was painted by Céline in an oval, with the corners blocked in and Thérèse's promise lettered around the outer edge: *Je veux passer mon ciel à faire du bien sur la terre.* The Carmel of Lisieux called this a "synthesis", claiming in it to combine the best and truest features of many photographs. But such an undertaking is doomed to failure at the outset, and the result is the rather wooden and expressionless face we all know so well. Contemporaries of St. Thérèse all appear to have considered her most attractive feature to be her eyes; in them lay depth of expression, they mirrored her love, her humour and her understanding, while at times their candid and penetrating gaze could be a source of discomfiture. The famous synthesis gives not the least indication of this expressiveness. I have never had the slightest suspicion that there was (as has often been hinted) any attempt to foist something on the public, or that the photographs were touched up merely in an attempt to make Thérèse look more attractive than she actually was. Had that been the object in view, it has failed miserably, and the result is, on the whole, to make her look less attractive, because inanimate. But in fact the retouched photographs and Céline's idealized paintings were only released in 1906. In the earliest editions of *The Story of a Soul*, the illustrations used were actual photographs, untouched apart from the fact that the figure of St. Thérèse had in many cases been "lifted" from a group of nuns; but no alterations to features or "expression" had been attempted.

At the time of the first publication of her manuscript, it was judged that certain portions should be suppressed, being considered unsuitable for the public of the time; and it is very probable that the same could legitimately have been claimed for those later photographs where she does look so desperately ill and, as her sisters well knew, totally unlike the Thérèse of *Les Buissonnets*. Those who are over-critical of the Lisieux Carmel in this matter would find, if they looked objectively at both sides of the question, that their criticism tends to rebound on themselves. Today we are apt to be scornful of those who fail to "move ahead with the times". But they are culpable on the same score who refuse to admit that when treating of an earlier generation one must "move back" to its time and tastes. A simple experiment proves this point. Take a random selection of the photographs of St. Thérèse, authentic and untouched; place beside them a similar selection of Céline's well-known portraits: "Thérèse with her Father"; "Thérèse and Céline"; "Thérèse on her First Communion Day", etc. It is most probable that the former group will appeal much more than the rather—to our eyes—unreal portrayals of the starry-eyed teenager with her carelessly-careful ringlets. But it does not need more than a second glance to realize why these made such an appeal in the first decades of this century. They were the approved and accredited style of portraiture, as every magazine and illustrated story of that period amply testifies. The public then were given what they wanted and what appealed to them. Today the same thing is being done by the publication of the original photographs and manuscript.

Céline's artistic talent was not great. She was a gifted amateur, and was fully aware of her own limitations. "I have painted this crucifixion with much love," she confided to Léonie. "However it is unquestionable that there are faults of anatomy which an expert would consider unskilful. Still, that is not important, for it will not hinder God's grace. Pray that the picture may accomplish much good."

It was to a large extent with this attitude that Céline painted the portraits of Thérèse, in an attempt to "incarnate" the spirit of the sister she knew so intimately. Her work was an interpretation, and many others who also knew the saint well did not concur with Céline's view. Surprisingly, however, most not only agreed, but were enthusiastic in their praises, claiming that to look at these portraits was almost to see Thérèse standing before one in the flesh.

There is no reason for us to claim that the untouched photographs are necessarily better likenesses than the so-called "synthesis" of all the photographs painted by Céline. Some people—and it seems that Thérèse was of their number— make poor subjects for the camera, and never appear on a photographic plate as they do in the flesh. Merely to turn a camera in their direction is a signal for them to stiffen, so that their faces assume a woodenness and their general expression becomes glassy-eyed, in every way unlike their normal appearance. Actually there is no reason why the originals should necessarily be "true" likenesses at all, and in any case, is there ever a studio photograph that is not touched-up? Missing teeth are carefully filled in, an untidy wisp of hair blotted out, and even surplus flesh is skilfully obliterated. Can the result be termed a true likeness? Many people firmly believe it to be so.

"She is so popular because she is so pretty," Abbot Chapman once said of Thérèse. It would seem that more nonsense has been talked about her physical beauty than almost anything else. Whatever Thérèse Martin was, she was not pretty in the generally accepted sense of that word. She had charm and personality, and was no doubt extremely attractive. Her features were strong, not pretty, and at the age of fifteen (see Note 3) hers was the face of one who had made up her mind about the direction her life was to take; and it was not to be that of a gentle piece of thistledown waiting to be wafted in any direction by the first breeze that chanced by. Her strong and rather large chin, the firm straight line of a wide mouth, the round face which a Carmelite coif does not flatter in the least, were all too indicative of character and determination to be merely pretty. Apparently she was a winsome child, with a round, soft

face, big blue eyes and long golden hair, which was daily
curled by Marie in order to please their father. Some of the
photographs taken when her illness was well advanced were
so obviously those of an extremely sick and feeble young
woman that one feels their touching-up was justifiable—up
to the point of removing the puffiness around her eyes, and
other signs of illness and exhaustion. To have published them
as they were would certainly not have given a true portrait
of the saint, and those who are most severe about this so-called
deception seem to take the view that the most unflattering
picture must necessarily be the most true likeness—something
which many people hope to the contrary when looking at their
passport photographs! For myself, I have been grateful and
interested to see the originals of the photographs, but they
have given me nothing of the essential Thérèse that I had not
already taken from her autobiography. (See Note 4.)

Céline also employed her talents on the negatives once it
had been decided to retouch them, and under her hand,
Thérèse's face became a smooth and vacuous oval. As Mother
Agnes had done with the manuscript, Céline worked on the
actual plates. But, as also in the case of the manuscript, the
restoration has been thorough. Modern research and chemical
treatment have restored them all to their authentic form, so
that we can now see the photographs as they actually looked
at the time they were taken.

There are in all forty-seven photographs of St. Thérèse,
forty-five taken during her lifetime and two of her body after
death before burial. All the originals have now been published
(see Note 5) but it is doubtful if these will increase or subtract
from the existing devotion to the "little Flower". The message
of the saints is so very much more important than mere outward appearance. St. Teresa of Avila, on seeing her portrait
painted by the Carmelite friar Juan de la Miseria, is said to
have exclaimed: "May God forgive you, Fray Juan, for paint-
ing me so blear-eyed and ugly!" Thérèse, on being shown one
of the photographs of herself, said wisely: "Yes, that is the
envelope. When will we see the letter? Oh, how much I would
like to see the letter!"

If we are wise, we too shall devote ourselves to the Christ-life as manifested in the soul of this self-effacing "grain of wheat," instead of wasting time in futile arguments.

(iii) Fact or Fancy?

Since the death of St. Thérèse, and particularly with the proliferation of pious pictures and edifying snippets from her writings, a whole apocrypha of littleness, childhood and artificial roses has sprung up. The accretions of devotional sentimentality with which her clients busily stuccoed over the strong and simple lines that were Thérèse's vision of spiritual childhood, led eventually to a violent reaction in the opposite direction. Exaggerations of another type would have her image hewn from rough granite or moulded in cast-iron. And as her own written words cannot be well reconciled with this stern-visaged and unsmiling caricature, such apologists rest their case on the fact that the writings as published were not as they left Thérèse's pen. But most of these arguments have of necessity to by-pass the poems she produced so volubly and effortlessly, as there seems no way of reconciling such effusions with the "other face" they have designed for Thérèse, "the ruthless perfectionist".

The poems composed by St. Thérèse have, in fact, been the subject of much discussion and adverse criticism. Their value as poetry has often been scathingly denounced, but whatever one's opinion on that score, their intrinsic worth cannot be seriously doubted. There seems no reason why any objection should be raised to their publication. St. Teresa of Avila, after all, wrote a considerable mass of doggerel, among which are embedded one or two gems of real poetry, but no editor has ever seriously considered omitting them from a publication of her complete writings.

In an address delivered in the chapel of the Lisieux Carmel on 30th September, 1947, the fiftieth anniversary of the death of St. Thérèse, the Abbé Combes, referring to Stanza II of her *Vivre d'Amour*: "O Trinity, you are the prisoner of my love!" stated that for this bit of verse he would willingly barter all the poetry of France.

It would appear that the opinion of most of her critics is the reverse, for many of them apparently would much more readily barter all the poems of Thérèse for one line of Racine; but of course the Abbé is here referring principally to the spiritual content of her lines, rather than to their value as part of the nation's heritage of literature.

There is, however, one factor which might be of assistance towards a better comprehension of Thérèse's poems. Carmelite nuns do not as a rule—and certainly did not in Thérèse's day—write poetry merely as a medium of self-expression; but it is a time-honoured custom, inaugurated by St. Teresa in the first days of the Reform, for the sisters to compose and sing "verses" in celebration of certain feasts and special anniversaries. As it is essential that the melody should be well known to those who are to sing it, and be as simple as possible, such verses are usually set to some familiar hymn-tune or popular song, so that the metre is thus confined and the poet's inspiration correspondingly limited. St. Teresa of Avila wished that the custom should be maintained among her daughters, and most of Thérèse's poems were without doubt composed for such occasions. She confesses that in writing them her aim was to express her feelings in response to the wishes of her sisters, and that, being more concerned with substance than form, she was not particular about observing the rules of versification.

As verses they are neither better nor worse than the average presentation, but certainly the ideals and spirituality conveyed in them are far loftier than most. (See Note 6.)

It is in this context, then, that the following words of St. Thérèse must be understood: "To judge by the sentiments I express in all the nice little poems I've made up during the last year, you might imagine that my soul was as full of consolations as it could hold; that for me, the veil which hides the unseen scarcely existed . . . No, when I write poems about the happiness of heaven and the eternal possession of God, it strikes no chord of happiness in my own heart—I'm simply talking about what I'm determined to believe."[1]

[1] A.S. p. 257.

The critics may therefore say that, this being the case, it is hardly surprising that Thérèse's verses are so bad. Yet actually the composition of those poems for which she felt neither the attraction nor the inspiration, was just another link in the long chain of heroic fidelity forged together by her hourly acts of submission and obedience and humility, and one which is a fundamental element of her little way. One can be a child of God with or without poetic gifts, but not unless one is "meek and humble of heart". Thérèse knew well enough that her sisters would not be over-exacting about the construction of her verses, and with her heart and mind filled with God, it is small wonder that her themes were solely spiritual and invariably lofty. Those who find them aesthetically unpalatable might try reading them as prose; they would, I think, find astonishing richness and depth of thought in them.

Thérèse was possessed of a sturdy, stolid French nature, a strong will and more than a touch of the peasant's shrewdness and stubbornness. Upon this natural equipment, God worked to produce a powerful instrument of love, and His work was accelerated because of her generous response to the promptings of grace. As Fr. Conrad Pepler, O.P., suggested, "the fundamentally sound 'sentimentality' of a pious Catholic family might have become a further instrument of grace, especially in the souls she was sent to help, the millions brought up in industrialized Europe, where poetry has so largely been replaced by sentiment".

St. Thérèse, intrinsically, is in fact St. John of the Cross presented in a more simple, practical way for the benefit of those who find his language too abstract or difficult to follow. It is only in her choice of words and metaphors that Thérèse parts company with him, and this is the outcome of her vastly different upbringing and environment. Thérèse could no more have written St. John of the Cross' poetry—or prose— than he could have produced hers. But in its essentials, her doctrine is the same, lacking none of the austerity or loftiness of the *Ascent of Mount Carmel* or *Dark Night*.

If we regard Thérèse as not being a mystic in the generally accepted sense of that much abused word, it is perhaps because we have an ineradicable mental picture of the notorious pseudo-mystics who abounded in the Spain of St. Teresa and John of the Cross; or because we erroneously link that state inseparably with the visions and extraordinary favours and revelations that were apparently the daily fare of some of the great medieval mystics. But of their elevated spirituality, their contemplation and union with God, she lacks nothing.

In the higher regions of the spiritual life, certain states of soul are called "mystical" because the soul penetrates the secrets of divine intimacy, and God's operations are as mysterious as the secrecy and intimacy itself. But such works do not require any particular framework, nor are so-called "mystical phenomena" essential. It is the interior operations which God performs in darkness and silence that constitute the mystical state.

The world mystic is out of fashion. Nowadays we want "doers"—people who accomplish something tangible in the material sphere. But there is an old saw which runs: "It is not the one who makes the most noise that does the most work."

The trouble is that we do not really expect a mystic to exhibit any capability in workaday matters, although we have the example of the extremely practical and energetic St. Teresa of Avila to demonstrate the possibility of combining the roles of Martha and Mary. Also there seems to exist in modern minds a tendency to confuse the two Teresas. Not long ago a Carmelite prioress was lectured severely on the fundamental selfishness of the enclosed contemplative life by a layman, who ended his homily by pointing to St. Thérèse of Lisieux as an example of what he considered a typical and useful member of the church militant, one who had achieved so much work in the active missionary sphere. Another stated that St. Thérèse of the Child Jesus was the foundress of the Carmelite Order.

There is in fact only one way to heaven, and that is the way of spiritual childhood. Our Lord has told us so Himself. We may give it various titles to suit our differing tastes or devotions, but only when it departs from the safe and sure way of the gospel can anyone say "Not for me!" And this one cannot

do, for the gospel is the pole and pivot of the little way, which
in no way departs from its teaching, its ideals or its principles.

"I've heard so much about saintly people who took on the
most rigorous mortifications from their childhood upwards,
but I'd never tried to imitate them . . . What I did try to do by
way of mortification was to thwart my self-will, which always
seemed determined to get its own way; to repress the rejoinder
which sometimes came to my lips; to do little acts of kindness
without attaching much importance to them; to sit upright
instead of leaning back in my chair. That wasn't much, was
it? But I did make these insignificant efforts to make myself
less unworthy of a heavenly bridegroom."[1]

Nobody could quarrel with this self-imposed programme,
except those self-styled "superior" souls to whom, as Bossuet
says, "the simple and common life is repugnant because, be-
guiled solely by the senses and far from a sincere conversion,
they will admire only what they regard as inimitable".

(iv) "Beauty and the Beast"

It is utterly unreasonable to attribute to St. Thérèse the
nonsense that has been spilled out in so many pages of print by
well-intentioned commentators no less than by adverse critics.
Her life was not rose-strewn, but like that of her model and
spouse, thorn-crowned. She had asked for the grace of martyrdom when, during her visit to Rome, she stood in the Col-
osseum, the scene of so many martyrdoms, and she felt deep in
her heart that this prayer had been granted.

"Jesus, I desire to die a martyr for your sake, a martyr in
soul or in body; better still, in both", was the petition she
carried on her heart during the day of her religious profession.
True, she was not permitted to shed her blood in witness of
her love. Apart from the wasting of illness and disease, she
suffered no violence in her body, any more than did Mary,
whose heart was pierced by seven swords and whom we honour
as the Queen of Martyrs. But there is still the martyrdom of
the heart, which is no less fruitful than the shedding of one's
blood, and which, according to St. John Chrysostom, consists

[1] A.S. p. 181.

in bearing patiently the sufferings and adversities of this life.
Physical martyrdom is a privilege granted only to comparatively few; but to live in the spirit of a martyr is open to us all.
St. Francis de Sales shrewdly points out that it is not of much
practical use desiring to die a martyr if one is not prepared to
live as one; if, failing the appearance of a persecutor, we are
in the meantime unwilling to suffer with patience the discomfort of a headache or a reversal of plans. And with amaz-
ing insight, Thérèse recognized the value of "martyrdom by
pinpricks", which becomes both more meritorious and harder
to endure because "it is seen by Jesus alone".

A martyr dies but once; Thérèse died daily, and at the end
of her brief life she could truly echo the wonderful cry of St.
Paul: "I am alive; or rather, not I; it is Christ that lives in
me." (Gal. 2 : 20.)

It is not, declares St. Augustine, mere suffering which makes
a martyr. Many invalids have suffered far more acutely for the
sake of health and in the hope of recovery than some of the
canonized martyrs have been called upon to endure in bearing
witness to their faith. Heretics have been burned at the stake
for their heresy; Christians have suffered the same torture for
their faith. Only the latter group are martyrs. It is the reason
for the death, not the death itself, that constitutes martyrdom.
To give one's life for the faith has always been precious in the
sight of the Church, while neither merit nor reward could be
won by spending one's life to defend error; although, no
doubt, those who died according to their own convictions, for
what they mistakenly believed to be the truth, will receive due
reward from God for their good intentions. St. John of the
Cross explains the martyrdom of the heart very thoroughly in
Chapter XIX of Book II of *The Ascent of Mount Carmel.*

Thérèse had no doubt that her desire was in the way of
being fulfilled, and God has given us striking confirmation of
this spiritual reality by the miracle which preserved the palm
branch placed in her hand by her sisters while her body lay in
the choir. When exhumed thirteen years later, it was found
that her body, her very bones had returned to dust—even as
she had predicted—also that the veils and habit in which her

body was clothed had rotted and perished, but that her martyr's palm was still green and fresh.

As regards the term "martyr of love" used by Thérèse in her Act of Oblation to the Blessed Trinity, however, care should be taken not to exaggerate its theological importance. This kind of "mystical inebriation", when genuine, is no more than secondary to the deeper action of grace purifying the understanding and memory in an "unfelt" way; and when undue prominence is given to it, people soon begin to imagine that it belongs to the essence of contemplation. Divine love disposes the soul for ever-greater perfection of virtue, but it does not threaten to overwhelm the human heart. Such "overwhelming" is due to the intensity of ordinary human emotion —sometimes combined with physical debility, but never an immediate effect of the divine action in the soul.

If we cannot see the depth and heroic inspiration of the little way, it must be that we are cutting it down to suit our own narrow ideas of spirituality instead of praying for the light necessary to grasp its meaning. The message given to us by God through St. Thérèse is the one most perfectly adapted to meet the needs of the world today. By means of it, even the weakest and most imperfect of us may hope to find strength for the conflict, and so to become capable of running in the way of true holiness. At the opposite extreme, however, let us not imagine that life in the Carmel of Lisieux was one long nightmare with Mother Mary Gonzaga going out of her way to torture the helpless Thérèse. Certainly the prioress possessed her full quota of faults, mostly of temperament, but she did not underestimate her daughter's virtues or capacity or aims. She knew that Thérèse was capable of heroic virtue and therefore she asked more of her than she would have demanded from one whom she knew was prepared to give less.

Thérèse always spoke of Mother Mary Gonzaga with deep affection. "Jesus is good to have brought us to such a mother as we have," she wrote to Céline. "What a treasure she is! If you could have seen her bringing me your letter at six this morning. I was deeply touched."

Is this, and many other similar expressions in Thérèse's

letters, to be explained as "tact" or "diplomacy"; that is, making untruthful statements, tongue in cheek, because she knew that Mother Mary Gonzaga would read her letters before despatching them? The person best qualified to answer this question definitely says "No". Mother Agnes has stated that Thérèse told her quite plainly that she dearly loved Mother Mary Gonzaga, and that the endearments *Mère bien aimée* and *Mère chérie* which she used in her manuscript expressed the genuine feelings of her heart. And there can be no doubt of the prioress' affection and esteem for Thérèse. "Of my good ones, she is the best. I am giving you a most fervent auxiliary who will neglect nothing that is for the salvation of souls. The dear little creature is all God's," she wrote to Père Roulland when introducing Thérèse to him as a "sister"-auxiliary. From her childhood Thérèse had been on affectionately intimate terms with the prioress, who had consistently encouraged her in her vocation and was eager to accept her as a postulant. When the time came she tried her utmost to persuade Canon Delatroëtte to give his permission for her entry. During the retreats Thérèse made prior to her clothing and profession, Mother Mary Gonzaga gave her full permission to unburden her soul in writing to Pauline and Marie, realizing no doubt that she needed this spiritual comfort and assistance at such times, especially in view of her difficulty in opening her heart to her prioress and novice mistress. This permission was quite exceptional, and Thérèse used it with utter simplicity for the time it was given, and afterwards lapsed again into silence without seeking any extension of the intimate contact with her two elder sisters, to whom alone she could speak freely and feel she was being understood in the matter of spiritual experiences and difficulties. "Pray for our Mother," Thérèse begged Père Roulland a few months before her death. "Her sensitive mother's heart cannot easily consent to my going."

The prioress showed herself stern and severe, and for this Thérèse was genuinely grateful. "My first memoir, which gave an account of my early days, will tell you what I think about the firm, motherly discipline I had from you. I thank you from the very bottom of my heart for not having treated me too gently. Jesus knew well enough that the little flower He had planted was in need of watering; only the waters of humiliation could revive it . . . and it was through you, Mother, that this blessing was bestowed."[1] She was, and Thérèse well knew it, the instrument chosen by God for forming her in the heroic cast. Mother Mary Gonzaga discerned in Thérèse obvious indications of high sanctity in the making, the desire to refuse nothing to God, and she treated her as one who wanted to give to God at her own cost, thus giving her the wings she needed to "fly away and be at rest".

"A soul of such mettle as hers should not be coddled," Mother Mary Gonzaga replied to a sister who pleaded that Thérèse was obviously tired and should be excused from Matins. "Dispensations are not for her. Let her be, for God sustains her." One may question her method, especially in view of Thérèse's extreme youth, but not her intentions.

Very soon after the entry of this young postulant, Mother Mary Gonzaga confided to the Guérins that she was amazed at the wisdom of the "little one". Writing to the Carmel of Tours shortly after the profession of Thérèse she mentioned the ceremony, and said that her new-professed had the judgment of an old and thoroughly formed novice together with the self-control of a perfect religious. "This angel of a child," she added, "is seventeen and a half years old."

It is apparent that life under the government of this gifted but erratic and high-handed superior did not always run so smoothly as could be desired. Thérèse was not blind to her prioress' defects, but she certainly never allowed them to influence her behaviour. As a person she liked Mother Mary Gonzaga and felt strongly attracted to her. As a superior she never looked on her as other than God's direct representative, the mouthpiece through which His expressed will came to her. "Never consider thy superior as less than if he were God, be the superior who he may be, for to thee he stands in the place of God," cautions St. John of the Cross to the nuns of one of the early Carmels of the Reform. "Keep thyself with great vigilance from considering his character, his ways or his habits

[1] A.S. p. 246.

or any of his other characteristics, for if thou do this thou wilt do thyself the harm of exchanging divine obedience for human, by being moved, or not being moved, only by the visible characteristics of thy superior, instead of by the invisible God whom thou servest in his person."[1] Thérèse confided to Mother Mary Gonzaga that she found no difficulty in recognizing God's voice speaking through her superior, for she saw not merely a loving and beloved mother, but beyond that Jesus Himself, alive in her soul and communicating His will through the prioress. "Of course, you treat me like a special case, like a spoilt child," she added, "so that obedience costs me nothing. But something deep down in my heart tells me that I should act just as I do, love you as you as much as I do, if you saw fit to treat me harshly. I should still know that it was the will of Jesus; you would only be doing it for the greater good of my soul."[2]

It is evident that Mother Mary Gonzaga's attitude and behaviour towards Thérèse after her first haemorrhage did not display neglect, disinterest, or even downright malice which has all too hastily been attributed to her. In the manuscript addressed to the prioress, Thérèse speaks with affection to her superior, and refers to this trial itself as a great grace, "one of the blessings which have come to me during your term of office." She then describes the scene when, returning to her cell after the vigil in choir on Holy Thursday night, she coughed blood for the first time. She waited until the appropriate moment came that she might have a chance of confiding to Mother Mary Gonzaga her "hopes and happiness"; adding that she felt no pain, and asking not to be dispensed from the Holy Week horarium or to be treated any differently from the others. To her relief the prioress agreed to Thérèse's taking part in the ceremonies and sharing the fast and penances of Good Friday. In her happy anticipation of soon standing before God, Thérèse made very light of this serious sympton, and her obvious joy seemed to have dispelled any momentary anxiety the prioress may have felt. Later when a hard, persistent cough

---

[1] Cautions against the Devil: The Second Caution.
[2] A.S. p. 263.

appeared, the doctors were immediately summoned, but even they failed to diagnose the complaint, and as their treatment got rid of the cough, the prioress felt no alarm about Thérèse who looked well, and whose demeanour completely hid what she was in truth suffering at this time.

"Since I've been ill, I've learned a lot about charity from the care you yourself have lavished on me. Letting me have the most expensive kinds of treatment, and never tired of trying fresh ones! And all the trouble you took when I still went to recreation, to keep me out of a draught! If I started trying to write it all down, I should never stop."[1] Nor does this, as might at first sight appear, cancel out Mother Agnes' testimony that Mother Mary Gonzaga had refused to allow morphine injections ordered by the doctor. This was done, not through unkindness, but because of the prioress' expressed conviction that it was shameful for a Carmelite to resort to the use of any form of "pain-killer". Any remedy ordered she would immediately have consented to, but not narcotics or drugs. This is still considered by many to be the normal procedure with slight inconveniences such as headaches; although morphia would not be forbidden by a superior today on such a ground, especially as we know nowadays that pain-killing is not the only consideration where there is danger of recurring haemorrhage. (See Note 7.) Mother Mary Gonzaga undoubtedly showed a lack of imagination in this affair, but that is not a capital sin. It seems quite certain that there was no heartlessness on her part. "You always treat me like a mother, not in the least like a prioress," said Thérèse, adding how touched she was by all the motherly attentions she received, so that she would never forget what she owed to the older nun, and her heart was full of love and gratitude.

This is not the way one speaks to a person one distrusts, and Thérèse obviously laid no blame on Mother Mary Gonzaga for any real or imagined neglect during the early days of her illness. Indeed she seems to take some pains to ensure that others should not do so. It is very probable also that Mother Agnes' grief at seeing her beloved little sister so obviously

[1] A.S. p. 293.

suffering and dying magnified in her eyes what appeared to be callousness or inattention, and she had been deeply hurt at not having been informed the previous year of the first blood-spitting. This is only natural. But here again it is absolutely essential that we should not examine the question from a merely natural point of view. The eighteen months of Thérèse's physical and spiritual martyrdom was the road chosen by God for her final perfection. Had she coughed blood a couple of months earlier she would have been obliged to make it known to Mother Agnes who was then prioress and who would immediately have lavished every care and attention on her in the hope of checking the disease. But God did not mean Thérèse to be either coddled or cured. Almost immediately after Mother Mary Gonzaga's re-election as prioress the sympton appeared; and she, knowing the courage of Thérèse and her desire to remain regular in the fulfilment of all her religious duties, was easier to reassure about the midnight haemorrhage than Mother Agnes would have been.

Mother Agnes herself suffered almost as much as did Thérèse merely in watching the appalling and long-drawn-out agony. It is not to be wondered at that she felt wounded at times by what appeared to be neglect or carelessness, for anyone who has had the experience of standing by, a helpless witness to the suffering of someone dearly loved, can appreciate the anguish of the elder sister, who had been a mother to Thérèse and loved her as one.

Thérèse on her part certainly never felt anything but deep gratitude for the fact that she had been treated with severity in the early days of her religious life when she might not have had the strength to resist the weakening effect of too much human affection, had she been petted or favoured by one for whom she admitted feeling a great natural attraction. The allegory of "The Shepherdess and the Lamb" which she wrote to console her newly-elected prioress in March 1896, proves beyond all doubt that Thérèse's relations with Mother Mary Gonzaga were right and perfect, wanting nothing in affection, loyalty or respect. And the prioress' attitude towards Thérèse could not have been any other than esteem and love, for had she despised and disliked Thérèse she would certainly not have confided to her the distress she felt over the results of the election, at which she had been returned to office only on the seventh ballot. Thérèse who must herself have been keenly disappointed that Mother Agnes had not been re-elected, put aside her own feelings on the subject, and in this letter she consoles and at the same time gently rebukes Mother Mary Gonzaga's too-natural disappointment at not having been unanimously chosen. It would have been an impertinence had their understanding and mutual trust not been deep and sincere.

After Thérèse's death Mother Mary Gonzaga wrote in the convent register against the entry of Thérèse's profession a long and effusive testimony to the virtues of her daughter, in which she described her as "a perfect model of humility, obedience, charity, prudence, detachment and regularity" who discharged her obligations as novice mistress "with sagacity and affection which nothing could equal save her love of God"; and mentioned the manuscript "which will edify the whole world while leaving the most perfect example to us all". This was no mere reflection of popular opinion, as Mother Mary Gonzaga herself went to join her daughter in 1904, many years before there was any hint of beatification or the "whirlwind of glory" which subsequently surrounded Thérèse and her Carmel.

Equally absurd is the idea that Thérèse was generally unpopular in the community and disliked by her sisters. Speaking to Mother Mary Gonzaga of her proposed transfer to Hanoï, for example, she says, "Here in Carmel I have your love and that of all the sisters, which means so much to me."

In a note to Thérèse in June 1897, Mother Agnes wrote: "Later, I think, it will be I who will console the others. They keep coming, one after the other, to tell me of their affection for you, and their expressions of grief touch me deeply. I can see that you are very greatly loved; even so, no one loves you as much as I do."

Her appointment over the novices is ample evidence of the confidence of her superiors in her virtue and wisdom beyond her years. Superiors know that the novices of today will be the community of tomorrow, and their formation is usually entrusted only to the most competent hands. Pope Pius XI, addressing the Major Superiors of Religious Orders of Men, cautioned: "Let the novices never forget that what they are in the novitiate they will be for the rest of their lives. If they once pass that time with little or no fruit, it will be a hopeless delusion for them to attempt later on by an awakening of fervour to make good the omissions of their novice days." This does not mean that on leaving the novitiate our spiritual growth stops, but that we are by then fixed in the habitual dispositions of soul in which our life will be spent. Mother Agnes appointed Thérèse as assistant to Mother Mary Gonzaga, who officiated as novice mistress during Mother Agnes' first term as prioress; and on Mother Mary Gonzaga's re-election Thérèse was left in this position—a clear avowal of what both prioresses thought of Thérèse.

The story has often been related that she was fed more or less exclusively on scraps of food and left-overs, and many biographers have either hinted or stated outright that this was because she was disliked by the lay sisters in the kitchen who deliberately and spitefully "took it out on her". Such a charge is a serious one, insinuating a complete lack of any sense of fraternal charity, and it is in fact wide of the mark. In a community where the food in the refectory is in common, there are invariably some left-overs, however hard the servers may try to gauge the requirements of the sisters, and the general working principle is that too much is better than too little. But left-overs have to be eaten by somebody. A Carmelite's vow of poverty prohibits waste, and food that is edible may not be thrown away. To use it up satisfactorily always presents a problem for the provisors, and when they know that a certain sister has neither fads nor indispositions, and will and can eat whatever is put before her, she is to them a heaven-sent benefactress, and they gratefully avail themselves of her services. The serving of heated-up remains from a previous meal in no way implies malice on their part, and as a rule it imposes no hardship on the obliging one. But to

Thérèse it did cause a very real difficulty, although nobody but she knew it. From the day of her entry into the Carmel, she had shown neither partiality nor dislike in the refectory, had cheerfully eaten whatever was served to her, little or much, ill or well prepared, so that even her neighbour at table, although she had endeavoured to do so, was unable to detect in her any preferences or aversions. As far as anyone could see she had neither, but the healthy appetite one would expect in the very young. A striking illustration of this is given in the incident of Sister Mary of the Sacred Heart, her eldest sister, who had so little knowledge of Thérèse's tastes and digestive capacities that more than once she prepared a special dish for her, which happened to be about the worst choice she could have made, but which Thérèse ate without demur, and doubtless with every appearance of relish.

We should not be surprised—but in fact we are often scandalized—that community life is frequently a very real penance. It is, and it is meant to be so, since the defects of character discernible in the members of every community are the precise means whereby we discover our own weakness and so are compelled to rely on the Sacred Heart for the strength we need. In the course of this, we shall find our own characters being modified considerably, with suffering perhaps but without conflict, since all the time our eyes will be fixed on Christ whose hand directs the process. In practice we are more ready to accept our role of sanctifying our neighbours than to admit that we are ourselves in need of similar treatment. Not so, however, with St. Thérèse. It is because she followed the teaching of St. John of the Cross in this matter of submitting herself to the action of her neighbours, accepting all the small rubs and discomforts of community life, and making of these little things the basis of a life of love, that she rose in so short a time to such high perfection.

(v) *"Little Mother"*

"You know all the innermost recesses of my soul—you alone." At the end of her life, this is what Thérèse said to her

sister; and it was indeed but a simple statement of the truth.
"Oh, little mother," she continued, "the *letter* is *yours*, please
continue to read it till the day when Jesus tears up the little
'envelope' which has caused you so much trouble since it was
made . . . are you not pleased that He is getting ready to read
it, the letter you have been writing this twenty-four years? . . .
If I have hidden a small corner of the *envelope*, I have never
hidden from you a single line of the *letter* . . ."[1]

Thérèse has told us in her own well-known words of the
excellent and wise training this "little mother" had given her,
and Pauline, generous in her own gift to God, understood the
magnanimity of Thérèse's heart. She was only sixteen when
she undertook this tutelage, and she was one of the few later
on who did not attempt to discourage her sister from entering
Carmel so young. Like Thérèse, Pauline was convinced that
this was a direct call from God, and that He had special
designs for her.

"As it was," said Thérèse, "I could only find one living soul
to encourage me in my vocation, and that was my own Pauline.
Every beat of my heart woke an echo in hers, and it was only
through her that I reached the coveted harbour . . . which had
welcomed her five years earlier. For five years, dear Mother,
I thought you were lost to me; but no sooner did my trials
begin than your hand was there to point me along the road
I must follow."[2]

To her as to St. Thérèse was entrusted a mission, although
necessarily a secondary one. In the words of Mgr. Picaud,
Bishop of Bayeux and Lisieux, who preached the funeral
oration for Mother Agnes of Jesus: "By a predestination incomparably precious, it was given to her to play an essential
part in the development of the holiness, sanctity and glory of
the greatest saint of modern times; so much so that in this hour
thousands of souls in the whole Catholic world whose thoughts
turn to her on the announcement of her death, see her only
within the radiance of the glory of St. Thérèse of the Child
Jesus."

[1] C.L. pp. 297-8.
[2] A.S. p. 137.

To nobody else was Thérèse able to open her heart as she was to her Pauline, who she felt drew her very soul. During the retreat prior to her clothing, Thérèse had permission to write freely to Pauline, but no dispensation was given from the rule of silence. In a note at this time, she exclaimed: "You cannot imagine what a privation I feel it not being able to speak to you."

In February 1884, Sister Agnes then a novice had begun to prepare Thérèse for her first Communion the following May which, to the delight of both sisters, was to coincide with her own profession. "I am so glad, darling, that your first Communion is to be on 8th May. What a joy for me to give myself to God on the same day as you. You must pray a lot for me, for to become the spouse of Jesus is such a great grace, and I am utterly unworthy of it." A little later she wrote again: "What a lot of work there is to do, what a lot of flowers have to be sown, and how little time there is to do it in! But look at nature; on almost the same day as you, she will be beginning to make herself beautiful; you can see the buds already on the trees in the garden, and soon the flowers will be there; by May all will be lovely to look at. Nature is only doing it to please us, but couldn't you do the same to welcome and delight the beloved Child at His first awakening in your heart?"

However, Pauline did not merely indulge in baby-talk. Nor did she make the mistake of talking down to Thérèse, and while accommodating her metaphors to the age and predilection of the other, she nevertheless gave her solid spiritual nourishment.

Thérèse recalls that if she had any confidences to impart, or doubts to be resolved, Pauline was the one to whom they had to be taken. On one occasion she was troubled by the thought that some souls had less glory in heaven than others, which, it seemed to her, must make them unhappy. Pauline solved the problem by a simple demonstration. Placing Thérèse's tiny tumbler beside her father's large drinking mug, she filled both to the brim with water, and then demanded which was the fuller. As neither could hold another drop, Thérèse had to admit that each was as full as the other. Then

Pauline explained her charade in terms of spiritual capacity, and showed Thérèse how in heaven each soul receives the amount of glory it is capable of accommodating and no more; so those in the lowest place have no envy of those in the highest.

"So," concludes Thérèse, "it wasn't only my body you looked after; you managed to attend to the needs of my soul, because you had the knack of bringing the most mysterious truths down to my level."[1]

Thérèse had chosen Pauline as her "little mother" after their mother's death, and that role Pauline fulfilled faithfully and lovingly, training her in her lessons, her duties, and in interior progress. From Carmel she continued to watch over her, and when her young sister joined her there, her influence in forming Thérèse as a religious was great, especially in fostering in her the simplicity and love of lowliness which are so characteristic of her spirituality and the source of her universal appeal. She received all Thérèse's most intimate confidences, mostly by means of notes as they were not as a rule in a position to speak together except occasionally by permission, and of course, during the three years when Mother Agnes was prioress. But in the last months when Thérèse was confined to the infirmary, Mother Agnes became her constant companion, and it was during this period that she made a record of all the reflections and conversations which were actually made by Thérèse in her presence.

In March 1888, a month before Thérèse entered Carmel, Pauline wrote to her: "Jesus may, if He wishes, play with a grain of sand, for the whole world is His. But why does He not play with a diamond rather than with a grain of sand? Jesus loves lowliness, He loves what the eyes of men do not notice, what they tread underfoot and despise. How beautiful humility is! I am sure my little grain of sand will understand me, and will never want to become a mountain, but to grow on the contrary smaller and smaller, lighter and lighter, so as to be the more easily carried off by the wind of love." This letter is very reminiscent of some of Thérèse's metaphors in her letters and autobiography, particularly her comparison of

[1] A.S. p. 70.

herself, the grain of sand, with the great saints, the mountains whose summits are lost in the clouds.

Pauline's spiritual motherhood produced the masterpiece which Pope Pius XI called "an exquisite miniature of holiness"; and although this miniature was the direct work of the Holy Spirit, it was the hands and the heart of Mother Agnes which became His principal instruments. She it was who guided Thérèse's spiritual life, and from her sprang the seeds which were to develop into the characteristic traits of Thérèse's spirituality: humility and confidence. She taught her littleness and humility, using the symbols of "the little ball of Jesus", and "the grain of sand"; and it was under this latter pseudonym that Thérèse invariably referred to herself in her notes to both her elder sisters, Mother Agnes and Sister Mary of the Sacred Heart.

"I think of my little girl very often," wrote Sister Agnes to Thérèse, preparing to join her in Carmel, "and I am ambitious for her! Jesus is too, for it is He who wants her to be a saint. Yes, indeed, a saint, a great saint, and at the same time *a little saint*, so small and so lowly that we shall always be able to read on her face and in her heart our Lady's words, that she must say to herself as she enters Carmel: *Behold the handmaid of the Lord.*"

Finally, as Thérèse stated, it was Pauline who discovered and directed her towards devotion to the Holy Face, which was to become the foundation of all her piety; and it was Pauline who, recognizing that her pupil had outstripped her, quietly slipped into the background, taking the position of disciple to her former charge.

(vi) *The Executrix*

Clearly, then, nobody was better qualified than Mother Agnes to take charge of the message and spirituality bequeathed by her sister. Had she not nursed it in embryo, watching it grow from a tiny spark in the soul of Thérèse until it had become a consuming fire? Although her own spirituality was undoubtedly not of the same height or calibre as Thérèse's, she understood perfectly what Thérèse meant by "spiritual childhood", and she knew both the extent and limitations of her metaphors of childhood. The efficiency with which she has fulfilled the charge bequeathed to her is witnessed by the simplicity and freedom from embellishment with which the little doctrine of Thérèse is held at the Lisieux Carmel today. In the glare of publicity which surrounded both the saint and her Carmel, frills and adornments could easily have been added, almost imperceptibly, until gradually the personality of Thérèse had been usurped by that of her sister. But the Thérèse of Lisieux Carmel today is the Thérèse who lived and died there sixty-seven years ago. Despite the difference in the individual spirituality of the two sisters, Mother Agnes' understanding of Thérèse could not have been more thorough.

"You have been, and always will be, the angel charged to guide me and announce the Lord's mercies to me . . . (you are) the angel that Jesus sent before me to *prepare the way* for me, the way that leads to heaven . . . You know that never shall I be able to tell you all my gratitude for the way you have guided me, like an angel from heaven, along the pathways of life; it was you who taught me to know Jesus and love Him . . . How proud I am to be your sister! And your little girl, too, for it was you who taught me to love Jesus and seek only Him . . . You, who are a flaming torch that Jesus has given me to light my steps in the dark pathways of exile, have pity on my weakness, hide me under your veil, that I may share in your light."[1] These are some of the expressions of admiration and gratitude that abound in the notes she wrote to Mother Agnes.

Surely some of the greatest joys and deepest sufferings in the life of this great religious must have stemmed from the same source. The immense glory that has surrounded her young sister, the power and universal homage accorded to Thérèse must undoubtedly have, at times, given Mother Agnes her fill of consolations, as indeed Thérèse had predicted that it would. But also there can be little doubt that it was not an unalloyed happiness, and one of her greatest sufferings in the latter years of her life was surely to see various writers vying to outdo each other in belittling the moral greatness of

[1] C.L. pp. 296, 295, 189, 108, 107.

Thérèse, apparently with the express intention of watering down her life and doctrine into insipidity and puerility. As has been noted, the good faith of Mother Agnes herself has been questioned; yet she continued on her way steadily, undeterred by either adulation or calumny, defending the message entrusted to her by her sister, and preserving it in all its integrity.

After the death of Thérèse, and particularly in the whirlwind of fame which descended on the Lisieux Carmel at the time of the canonization and since, Mother Agnes was the one to whom fell practically the sole responsibility for safeguarding the spiritual life of her own convent, without allowing the inevitable publicity and worldly incursions to ruffle the surface or upset the routine observance of community life; and as well it was for her to preserve intact both the spirit and the letter of Thérèse's message. One has only to consider the amount of misrepresentation and distortion that has crept in among even the well-meaning but indiscreet clients of the saint to realize that this was no easy task. If Mother Agnes herself had not been so familiar with the doctrine, understanding perfectly both it and Thérèse, the preservation of anything so utterly simple, yet so evanescent that it almost eludes the grasp and wellnigh defies definition, would have been quite impossible.

A typical example of this understanding watchfulness is given by the Lisieux Carmel. When the text of the contracted lessons for the office of St. Thérèse was sent from Rome, Mother Agnes was distressed to find it read: "Inflamed with the desire for suffering, she offered herself as a victim to the merciful love of God." This seemed to her merely a parody of Thérèse's oblation, and she made every effort to have it rectified. After much correspondence with the Sacred Congregation of Rites, she obtained from them an amendment of this clause to read: "Inflamed with divine charity, she offered herself as a victim . . ."

"If one encounters such misrepresentation of Thérèse's thought in our own lifetime," she remarked, "what will it be like after our death?"

On 7th September, 1941, the eightieth birthday of Mother Agnes, the Holy Father, Pope Pius XII wrote the following letter to this "beloved daughter" in his own hand: "How many constant and merciful favours has not our divine Master showered on this noble and fruitful life, in which destiny set, like a peerless diamond, that angel of prayer and charity whom generations of Christians will ever hail with the blessed name of St. Thérèse of the Child Jesus! . . . Certainly the remembrance of those tender ties which attach us to Lisieux and through you to St. Thérèse is not the least among our comforts . . . and it is to your saintly little sister, so powerful over the hearts of Jesus and Mary, that we confide our immense cares."

That the gentle strength and real virtue of Sister Agnes were appreciated by her community was proved by their electing her to the office of prioress at the age of thirty-one—"that golden day when you were elected" Thérèse recalled later, rejoicing that Pauline was now officially her "mother" and would be for all eternity.

Certainly when one takes into consideration its subsequent effects, unforeseen at the time, the most important act during her first three-year term of office was the order given to Thérèse to write the memoirs of her early years. Later it was she who realized that the manuscript, although valuable, was incomplete, as it gave practically no details of Thérèse's religious life; and it was she who obtained permission from Mother Mary Gonzaga, once more prioress, for Thérèse to complete it by writing the final pages. These form Chapters IX to XII of the *Autobiography*, and Book III, Chapters XXI to XL of *The Autobiography of a Saint*. It is also to Mother Agnes that we owe the recording of the conversations of Thérèse during her last five months in the infirmary, which have been published under the title *Novissima Verba* (Last Words). Many of the remarks made by Thérèse to her elder sister were not published in this little volume, due no doubt to reticence or modesty on the part of Mother Agnes, and it was not until after her own death that they saw the light of print. What she was to Thérèse and how much her young sister appreciated her is beyond doubt. "If you but knew all you are for me," Thérèse exclaimed. "You fill my last days with sweetness. It was you who threw the seed of trust into my soul. What a debt I owe you! But when I am in heaven I shall tell the saints: It was my little mother who gave me all that you find pleasing in me."

Under the circumstances, the task of editing the manuscript could hardly have been entrusted to anyone except Mother Agnes, and Thérèse apparently had taken it for granted that she would be the one to undertake it. Certainly it was for her a labour of love. In September 1898, a year after the death of Thérèse, the first edition was published. In 1902 Mother Agnes was prioress once again, and before the end of her six-year term of office in 1908, the Carmel of Lisieux was being inundated with requests for copies of *The Story of a Soul*, for relics, for prayers—Thérèse's prediction that it was in the letter-box that Mother Agnes would find her consolation was being fulfilled rapidly.

In 1909 Mother Agnes was elected prioress once more, and this office she filled successively for forty-two years until her own death in 1951. She continued to be re-elected by her community, and even after the customary six-year term, when normally she would not have been eligible for re-election, she was retained in office by the superiors of the Carmel who considered it expedient to keep her there during the beatification processes. In 1923 she was appointed prioress for life, being confirmed in that office by Pope Pius XI, in token of his esteem for her virtues, prudence and capability. She was, of course, an active instrument in the processes for the cause of St. Thérèse and her depositions were of major importance. Her prestige was high in Rome and it has always continued to be so.

Mother Agnes became a well-known figure in the succeeding years. Thousands of pilgrims yearly sought an interview with her in the Carmel parlour; she was the confidante, spiritual director and adviser of many; the friend and respected correspondent of bishops, cardinals, and even of popes. People from every corner of the world and from all walks of

life applied to her, inundating her with requests for prayers
and intercession with St. Thérèse, and throughout it all she
remained simple and humble, calm and at ease, never over-
whelmed by the enthusiasm and splendour which at times
broke like a tidal wave over Lisieux, as pilgrims poured
in for the beatification, canonization, jubilee celebrations,
dedication of the basilica, and for many anniversaries of
the saint.

Her tact and discretion were remarkable in the way she
handled the influx of requests that came to the Carmel for
intercession and intervention on her part. She had the confidence of both Popes Pius XI and Pius XII; from the latter
she has received the rare honour and mark of high esteem of
letters written or signed in his own hand. As Thérèse became
the child loved by the whole world, so her little Mother became the little Mother of the whole world. Truly she shared in
the glorification of Thérèse, but she never appropriated to
herself any of its lustre; hers, she always felt, was the portion
of living in the reflected rays of her sister's glory, and she
longed to remain—and succeeded in so remaining—always
little and humble as Thérèse would have had her to be.

In 1944 after the Allied landings in Normandy, Lisieux
underwent bombardment. Mother Agnes was now old, and at
eighty-three, another sacrifice was asked of her, which would
have constituted a difficult decision for any superior. She was
called upon to lead her daughters from their enclosure, and
with them to take refuge in the crypt of the basilica: an exile
which was to last eighty days. Her happiness at seeing the
basilica at close quarters was hardly likely to have exceeded
her joy at leaving it, and being able to return with the entire
community to their Carmel in August. The great basilica,
whose architecture and "sugar-cake" adornment are deplored
by so many, was one of the consolations of her old age, for her
a tangible expression of the power of spirit over matter.
Mother Agnes was no artist, but even had she been, the basilica
would have lost none of its wonder for her, as it typified one
thing: the magnanimous response of God in "filling the
humble with good things". And to people of all countries and

classes, Mother Agnes represented the palpable link between them and St. Thérèse.

During the Apostolic Process conducted in 1915 to investigate the cause of Thérèse, Mother Agnes stated that she wished for the beatification of her sister, for she was firmly convinced that Thérèse had been chosen by God to make known on earth the fatherly love which He has for His children, and His will to be repaid by a tender and filial love on their part. Saints canonized by the Church have been, for the most part, models of behaviour for relatively few; their mission has not been to inspire all men to imitate them, for their lives have contained so much of the superhuman and extraordinary. The number of *little souls*, on the other hand, who walk with Jesus and Mary in simple faith and hope, is beyond our power of reckoning.

CHAPTER FOUR

THE BLESSEDNESS OF BEING LITTLE

His overthrow heap'd happiness upon him;
For then and not till then, he felt himself,
And found the blessedness of being little:
And, to add greater honours to his age
Than man could give him, he died fearing God.
                                        (*King Henry VIII*, Act IV, Sc. II)

(i) Concept of a "little" soul

The criticism has often been raised that St. Thérèse did not "discover" spiritual childhood, and this is perfectly true; she never made any claim to have done so. Our Lord taught it to His apostles and disciples, and many have trodden that way before her. Pope Pius XII, in a letter to the Carmel of Lisieux in 1947 referred to "the way of spiritual childhood which she *like many other saints* has been sent to recall to us, the way which was given by our Saviour to His apostles: 'Amen, I say to you, unless you be converted and become as little children, you shall not enter the kingdom of heaven'." Truly the gospel principles and those of the spiritual life remain the same today as they were in the beginning and always will be until the end of time, but the critics rarely follow this out to its logical conclusion. If they did they would recognize that St. Thérèse—in re-discovering a way already known, a doctrine already formulated—has taken it to herself, made it her own, and given it back to us with certain elements which are strikingly original, being invested with a significance and application entirely new. In other words, Thérèse was, under the Holy Spirit, instrumental in bringing to the notice of the modern world the age-old secret of living in Jesus and Mary by means of the theological virtues. Only thus can it be claimed that she designed a new

pattern of heroic sanctity; never in any way did she depart
from the teaching of the gospel. For her, Jesus was the teacher,
and she listened to His words with reverence and love, and
after pondering them well in her heart—"meditating day and
night on the law of the Lord" as her holy Rule bade her—putting them into literal practice, she then gave us the outline
of her method of applying them to her life. Jesus taught her
the little way, she affirms. It was from Him alone, and not
from any book or theologian that she learned it. In the Communion prayer of the Mass of her feast, the Church applies to
Thérèse the words of Deuteronomy *Dominus solus dux ejus
fuit* ("The Lord alone was her leader").

Whether St. Thérèse ever studied the *Ascent of Mount
Carmel* cannot now be ascertained. Abbé Combes states that
the only two works of St. John of the Cross available in the
Carmel of Lisieux in her time were the *Spiritual Canticle*
and *Living Flame of Love,* and that therefore she never read
either *Ascent of Mount Carmel* or *Dark Night of the Soul.*
The Carmelites of Liseux, however, have told me that this
statement is *"trop categorique",* and that it is not now possible
to say definitely whether this was, in fact, the case. However,
even if she never saw that great composite-treatise on asceticism
and essential mystical experience, she knew and understood
well enough what his teaching was.

But Thérèse felt that she had something further to say on
this. Although in the first place her pages were written for
her sisters and her prioress, she was quite aware that she was
leaving a message for her "legion of little souls", and the many
references in *Novissima Verba* to the importance of her manuscript puts this beyond doubt. Thérèse knew quite well that
she must re-draw the map. She realized that St. John of the
Cross was not likely to be read by those whom she designated
"little souls", and that it was for her to provide their directions. But her little way is more than a map to the way of
salvation. It is a way of perfection, that is to say it is a guide,
profuse with illustrations from daily life, to the practice of
heroic virtue. For the little way as St. Thérèse envisaged and
lived it, postulates heroic virtue and the attainment of union

with God in this life, not merely by habitual charity, but through progressive union with Christ in faith and hope. She had a form of intuition (what theologians call the Gift of Understanding) which enabled her to go direct to the heart of the subject, reducing everything in the spiritual life to its first principle; but although this made things genuinely "easy" for herself, as it does in the case of any soul assisted by this kind of supernatural intuition, none but God can bestow the gift. All we can do to prepare for it is to exercise ourselves in the virtue of faith and avail ourselves of the practical advice which St. Thérèse has laid down for our guidance.

Her teaching runs parallel in every respect with that of St. John of the Cross, the only difference being that the language of St .Thérèse is easier to understand. But *do* we all—or even the most of us—understand Thérèse? I think not. It is one of the many paradoxes attaching to her that she is often least understood by those who love her most. And they do really love her, these clients who have not even begun to grasp her doctrine. Her language is so guileless and simple on the surface that it requires attention and care if we are to discover the profundity of thought it clothes. All this talk about "little souls" is misleading further. This way is not for little souls if by that expression we mean the mediocre, but it is little in as much as it can be insignificant and unnoticed; that is to say, heroic virtue really can be practised amid the trivial incidents and duties of daily life.

Or again we can say it is intelligible to little souls—but there once more is the rub, for most of us resent being told we have little souls, even when, alas, we all too obviously have. Again Thérèse corrects our thinking, pointing out the folly of wishing never to fall. What does it matter, she says, if I fall at every instant, "for thereby *I see* my weakness, and that for me is great gain".

Today perhaps more than ever before in the history of Christianity we are called to live our lives on an heroic level, to be the leaven of the mass, and at this crucial time many of us utterly fail to comprehend the heroic element in the life of Thérèse, and consider that her "way of childhood" is for the

spiritual Peter Pans, removing even the possibility of heroism
from daily life, and reducing everything it touches to a banal
sentimentalism. On the contrary it is the only way that puts
within the reach of the average person in ordinary conditions
the opportunity of attaining heroism without removing from
his natural scope or sphere. The little way can charge with
supernatural life the trivial duties and humdrum chores that
are the portion of most of us; it is a "Midas touch" to transform such a humble object as the cobweb that must be swept
from beneath the staircase, so that without departing from our
daily round we can begin the ascent of the mount of perfection
by simple fidelity in little things within our reach, instead of
awaiting placidly the opportunities for greater achievements
which may never come across our horizon.

Few of us have the opportunity of offering anything but
trifles: wounded vanity, disappointments, minor aches and
pains, uncongenial surroundings, companions who misunderstand or embarrass us, monotony and discouragement. Can
God *really* accept these, we are tempted to wonder; do we give
Him *pleasure* by our headaches, our weariness, the very futility
of our life?

Thérèse herself knew this experience. Sometimes she felt
her "treasures" were not worth the trouble of amassing; there
were difficult moments when she felt tempted to throw in the
sponge and admit that she was achieving nothing and getting
nowhere. But instead of growing disheartened, she found
that "in an act of love, even *not felt,* all is restored and
more".

On every page of her writings St. Thérèse insists upon the
reality of the truths of faith over those of the material world
about us. "Life is not dreary," she corrected a novice who made
a statement to that effect. "Had you said 'Exile is dreary' I
could understand. But the word 'life' should be used only of
the eternal, unfading joys of heaven, not for that which must
end. And in this true meaning, life is far from dreary; on the
contrary it is extremely gay." If we can but follow her she holds
out to us the possibility of rising to meet what is, perhaps, the
greatest challenge that has ever been held out to Christians

since the days of the infant Church, the precious opportunity
of "gathering diamonds with a rake".

All Christians know quite well from our Lord's words that
there is no easy way to heaven; no easy way even of being His
disciples. We are not bidden to endure the cross, to make the
best of a bad job and put up with what cannot be avoided, but
to take it up willingly and follow in His footsteps, after first
having given away all that we possessed. Thérèse never
attempted to water down or sugar-coat these great gospel
truths, although she did believe she had received new light
on them. She did not write another treatise on perfection, she
simply told the story of her own soul, letting us see how
naturally the following of Christ works out in practice. She
invites us to follow her up the steep incline by a short way, a
little way, but one which is every bit as toilsome as the old one,
in so far as it necessitates the same abandonment of self and
possessions and will as do the maxims of our Lord, and of every
teacher of asceticism and mysticism since. It is a short-cut only
in as much as it takes the ascent more rapidly. It is unremitting
climbing every inch of the way, for, as St. John of the Cross
says, on this road not to go forward is to turn back, and not to
be gaining is to be losing.

It is unfortunately a common mistake to read into Thérèse's
words a meaning which she never had in mind. She tells us
that everyone can do what she has done. She does not mean to
imply that anyone can do it without taking the pains she took
over it, without departing from the comfortable motor road
that winds gradually around the lower slopes of the mount of
perfection. One of the reasons for misunderstanding her,
possibly, is the gaiety and happiness and matter-of-fact cheer-
fulness she diffuses through her pages, while her habitual
disposition to hide her sufferings beneath a smile has deceived
some readers, who have failed to see beyond the gaiety, suspect-
ing nothing of the anguish underlying the smile. The little
way is essentially simple. It is based on the fact that it is not
what we do, nor how much we do, nor even how difficult are
the things done that really counts, but the love with which we
do them. Our Lord has no need of our works, we can accom-

plish nothing, add nothing to Him, nor take anything away; but He wants the complete abandonment of our minds and wills to His sanctifying power. "Our Lord has seen fit to show me the only way which leads to love, and that is the unconcern with which a child goes to sleep in its father's arms . . . If all the weak, imperfect souls in the world could only feel as I do about it . . . there'd be no reason why a single one of them should despair of scaling the hill of charity and reaching the very top. Our Lord doesn't ask for great achievements, only for self-surrender and gratitude."[1] He never refuses the grace to take the first step, and on the road to self-abandonment it is the first step that costs. "You must practise the little virtues," Thérèse constantly exhorted the novices.

What are the "little" virtues? St. Francis de Sales repeatedly stressed their importance in the spiritual life: courtesy, the "fine flower" of charity, patience, considerateness, kindliness, which are very far from mere social grace or suave *politesse*, an outward façade which often conceals deliberate rancour and ill-will. For the holy Bishop of Geneva these little virtues were the outward manifestations of an inner simplicity of heart, the love of one's neighbour for Christ and Christ in one's neighbour. From this point of view there is nothing "little" about any such act of virtue, apart from the fact that it is exercised for the most part in a small way, and never bears any of the classical outlines of the heroic or adventurous.

As long as we co-operate with the graces as they are given to us and make a consistent effort, God will accept our good will and achieve for us the deeds we can do no more than envisage; but we must keep striving and never allow ourselves to be beaten into discouragement. By practising the virtues, says Thérèse, we persevere in lifting our foot to climb the hill of perfection. But of ourselves we can never succeed in taking even the first upward step. God who asks nothing of us but good will, watches our fruitless attempts, and eventually He will stoop down and carry us in His arms to the top. "But if you leave off lifting your foot, your stay at the bottom will be a long one."

[1] A.S. pp. 228-9.

When we have learned to recognize the will of God in every event of daily life, we will receive everything from His hand with love and joy. Little sacrifices or sweeping renunciations, pleasure or pain—all are welcomed as expressions of His will for us and means of drawing us ever closer to Him, stripping us of those attachments which keep Him, as it were, at a distance.

"Let us travel with our Lord, in whatever sphere of life we are in; and we must travel light in His company. If we hasten on the road, we mustn't have a load," said Fr. Vincent McNabb, O.P. "We travel light that we may travel fast. One requires so little with God; and what a glorious thing it is to see how little one needs for any great things—very little beyond the human hand, the human brain, the human heart. There is no life which could not get rid of quite a number of things. There is perfection in simplicity. Simple lines have always to be the essence of the spiritual life. They are lines of strength. If God is our great defence, we are very strong, and the less we ask from the world, the stronger we are. I want you and myself to go about with our Lord, fancy free, having hardly any load in His sweet company. May we be among those "little ones", not "wise and prudent", but those who strip themselves of almost everything in order to clothe themselves with HIM."

(ii) A Theory of Littleness

"God is so pleased with the confidence of a soul who relies on Him and looks to nothing else, that it may truthfully be said of her, she receives as much as she hopes for." (Maxims of St. John of the Cross.)

By surrender and self-abandonment, Thérèse takes for granted that we understand total dedication that stops short at nothing. Nowadays we are inclined to question the word abandonment, and feel that in speaking of an "abandoned soul" we might be indicating one in the last stages of depravity. Also we find the same word used for the soul abandoned to God as applied to her who is (to all intents and purposes) abandoned by God. But there is no word which replaces it, and in his translation of Père de Caussade's treatise, Algar Thorold adopted, as the nearest English equivalent, the compound word "self-abandonment"—though even this fails to convey the full sense of the untranslatable *l'abandon*. There are many features which we familiarly associate with Thérèse, for instance her charming *naïveté* and innocent ignorance of the world and its ways, but there is only one element which is essential to spiritual childhood, and that is the recognition of one's own nothingness, the deliberate referring of all things to God. This is the abandonment of spiritual childhood, wherein one turns with confidence and hope to the heavenly Father in whom alone can our trust be placed, surrendering to Him all responsibility for our welfare. In no sphere of life, least of all that of the spirit, can we have our cake and eat it. "The measure of our love of God," according to St. Bernard, "should be to love Him without measure."

Mgr. Gay speaks of spiritual childhood as being more perfect than the love of suffering, in that it kills pride much more surely than does the spirit of penance. Nothing so immolates man as to be sincerely and peacefully little. A child surrenders itself, it can do nothing, it knows nothing, it has neither pretences nor affectations. It is a being who lives a supervised life. However, the process of becoming little (in the real, supernatural sense of the term) is not the outcome of any efforts of our own, but is a gratuitous effect of infused faith on our ordinary consciousness. When people try to produce it themselves they merely make themselves look unnatural, childish, or—very often—plain ridiculous.

St. Thérèse well understood the true value and intrinsic worth of so-called little sacrifices. They can be just as costly as nobler deeds, but their very pettiness robs one of any sense of complacency in achievement, which heroic penances could breed. One is not liable to boast of such performances, nor is anybody else likely to notice them.

There have been numerous attempts at interpreting Thérèse's use of the word "little", and as many at translating her idiom—some taking it to mean mediocre, others babyish and undeveloped, others ordinary or average. My belief is that

what Thérèse really means to convey is the same kind of littleness or dependence on grace of which our Lady spoke when
she said: "He hath regarded the humility (i.e. dependence on
Himself) of His handmaiden." (Luke 1 : 48.) In her own eyes,
Mary was nothing, and she humbly acknowledged that all that
had come to her was the gift of God. He had exalted her, the
lowly one; He had done great things in her, and she did not
possess that perverted pride that sometimes parades itself as
modesty, refusing to acknowledge the great work He had
wrought in her. From henceforth, she declared, all generations
would call her blessed; and Thérèse too recognized, like a true
child of Mary, that God had done great things in her, the
greatest of all being, as she claimed, "to make me conscious
of my own littleness, my own incapacity".

Thérèse's littleness was that of Mary, on whose hidden life
she had some very penetrating things to say, and this life of
littleness has been lived by St. Thérèse with a sincerity unsurpassed by anyone, with the exception of our Lady herself,
who is of course the supreme exemplar of the little way, in
whom we see the first and greatest demonstration of "the
blessedness of being little".

"What then," asks Père Grou, S.J., "is solid devotion to the
Blessed Virgin? It is imitation of her interior life, of her lowly
opinion of self, of her love for a hidden life, silence, retire-
ment; *of her attraction to little things*; of her fidelity to grace,
of the simplicity of her recollection and prayer, the only object
of which was God and His holy will, Jesus Christ and His
life."

When asked what she meant by always remaining a little
child before God, Thérèse made the now-famous statement:
"It is to recognize our nothingness, to look for everything from
God as a little child looks for everything from his father; it
is to be disquieted about nothing, and not to be set on gaining one's fortune. Even amongst the poor they give the child
what is necessary for him, until he grows up, then his father
will no longer support him, but says to him: 'Go and work
now, for you are able to look after yourself'. It is to avoid hearing that, that I have not wished to grow up, because I realized

I should never be able to gain my living, the eternal life of heaven! I have, then, always remained little, and have had no other occupation than that of gathering flowers, the flowers of love and sacrifice, and offering them to God for His pleasure. To be little is not to attribute to oneself the virtues one practises, believing oneself capable of something, but to recognize that God puts the treasure of virtue into the hands of His little child to serve Him when there is need of it; but it is always the treasure of the good God. Finally, one must never be discouraged by one's faults, just like little children who often fall, but are too small to do themselves much harm."[1]

This emphasis on abasement, helplessness, nothingness, and —which seems even worse—the desire to remain so, has an alien ring to modern ears, accustomed to eulogies on the virtues of independence, self-reliance and autonomy. Even before the dawning of his reason, the modern child must be allowed to express himself, his latent powers given scope to develop freely, removed from the danger of inhibitions which punitive checks on his attempts at self-expression might engender. I was once told by a priest of a young pagan whom fate or grace had drafted into his catechism class, and who was extremely disconcerted by the novel suggestion that God was everywhere and in everything.

"Is He here, on my left, and on my right as well?"

"Yes."

More incredulously: "Here in front of me?"

"Yes."

"Behind me as well?"

"Yes."

It required a little time and effort to digest this.

"Well," was the eventual pronouncement. "I only hope that He's not going to make a nuisance of Himself."

Many of us, like that young man, face the potential danger of becoming so free that we might be allowed to fall out of existence.

Our own natural intelligence will never lead us very far on the spiritual road unless it is trained to grow and develop in

[1] N.V. 6th August.

the light of faith. But how are we to make faith grow and strengthen in us? Christ, contemplated in faith becomes, as He promised, the way, the truth and the light, through which we pass into the mystery and divine life of the Blessed Trinity. It is essential, in order to attain to God, to keep our eyes, illumined by faith, upon Christ; and it is faith alone that makes it possible to do so. Faith is the door, the entry which gives access to God, and faith only, St. John of the Cross reiterates many times, is the proximate and proportionate means whereby the soul is united with God. Indeed he, the mystical doctor, reduces the whole doctrine of contemplation to an exposition of the role of living and active faith—that is faith animated by charity.

The natural intelligence can prove for itself the existence of God and discover some of His perfections, merely by attributing to Him the beauties and excellences that are constantly before us in the works of His creation. Such natural knowledge, although it leads us to a love of the Creator of these wonders, is very far below the supernatural knowledge of Himself that God offers us, calling us to know and love Him as He knows and loves Himself. Our intellectual knowledge of God reveals Him to us as the author of all in the natural order, and attributes perfections to Him by reason of the proportion of perfection He has bestowed upon creatures—"leaving them, by His glance alone, clothed with beauty". But it is a finite power and could never, by itself, come to know God as God, had He not revealed Himself and given us a supernatural power capable of receiving His light. That power is the virtue of faith, which is an aptitude for possessing Him according to the gifts of the Holy Spirit, in wisdom and understanding especially.

Thérèse knew what true power, and also what true freedom were; and because she understood God's rightful place she was able to see her own quite clearly. He is all; she is nothing. All she has has come from God and without His grace she can do nothing. On this scale of values she built her life of love, an edifice with the two foundation-stones dovetailed into each other: knowledge of her own powerlessness, allied with unshakeable confidence in His strength. Resting on the firm bases of humility and trust, she was able to raise her soul to the heights of sanctity. It is interesting to compare her definition with the following letter of spiritual direction from the great Abbot Marmion: "It is a great grace to see our miseries and our littleness which are really much greater than we imagine; but this knowledge is real poison unless it be coupled with an *immense* faith and confidence in the all-sufficiency of our dear Lord's merits, riches and virtues, which *are all ours.*"

It would be an error to assume that, because Thérèse preached to her novices in season and out the necessity of confidence and absolute trust (even to the point of audacity) in Almighty God, and because her own tranquil confidence never wavered however high the dark waters rose in her soul, this childlike trust came naturally to her. She had to fight down temptations against this virtue—that is abundantly clear from her own evidence and that of other witnesses. The most important of these, Mother Agnes of Jesus, related that during a community retreat, in which the preacher constantly dwelt on the inexorable justice of God and the judgment of the soul, impressing on them the ease with which one might fall into grave sin (and that even a religious was by no means exempt therefrom), Thérèse's anxiety and fear were so great that she was in danger of becoming really ill. "I was serving in the refectory at the time," said Mother Agnes, "and I was struck by her anguished expression. She could not eat. I think she would have died had the spiritual exercises been prolonged, for they were based principally on fear, and our St. Thérèse, whose soul only expanded in confidence, felt stifled by them." Thérèse herself states in her autobiography that her fear of having gravely offended God was so great that she could find no peace for many months; that the way of trust and confidence had long attracted her, but she had not ventured to embark upon it until the retreat of 1891, when the Franciscan, Père Alexis Prou, diagnosed and dismissed her fears, and launched her "in full sail on the ocean of confidence and love".

Her child's confidence in the infinite mercy of God was, then, something on which she had to exercise her faith. It was not, despite the metaphor she so often employs, merely a hang-over from her physical childhood, and the absolute trust she had had as a small child in her own parents. But she uses that figure, because such a confidence expresses aptly what should be the attitude of the "little" soul, abandoned to its heavenly father. It was something that had developed in her, something she visualized as a way of perfection and which—although it attracted her powerfully—was not, as might be inferred, as natural to her as breathing. She needed reassurance before she could be certain that her attraction was sound and could be relied on.

This confidence need not always be felt, at least not sensibly, for it to become an habitual disposition of the soul. "If the night terrifies you," she advised Sister Mary of St. Joseph, "if you complain at not *seeing* the one who bears you up, *close your eyes*; and *willingly* make the sacrifice asked of you. So you will remain at peace, and the night, which you can no longer notice, cannot frighten you; soon serenity, if not joy, will be born again in your heart."[1]

Weakness and littleness, when permitted by God, are the beginning of spiritual strength, for they compel His merciful love. St. Paul said this quite clearly: "When I am weakest, then I am strongest of all"; (II Cor. 12:10) and "God has chosen what the world holds weak, so as to abash the strong". (I Cor. 1:27.) And countless souls between him and St. Thérèse have made spiritual capital of it. St. Francis de Sales points out that, among the poor and beggars, those whose wretchedness and poverty is greatest may be considered in the best position to receive alms because of their piteous state. We are the poorest of the poor, and, as the more miserable have the greater claim, the mercy of God will stoop more willingly to us.

Commenting on the text "Master, we have toiled all the night and caught nothing" (Luke 5:5), Thérèse observes: "Maybe if he had caught a few *small fish*, Jesus would not have worked a miracle, but he had *nothing*, so Jesus soon filled his net so that it almost broke. There you have Jesus' *charac-*

[1] C.L. p. 284.

ter: as God He gives, but He requires *humbleness* of *heart*."[1]
This is her conception of littleness and helplessness. It is a
mistake to think that she suffered from some sort of child-
complex—a refusal to grow up, a desire to remain a "baby",
and therefore to read into her spirituality something puerile
and coy. She used the words of childhood only in an attempt
to define what she could otherwise not express, and did not
mean "children" in the literal sense of the word. "The Holy
Innocents are not infants in heaven," she said to Mother
Agnes. "They only have the indefinable charm of childhood
and are represented as children solely because of our need of
images to comprehend invisible things." And Mother Agnes
adds that in adopting the terms of childhood to explain
spiritual realities, Thérèse used them solely as a comparison,
to expound her thoughts more easily.

Spiritual childhood is not infantilism or retarded growth,
certainly not a child-complex. It co-existed in Thérèse along
with real maturity of soul. Everything which is incomplete or
imperfect as a way of spiritual life is directly opposed to the
way of childhood.

Despite her love of diminutives and fanciful metaphors,
there was nothing childish about Thérèse's conception of God.
She spoke to Him in the way that came most naturally to her;
and if He was "Papa, the good God" to her, there was no lessen-
ing in her mind of the omniscience she was presuming thus to
address. She knew that God, the all-holy, all-wise, is a most
tender Father, who wishes His weak and foolish children to
be completely themselves when approaching Him; and since
we, however lofty our wisdom or learning, can never raise ourselves to God and speak on equal terms with Him, He in His
infinite condescension and courtesy, stoops to listen to what
we are trying to say. Thérèse had an inherent dislike of for-
mality in prayer, and certainly it is difficult to enthuse over
rigmaroles bearing no resemblance to our normal mode of
speech. We would not ask a favour from our own father by
making a ceremonious bow and begging him to deign to listen
to our petition and vouchsafe to grant us permission to borrow

[1] C.L. p. 196.

his car for the afternoon; and we should avoid as far as possible the use of such expressions in our private converse with God. Why should our heavenly father be any more favourably disposed when we behave so unnaturally? When we speak and think of God like this, our prayer is in danger of becoming mechanical, artificial and impersonal, a mere pigeonhole to be used at certain specific times, not, as it should be, something that pervades our whole lives and influences everything we do. Of course, it is equally misguided to go to the opposite extreme of despising the sacred liturgy, but certain "consecrated phrases" do not normally find their way into everyday speech. The public prayer of the Church is one thing, and more or less on a par with formal modes of address; one's private relations with God are quite another matter, and simplicity should always be their keynote. I remember as a child being given a book of thanksgivings after holy Communion, one for each day of the week. Among them I found what seemed an extraordinary request—taken, though I did not know it at the time, from Psalm 25—that God should "burn my reins and my heart". As a consequence, most of my thanksgiving was spent in wondering what my reins were, and why on earth they should be burned, and what good it could possibly do either to God or myself. Mgr. Knox has translated this verse: "Assay my inmost desires and thoughts"; but even this would hardly comprise a very heartfelt or fervent prayer for a seven-year-old.

Referring to her lack of sensible consolation at holy Communion, Thérèse says that she imagined her soul as a vacant site littered with rubbish, which she asked our Lady to clear away. Then she asked her to erect a pavilion worthy of the reception, and decorate it with all the finery she had at her disposal, and then invite all the saints and angels to come and assist at the entertainment. "I think this is all the welcome our Lord expects from me when He comes to visit my soul, and if He's satisfied, then I too am satisfied."

This was Thérèse's personal approach to God, but in telling us of her interior dispositions, she does not propose that we reproduce them literally. Only in such slavish copying does one find anything that could be considered repellent, and we do not have to imagine ourselves as little balls or children with soiled pinafores in order to follow the little way in all its essentials. These are sound and wholesome and for everybody, for they are, after all, what our Lord Himself has recommended. We can fill in our own details, but still follow the essential pattern none the less faithfully.

Thérèse herself, in using the terms of childhood to express her thoughts, often found it necessary to correct the picture of infancy by qualifications. She was never silly. She never lowered her ideal. From her earliest years she dreamed of becoming a saint, and although at the end of her life she saw herself still no more than a helpless child, a "little soul", she never called herself a "little saint" (see Note 8) except in the sense of being one who desired to attain sanctity through the practice of little and hidden virtues. She has explained this in speaking of Théophane Vénard as a *little* saint whose life was quite ordinary. "His soul and mine resemble each other, and his words re-echo my thoughts." Her self-chosen title of "little Flower" was borrowed from this young martyr, and when she wished to leave a "souvenir" for her sisters, she copied for them extracts from his letters: "We are all flowers planted upon earth, and God will gather us in His own good time— some sooner, some later. I, a *little flower* that has lived but one day, am the first to be taken! But we shall meet again in Paradise where we shall enjoy unending bliss."

The attitude of childlike confidence was not the outcome of a psychological disorder. It was the fruit of that change of heart our Lord counselled to the apostles: "Unless you be converted and become as little children, you shall not enter into the kingdom of heaven." (Matt. 18: 3.)

"The Son of God was not content with merely stating that the kingdom of heaven was for children, or that whoever became a little child would be greatest in the kingdom of heaven," said Pope Benedict XV. "He went so far as to exclude from His kingdom those who did not become as little children . . . It would be absurd to dream of resuming either the outward appearance or feebleness of the state of infancy, but it is not unreasonable to discern in the words of the gospel a counsel given to those who have attained maturity to return to the virtue associated with spiritual childhood."

Thérèse had always been the baby of the family at home, and as a Carmelite, although the senior novice, she was destined to remain the "youngest", being permanently excluded from the chapter where she would automatically have taken her place at the end of her canonical novitiate, because of the presence of two elder sisters. Always she had been and thought of herself as "little Thérèse", and as such she remained, not through spiritual or emotional immaturity, but as the fruit of a grace that made her understand completely the ideal which Jesus proposed to His disciples.

It was a natural tendency, however, that made her cling to the language and symbols of childhood. But these are not essential to spiritual childhood, and can easily become a hindrance if they are studiously copied, in the same way that any artificiality is detrimental in the spiritual life. In point of fact there is only one way to heaven, and that is the way of the gospel. We may call it by whatever name we please, but in the end it reduces itself to one formula: spiritual childhood. No Christian may say that the way of the gospel is not the way for him. Whether we picture ourselves actually as children is neither here nor there; what we must do is to recognize our own nothingness and powerlessness, look to God for everything as a child looks to his father, let nothing disquiet us, and be content to remain always poor. It is this child that is to grow within us, the child who knows that its only prerogative consists in dependence and trust.

This is the meaning and strength of spiritual childhood. When it is fully attained it cannot be anything less than sanctity, which does not lie in "this or that practice"; but is *a disposition of the heart* which "makes us always humble and little in the hands of God", fully alive to our own helplessness, but confident to the point of audacity in the goodness and power of our father. Genuine humility is an unfailing protection against the anxieties consequent upon daily human encounters, for the truly humble person not only acknowledges her own weakness and dependence on God's grace, but also her interior peace remains undisturbed when her deficiencies are recognized by others as well.

In the words of Père Grou, S.J.: "God has at His disposal infallible means to save me; in spite of my weakness, in spite of my miseries, in spite of my inclinations to evil, He will infallibly succeed, if I never lose confidence in Him, if I expect all from Him, if I keep always united to Him."

(iii) "Little and Humble in the Hands of God"

There are today many Catholics in search of a simple method of spirituality by which they can grow in devotion to our Lord and His blessed Mother. Such a method, above all, must be closely associated with everyday events, and it is here that St. Thérèse gives the lead. She herself never went beyond the common order of things. In her home as a child or in her convent as a religious, she followed the ordinary routine, and fulfilled her vocation, but as Pope Pius XI said, with such readiness, generosity and fidelity, that her virtue reached a heroic degree.

As has been pointed out, there is no easy ascent of Mount Carmel, but that was not what Thérèse had in mind when she spoke of a "lift". This is another case where a lot of nonsense is talked about the little way, almost as if the lift in question were a mechanical device designed to carry all the toddlers to the top floor, whilst they sit in comfort, merely allowing themselves to be conveyed thither. Idiotic though it be, this sort of childishness finds its way not only into conversation but even into print, from which one can see how detestable to the devil are the secrets of God's intimate friends. The original words of St. Thérèse were as follows: "I've always wished that I could be a saint. But whenever I compared myself to the saints there was always this unfortunate difference—they were like great mountains, hiding their heads in the clouds, and I was only an insignificant grain of sand, trodden down by all who passed by. However, I wasn't going to be discouraged; I said to myself: 'God wouldn't inspire us with ambitions that can't be realized. Obviously there's nothing great to be made of me, so it must be possible for me to aspire to sanctity in spite of my insignificance. I've got to take myself just as I am, with all my imperfections; but somehow I shall have to find a little way, all of my own, which will be a direct short-cut to heaven . . . Can't I find a lift which will take me up to Jesus, since I'm not big enough to climb the steep stairway of perfection?'."[1]

The concept of herself as "a grain of sand, trodden down by all who pass by" is taken directly from the prayer composed by the famous General Louis-Gaston de Sonis, a French Carmelite tertiary whose cause for beatification was first introduced in 1928, and which, as was seen in the previous chapter, must have been very familiar both to Mother Agnes and Thérèse. The meaning of the term "lift" is given in Holy Scripture: "Is anyone simple as a little child? Then let him come to me," (Prov. 9: 4) and "I will console you like a mother caressing her son; you shall be like children carried at the breast, fondled on a mother's lap," (Isaias 66: 13,12). And we know from Thérèse's comment on these passages what she meant by being little: "Never were words so touching . . . I could, after all, be lifted up to heaven, in the arms of Jesus! And if that was to happen, there was no need for me to grow bigger; on the contrary, I must be as small as ever, smaller than ever."

For Thérèse love was not a goal to be won through the practice of asceticism; it was the starting point. With love to spur her on, the practice of the virtues seemed easy, and the desire to give pleasure to Jesus, the sole object of her love, predominated in everything; for it is through love alone that we can become pleasing to God and our works acquire merit in His sight. The love of God—charity—is the supernatural predisposition that enabled her to correspond to the minute-by-minute graces of every day, thus finding herself "in God's sunlight", receiving more and greater graces in proportion to her acceptance and co-operation with those already given.

"In the onset we must act with courage," she told a novice. "By this means the heart gains strength and victory follows victory . . . the more you advance the fewer the combats, or

[1] A.S. p. 248.

rather, the easier the victory, since the good side of things will be more visible."

This is little, but it is not easy. It is easier for nature to bear a sweeping renunciation which would at least provide some consolation, the knowledge of having achieved something worth while. But these pinpricks, seen by God alone, are for that very reason most important rungs on the ladder of humility, and the steps that go to make up the little way.

St. Thérèse, says Père M.-M. Philipon, O.P., throws a clear light on an aspect of the gospel that has been somewhat disregarded: the utilization of our faults and failings to help us in our approach to God. This is no new doctrine, but in line with St. Augustine's well-known comment on St. Paul: "Everything co-operates to the good of those who love God, *even their sins*"; and St. Thérèse's reminder of it is of prime importance. "There are faults," she says, "which do not offend God, but merely have the effect of humbling the soul and making love stronger." What director has not met countless souls entangled in a maze, fumbling in their confusion deeper into the labyrinth, always turned inwards on themselves and their misery, and unable to fly upwards to God and find release and rest in Him? A full and humble avowal of their weakness would set them free for ever. Thérèse comes at the crucial moment to remind them of the potential value of their interminable falls and backslidings. "Look at little children, who never cease falling down, breaking things, tearing and soiling their clothes, and all the while loving their parents very much. When I fall thus, like a small child, I realize at once my nothingness, and I tell myself: 'What would happen to you if you tried to support yourself on your own strength'?" This is one of the most significant subjects in the teaching of Christian spirituality: the ability to accept our own worthlessness and even to rejoice in it. "Grief that depresses us comes from self-love," St. Thérèse once admonished Sister Mary of the Trinity. "The more humbly we admit our weakness and helplessness, the more readily will God stoop down and pour out His gifts lavishly on us."

One cannot follow the little way, become a child, practise

spiritual childhood, without humility which is the root and stock of all the other virtues, and without which no virtue can flourish. "Jesus takes pleasure in teaching me how to glory in my infirmities," Thérèse wrote to her uncle, M. Guérin. This does not mean that she accepted them complacently, content to do nothing about it. She tells us that we must be patient with ourselves, acknowledge our weakness and indigence, but never yield to discouragement, suffering sweetly and lovingly God's blows on our pride and self-reliance. Nobody who is really trying to live a Christian life refuses God his confidence, but we do not always realize how deep-rooted and almost instinctive are our self-assurance and independence. In practice, many of us behave as though we considered ourselves endowed with considerably more commonsense and sound judgment than God. The metaphor of the shepherd who abandoned the ninety-nine sheep in order to go seeking one stray is so familiar that we hardly ever consider it apart from its poetic scriptural setting. But in daily life, our admiration would seldom be reserved for anyone so unreliable and impractical as that shepherd. On the contrary we would dismiss him on the spot. How could we be easy in our mind about our property if it were in the care of anyone with so little sense of proportion? Only God can give us light on this, and it was from Him that St. Thérèse was always "making fresh and salutary discoveries" of her weakness.

For her remaining a little child meant acknowledging her incapacity and looking for everything from God, never becoming discouraged by her faults, which were like the frequent tumbles of the very young, who however are too small to do themselves much harm.

The humility which characterizes the child of God is a much more attractive form of this virtue than that which is based on scrupulous and meticulous self-examination. To be incessantly preoccupied with oneself, even though it be in order to discover one's failings, can be a form of egoism, and it is carried to such lengths at times that one's soul might well be the only one in the world. To be little, to be forgotten, we must first be so in our own eyes, and the way to achieve this is by self-forgetfulness, turning to God in faith and referring all to Him. In this way we acquire not only a more attractive but a more true humility, which relates all things to God and enables us to see ourselves in the light of His scale of values, instead of measuring everything by own own standards and endeavouring to limit the Infinite to the capacity of an inch-rule. We cannot even perceive ourselves when we try to view our lives against the backdrop of people and places that move across the stage of daily living. It is not how we appear in our own eyes, nor how we hope we appear to other people that matters, but how we really stand in the sight of God. "Yes," said Thérèse, "it does seem to me that I am humble. God shows me the truth, and I see so clearly that everything comes from Him." And again: "Do not believe that humility would keep me from realizing the gifts of God. I am aware that 'He has done great things in me', and I thank Him and praise Him for it daily."

When she was still a child, Thérèse felt certain that she was destined for greatness, although she did not see how she could ever achieve it. Like so many people, she still laboured under the delusion that extraordinary feats were required to qualify for greatness, and she knew that she could never manage them. Then the idea dawned on her that her glory would never be discernible to human eyes, but was to consist in devoting her energies to becoming a great saint. A presumptuous thought? Hardly, since we are all "called to be saints", and nobody will accomplish it without trying, or in fact working hard and consistently. But what Thérèse had grasped intuitively was the difference between the two criteria of greatness: that of the supernatural standard, and the yardstick of this world. As well as the greatness that belongs by right to a noble deed or a great sacrifice, there is the greatness bestowed by desire and love on things that are in themselves insignificant and commonplace. The greatness of the world's measure is quantitative; that of the spiritual realm is qualitative only. This was one of the most significant discoveries of her formative years. "The only true glory is the glory that lasts for ever; and to win that, dazzling exploits are not necessary. What is needed is to live a hidden

5*

life, doing good so unobtrusively that 'the left hand does not
know what the right hand is doing'." A child is totally dependent upon its father; Thérèse, therefore, wished to remain in
spirit always little and dependent, acknowledging her incapacity to earn her livelihood, the eternal life of heaven.

A few hours before her death, Thérèse asked Mother Mary
Gonzaga to present her to the Blessed Virgin, and prepare her
to die well. The prioress told her that she had always understood and practised humility, therefore her preparations had
all been made in advance. Thérèse replied simply: "I have
understood humility of heart, and have never sought anything
but the truth." This is the reason why she could, with no detri-
ment to her humility, relate with absolute simplicity and can-
dour the story of her astonishing holiness. In her eyes, as in
truth it was, all her story was the action of God's goodness and
mercy on one of His creatures who fully responded to grace.
Despite the intimate nature of her memoirs, she was able to
get outside herself, as it were, view herself objectively and,
seeing clearly that God had done wonderful things in her, give
Him all the credit for it. As for herself, she said she had become
so detached that she could not even bother searching for words
that would sound appropriately self-effacing.

The most common mistake is to equate humility with abasement. However the abasement that is needed is not mere
self-depreciation, but the attitude in which one holds oneself
with regard to God. Once He becomes our real objective, we
can perform the highest and most important actions and hold
responsible offices "with anxious care", while remaining
simple and humble children of God, recognizing ourselves for
what we are, with our failings and insufficiencies, but also with
our gifts and graces, whether physical, moral or intellectual,
and acknowledging them as gifts of God to be used in His
service. For in relation to God we remain little because we
are—and know ourselves to be—dependent always and for
everything on Him. Actually when we have once got our perspective correct, the greater stature we attain to, the greater
will grow the conviction of our creaturely dependence; for the
more we receive the greater becomes that dependence.

Thérèse knew that everything she had was from God, and she simply and frankly admitted that He had lavished great graces, all undeserved, on her.

Mother Agnes reminded her of St. John of the Cross' words: "Perfect souls can gaze without danger at their own supernatural beauty", apparently in the hope of drawing her on the subject. But Thérèse replied quickly: "What beauty? I assure you I do not see my beauty at all, but only the graces I have received from the good God."

This, then, is the ordinary way of love, humility and confidence in God, of simplicity, the way of a little child, dependent and lovingly trustful in its father's arms. It presupposes deep love, and that primary disposition, humility, the basis that must be well consolidated before an other virtue can even begin to raise itself. As St. Teresa of Avila put it : "The foundation of this whole edifice is humility, and if you have not true humility, the Lord will not wish it to reach any great height; in fact, it is for your own good that it should not; if it did, it would fall to the ground . . . By meditating on God's humility, we shall see how far we are from being humble."[1] Genuine humility is inseparable from trust in God; the two virtues are complementary. Thérèse defined the *only way* that leads to divine love as "the unconcern with which a small child falls asleep in its father's arms".

There is nothing essentially new in this way, for Thérèse is but reiterating the stipulation made by our Lord that unless we became like little children we could not enter His kingdom. She could, then, be lifted up to heaven in Jesus' arms. And for this, it was not necessary for her to grow big, but rather to remain small, or even become smaller. Thérèse is indeed digging deep, building on a foundation of rock. Pride and self-reliance are the barriers that block most of the light that otherwise would come flooding into the soul. Thérèse declared that she had light only to see her own nothingness, but that did her more good than lights concerning faith—in fact, such a revelation prepares the soul to receive lights on faith.

[1] I.C. Mans. VII, Ch. IV, Mans. I, Ch. II.

We have only to work at breaking down our self-love and self-will which hinder the action of God in our souls; He will do the rest. "Give me a humble soul," is one famous dictum, "and I will give you a saint." When Jesus finds us emptied of all self-sufficiency, He will come and occupy the space we have cleared and prepared for Him; but, as St. Teresa of Avila tersely points out, we cannot expect His Majesty to take up His abode in a dwelling that is not in order. "If we fill the palace with vulgar people and all kinds of junk, how can the Lord and His court occupy it? When such a crowd is there, it would be a great thing if He were to remain even for a short time."[1]

(iv) Seed of Glory

When Sister Mary of the Trinity confided her discouragement at her failure to meet setbacks with the courage that would draw profit from them, Thérèse counselled her to offer to God the sacrifice of never gathering any fruit from her tree. "It may be His will that throughout your whole life you will feel nothing but repugnance at suffering and humiliations." Well, if He permits every blossom of desire and goodwill to fall to the ground before any fruit appears, there is no cause for worry. "At the hour of death, in the twinkling of an eye, He will cause ripe fruit to appear on the tree of your soul."

This is sound but singularly unpalatable advice. Most of us know the frustration of seeming failure. If we had the assurance that our disappointments were in fact spiritual successes, the consolation would remove the sting and suffering. But Thérèse knew what she was talking about. She herself had never achieved much visible success despite all her persistent and wholehearted efforts. As we have seen, she was considered by her sisters as a good religious but quite ordinary; not one of those seemingly indispensable persons who can capably fill any office. She was slow and apparently none too deft with her needle or at the various domestic chores which fell her lot. It did not occur to the others that up to the time she left *Les Buissonnets* at the age of fifteen, Thérèse had never even made her own bed, let alone done her share of the housework; and

1 W.P., Ch. 28, p. 118.

many of her sisters considered her inaptitude a sign of slovenli-
ness and disinterest. Very few even suspected her interior progress or sanctity. She knew all this and rejoiced, feeling herself
to be in good company. How many of the saints have been, to
all intents and purposes, complete failures? Think too of our
Lord, whose earthly life was crowned by the greatest failure
of all in the eyes of men, the ignominious death of a criminal;
yet the smallest and most indifferent of His actions were of
infinitely more value in the sight of the Father than the combined sufferings of all the martyrs from the beginning to the
end of the world. Truly, it is not so much the greatness of our
acts, nor even their difficulty that counts in the final analysis,
but only the love which prompts us to do them.

Holiness consists of three principal stages. First there is our
habitual union with God effected by sanctifying grace in the
depth of the soul. Secondly (that is to say, springing from this
habitual union) is the attainment of actual conformity between the human will and the will of God. Thirdly (except
we wish to be detained in purgatory) there still remains the
task of sanctifying our natural intelligence and memory, and
in this we are helped principally by theological faith and hope.
Usually when we have attained to humble conformity with
the divine will, we are offered the grace of entering upon the
way of spiritual childhood; but we cannot be described as
following in Thérèse's footsteps until we have made the sacrifice of our natural excellence as well. It is moreover in the little
things that we give proof to Jesus of our sincerity, because here
alone there is no room for self-love. Holy Scripture warns us
that the one who despises small things will fall gradually to his
own ruin. Our Lord confirms this when He says: "He that is
faithful in that which is least is faithful also in that which is
greater" (Luke 16: 10); and He has promised to reward the
least service, even a cup of cold water if it is only given in His
name and for His sake.

"Do unto other men all that you would have them do to
you." Our Lord, towards the end of the Sermon on the Mount,
gave us a positive direction, which for the most part we trans-
late into negative terms, such as not inflicting on others what

we would not like done to ourselves in similar circumstances; refraining from making comments that we would dislike hearing about ourselves; avoiding inconveniencing others unnecessarily, and trying not to misinterpret their actions or think unkindly about their foibles.

Such an interpretation falls short of our Lord's requirements, and is more in line with the old pagan axiom—the golden rule of neighbourliness—expressed under many forms. The Persians knew it in the seventh century B.C. "That which you find unpleasant to yourself, refrain from doing to your neighbour." A century later Confucius propounded it not as a religious tenet at all, but as a principle of moral and social philosophy. His contemporary, the Buddha Siddhartha Gautama, counselled: "Wound not others with that which causes pain to yourself."

Nearer to our own time Mahommed declared that "one is not a believer until he desires for his brother that which he desires for himself". This is also a closer approximation to the Old Testament commandment: "Thou shalt love thy neighbour as thyself" (Lev. 19: 18). The demands of such a precept would literally be satisfied simply by refraining from doing our neighbour any harm we would not like inflicted on our own person or property, as we read in Tobias 4: 16: "Never use another as thou wert loth thyself to be used." But Christ has promulgated a new law which superseded all that went before. From now onwards, He says, "you are to love one another *as I have loved you.*" Twice He repeated this injunction at the Last Supper.

"Well," asks Thérèse, "how did Jesus love His disciples?" She then points out that loving our neighbour as ourselves was the criterion God demanded before the Incarnation, because He knew what a powerful motive self-love is, and could lay down no higher standard than the esteem and solicitude we have for our own person and opinions. But this was not Jesus' measure. "I am not just to love my neighbour as myself; I am to love him as Jesus loves him, and will love him till the end of time."

Her paraphrase throws into clear relief the essential

difference between our Lord's definition and those which preceded it. All the pagan philosophers, as well as the Old Testament commandment, are negative, and can be reduced to a perfectionist attitude towards exterior actions. But Christ's teachings are always positive. It was the old law that consisted of a long list of wearisome prohibitions. Jesus simply says "*Do* to others that which you would like them to *do* for you."

These positive good deeds need not be sweeping benefactions, which in any case most of us could not afford. A smile when we are more inclined to show displeasure or boredom is often the most welcome alms, and not infrequently the one that costs us most! The "new commandment" is as new today as it was two thousand years ago. For most of us it has lain in its box, carefully folded in tissue paper, to be taken out and admired occasionally as an edifying text, but never pressed into hard service in daily life.

The whole question is not so much what it is sinful to omit, but rather to find what extra we can do, over and above that which is of strict obligation, for the love of God, expressed through service to our fellow-men. What a happy place this world would be, how remote the threat to domestic or world peace, if we only took the trouble to be pleasant to each other. It is the unexpected word of praise, the unlooked-for encouragement, the word of comfort instead of censure, that is as a cup of cold water to a thirsty traveller. When it comes from the heart and is accompanied by a smile, it identifies the genuine follower of Christ. Not doing any positive kindness, on the other hand, means that we are losing countless opportunities of grace, precious chances of putting happiness into the lives of others and enriching our own with joy on earth and additional degrees of glory for eternity. This is the meaning of all the "roses of Lisieux", exploiting all those little opportunities for inconspicuous service that fill everyone's day.

The Christian law of charity has abolished the rigid interpretation of the law as so many commands to obey, so many prohibitions to remember, fasts to be observed and prayers to be recited, and instilled instead into the heart of man a spirit of love, so that if properly understood and practised, commandments should be superfluous. The habit we must eventually acquire is to do, actively and positively, those things that we would like to receive, while at the same time expecting no return, because we are doing them solely to demonstrate our love of God. We have His guarantee that not one of them will pass unnoticed or unrewarded—not even a cup of cold water so long as it is given in His name and for His love—because each and every one of them, however insignificant in itself, has been a personal service rendered to His son.

It was our Lord Himself who first demonstrated the principle of "littleness"—that perfection in charity and all the other virtues is to be sought in the humdrum incidents of daily life. The mysteries of the kingdom were presented in familiar, homely wrappers—fishing tackle and vineyards, leaven and seed and harvests, marriage-feasts, birth and death. All our trials are ingredients for sanctity—we are blessed, happy, when we exercise patience, mercy, poverty of spirit, when we are attacked and do not seek to retaliate, when we suffer injustice without succumbing to the temptation to pass it on to others. But charity—the first and greatest of the commandments—does not figure in the list of beatitudes at all, for it contains and sustains them all.

Completely detached from creatures, Thérèse lived only for Jesus and the spread of His kingdom in souls. That she herself was quite aware of the intimacy of her relations with Him is clear from her statement that she did not see what good she would enjoy after death that she did not already possess on earth. She would see God face-to-face, but as for being with Him, that she already enjoyed. This was during her "dark night" when, as she confessed, all joy in the belief of God and heaven was gone and she clung only in faith, hope and charity to the certainty that she was still beloved.

St. Francis de Sales' judgment: "A sad saint is a sorry sort of saint" is well known; and St. Teresa of Avila has expressed it even more forcefully and characteristically: "God preserve me from gloomy saints!" St. Thérèse was not sad, and certainly

not gloomy. Childhood is full of joy. So should spiritual childhood be if it is correctly understood and practised. "Tears for
God—that will never do!" she reproached the weeping Sister
Mary of the Trinity. "Far less to Him than to creatures ought
you to show a mournful face for He comes to our cloisters in
search of rest. Jesus loves the glad of heart, the children who
greet Him with smiles and joyous countenances." And on
another occasion she told this novice that the face being the
mirror of the soul, hers, like that of a contented child, should
be always calm and serene.

Spiritual childhood, it must be insisted, does not imply
mental or spiritual immaturity. To interpret it so is to confuse
the terms "childlike" and "childish". Many of us have doubtless encountered nuns whom we would be obliged to label
"childish", but these have nothing whatever in common with
St. Thérèse of the Child Jesus. Childishness in an adult is an
imperfection, a state of arrested development manifesting
traits which long ago should have been outgrown. The quality
of being childlike, on the other hand, is the result of development, and development in the right direction; it is something
one has become. To do this we have to go back to the beginning and start all over again with the attitude of a child, knowing ourselves to be unable to do anything of ourselves, "casting all our care on Him who cares for us", contentedly leaving
all to God who never ceases to watch over us and forestall all
harm, accepting everything from His hand as His own choice
for us and therefore the very best thing that could happen to
us. St. Thérèse illustrates this by one of her own characteristic
"parables".

Supposing, she says, a doctor's son trips over a stone and
breaks his leg. Thanks to his father's skill the bone is set and
soon completely healed. Rightly the boy is grateful. However,
had his father noticed the stone and removed it beforehand,
the boy, unconscious of the danger his father's consideration
had averted, would be less grateful, less moved to affection,
than he was for the cure. But should he learn later what he
had been spared, the boy would love his father more than ever.

And, Thérèse declared triumphantly, that is precisely what

God's loving providence had done for her, so that she realized what she owed to His tender foresight, and "loved Him to distraction".

Thus God had always treated her. She felt His preventive grace had gone before her, removing possible occasions of falling, so that in all humility she admitted that He had forgiven her more than the greatest sinners because He had not waited for her transgressions in order to pardon her. Instead He had taken from her the occasion of falling into sin, thus "forgiving" her in advance the offences she would otherwise have committed. "He hasn't waited to make me love Him much, like the Magdalen," she confessed.

Obviously then one who sees in Thérèse something merely winsome and "pretty", and her little way as a childish or fanciful metaphor unrelated to the hard facts of life, has not read her story aright, and has failed to grasp what she says in so simple a manner. She was not in some miraculous way preserved from the sufferings and agonies that are part and parcel of the way of perfection. Sanctity was purchased by Thérèse at no half-rates. It costs her the same expenditure of heart's blood, a similar outlay of all her resources of courage and endurance as that which every saint has had to pay for this "treasure that is hidden in a field".

"It has to be won at the point of the sword," she warned Céline. "One must *suffer*, agonize!".

CHAPTER FIVE

ALL GOD'S CHILDREN

"Sincere humility of heart, utter fidelity to duty, whereso-
ever God has placed us, readiness for self-sacrifice, affectionate
surrender to God's loving guidance; charity, above all the
charity that is genuine love of God and a tender affection for
Jesus who has loved us so tenderly, a charity which 'is patient
and kind . . . beareth all things, hopeth all things, endureth
all things' . . . such is the 'Little Way'."

(H. H. Pope Pius XI)

(i) The Pathfinder

In the last lines of her letter to Sister Mary of the Sacred
Heart (which now forms Chapter XIII of the *Autobiography*
and Chapter XXX of *Autobiography of a Saint*) addressing
herself to our Lord, Thérèse implored Him to look down in
mercy on the great multitude of souls who share her littleness,
and to choose out for Himself a whole legion of victims, "so
little as to be worthy of your love".

On the occasion of the promulgation of the decree concerning the heroic virtue of St. Thérèse (the first step towards
canonization), Pope Benedict XV said: "There is a call to the
faithful of every nation, no matter what may be their age, sex
or state of life, to enter wholeheartedly into the little way
which led Sister Thérèse to the summit of heroic virtue." At
the canonization in 1925, Pope Pius XI ended his sermon with
the exhortation: "If the way of spiritual childhood became
general, who does not see how easily would be realized the
reformation of human society which we set ourselves to accomplish at the commencement of our pontificate . . . we, therefore,
adopt as our own the prayer of the new St. Thérèse with which
she ends her invaluable autobiography: 'O Jesus, we beseech

Thee to cast Thy glance upon the vast number of little souls, and to choose in this world a legion of little victims worthy of Thy love'."

The two popes draw attention to the fact that sanctity is the vocation of every member of the Church, and that the little way of spiritual childhood is not just another way, but *the* way *par excellence*, which is within the scope of everyone, to attain perfection. Just as each of us is called to sanctity, so the Church in order to fulfil her vocation in the world requires the sanctity of her members. Unless there are Catholic saints there can never be fruitful Catholic Action. "There are many saints whom God raises up for the salvation of souls and from whose countenance He causes rays to proceed which enlighten the feeblest souls. Such were the prophets and apostles, and indeed such are all the saints when God chooses to place them, as it were, in a candlestick. There always will be, as there always have been, saints like these as well as an infinite number of others in the Church who are hidden, who, being intended to shine only in heaven, send forth no light in this life, but live and die in profound obscurity."[1] These "hidden saints" are the "legion of little souls" whom Thérèse calls to follow her along the way of spiritual childhood.

But if perfection is to be attained by all, a simple means which places it within the reach of all is essential. Nobody must be able to say that because of inability to reach a given standard of education, a certain state of life was unattainable, and therefore he could not even aspire to sanctity. It is not of much practical use to point towards the Mount of Perfection towering above us, its peak lost in the clouds and its sides pitted by deep ravines which only a skilled mountaineer equipped with every necessary piece of apparatus could even attempt to negotiate, and bid those who have never left the level plains to scale it. There must be a short-cut for the non-professional. But how is it to be found? There were innumerable scale-maps of this inaccessible but well-chartered mountain, but again they were only for the experts, needing

---

[1] Père de Caussade, S.J., *Self-Abandonment to Divine Providence,* Bk. II, Ch. I (5).

skilful guidance step by step. What busy mother or father could possibly neglect home and family, or take time off from earning their livelihood, to undertake such a strenuous and full-time task? Similarly in many, if not most, walks of life for lay-folk. Yet perfection is not the exclusive prerogative of religious. What is the solution?

"Men seek methods of learning how to love God," said Brother Lawrence in his little treatise *The Practice of the Presence of God*. "They try to reach their goal by I do not know how many different practices. They go to a lot of trouble to stay in His presence in a great number of ways; is it not much shorter and far more direct to do all things for His love, to make use of all the duties of one's state to express our love for Him, and to maintain His presence in us by our heart's commerce with Him? We need not go about this in any subtle way. All we must do is *simply to do what we do*." (Italics mine.)

To live in the present moment is to live in the presence of God, to see Him in all situations, interests or contacts. Every moment of the day or night the Blessed Trinity dwells in the soul which is not separated from God by sin. Continually united to God as we are by grace, this union becomes *communion* when we advert to it, turn our attention to Him; and although usually this awareness only comes in spasms, or when something or someone reminds us of it, we can train ourselves to become conscious of it much more often by aspirations or acts of recollection, until gradually we achieve a state of continual awareness of the divine indwelling. This permanent and uninterrupted communion is given various names, the best known being "the practice of the presence of God".

As well as keeping us in a state of grateful awareness of our dependence on Him, the perpetual "spiritual communion" of the presence of God should be a powerful aid to preserve us from daily sins and faults. Who could dare to offend God deliberately if he realized that the same all-powerful and all-holy God was present within him, actually conferring on him the power and strength he uses in opposing his will and desires to the divine will? Certainly we could not speak or act unkindly were we conscious of this fact, but could we even think uncharitably?

Again, what a powerful motive for confidence in our trials and sufferings, be they in the form of physical pain or mental anxiety. He who rules all things wisely and guides them to their appointed ends not only knows our need, our sorrow, but He is actually within us strengthening us to bear it, directing its work in our soul. What suffering could be unendurable in the light of such knowledge?

Nearly four hundred years ago St. John of the Cross compiled a detailed and careful map of the Mount of Perfection. He showed us that there were two roads by which one might travel. The first was a slow and winding track, which broke the steep gradient by its tortuous curves, and which the most pedestrian could not only climb, but also manage to carry along with him all the provisions and impedimenta he could possibly require for such a slow and unadventurous journey. By that route, he said, they arrive at their goal exceeding late and with greater labour, yet with less merit, some of them never attaining it at all during this life. The other road cut straight up the side of the mountain in a direct, undeviating line, but to travel by this way one needed to strip oneself of all encumbrances and go into training. "For this path ascending the high mountain of perfection leads upward, and is narrow, and therefore requires such travellers as have no burden weighing upon them with respect to lower things, neither aught that embarrasses them with respect to higher things; and as this is a matter wherein we must seek after and attain to God alone, God alone must be the object of our search and attainment."[1] He wrote, as he himself said, only for those who intended travelling by the short way, and going *all* the way, in order to give them the necessary directions for doing so.

The direct route was the one Thérèse chose, but it was for her to discover and plot the short-cut. Since the industrial revolution we have entered the age of inventions, and surely she could benefit from the general ingenuity of mankind in devising efficient labour-saving devices? Lifts had been in-

---

[1] *Asc.*, Bk. II, Ch. VII, para. 3.

stalled to save people the trouble of climbing stairs. Well then, if the rich could provide themselves with such conveniences, she would find a lift to take her up to Jesus, since she was not big enough to climb the steep stairway of perfection.

Although Thérèse does not actually define the "little way", she has given us ample illustrations of it in practice. In *La Morale de l'Evangile*, Père Garrigou-Lagrange, O.P., pointed out that Christ did not formulate a hard and fast system of spiritual and moral teaching. His spiritual doctrine is everywhere in the gospels, but nowhere is it systematized. As the opportunity arose, according to the circumstances and spiritual interests or capacity of His hearers, Jesus resolved their problems by sketching "the patterns of particular solutions" rather than by laying down principles. This is the only "system" that can be attributed to St. Thérèse. Her writings are full of it, but while setting before us a teaching applicable to all, nowhere does she attempt to write a formal treatise; she merely tells us how she found it worked out in daily life for her, and invites us to follow her. And it is this informality or lack of systematization that makes her teaching so readily available to all, and is in part the reason for the popularity of her autobiography, particularly among those who are inclined to be wary of treatises on perfection; for it bears a character of universality in which one might, with no irreverence, find a striking similarity to the writings of the evangelists.

Now and then in this world, where people have grown so accustomed to the familiar words of the gospel that they seldom stop to consider their meaning, some soul appears and— taking them quite literally—astonishes everyone else by putting them into practice. St. Francis of Assisi and St. Thérèse of Lisieux are, perhaps, two of the most striking examples of this, yet one can say without exaggeration that no two saints are more often misrepresented by their own devotees.

Abbé Combes compared St. Thérèse with the great Newton because he claims she did in the spiritual life what Newton did in the material, that is discovered and formulated with greater simplicity, clarity, depth and comprehensiveness "the principle of universal gravitation in the world of spiritual

reality". And he claims that so far as the world of spirit is
above that of matter, her achievement surpasses that of Newton. In his book *St. Thérèse and Her Mission*, he offers her to
us as "the saint of the atomic age". Her spiritual doctrine can,
I suppose, be compared with the splitting of the atom, in as
much as the release of the force concealed in the atom seems
to be in the field of material science parallel to the "science of
love" which Thérèse has acquired and released, which utilizes
to the full all the forces of supernatural energy that can lie
buried and latent in the heart of a very little thing—so insignificant as to be almost microscopic. For instance, she says
when she *feels* nothing, and is actually incapable of praying
or practising virtue, that is the time when she looks for *nothings*, atoms, small occasions of giving to Jesus at her own cost:
a smile, a friendly word when she would prefer to remain
silent or look bored. And when even these occasions did not
present themselves, at least she *wanted* to keep telling Him
that she loved Him and thus found a few straws to keep the
fire alight. "Don't be afraid to tell Him that you *love Him*,"
she told one of the lay-novices, Sister Marthe of Jesus, "*even
though you have no feeling of love*; that is the way to *force*
Jesus to come to your help, to carry you like a little child too
weak to walk . . . *let us be small, so small that everybody may
trample us underfoot*, without our having the least air of
noticing or minding."[1]

The immense power which this nothing, this "atom" has
released is love, which grew with her growth until it became
the great abyss whose depth was past sounding, reaching finally
a sublimity which broke out in the burning cry of love in her
letter to Marie, which forms part of her autobiography.

Thérèse's love of God was not mere devotional sentiment,
the outcome of her pious and sheltered home-life. It was a
deliberate election, the love of choice. She knew she had been
first loved, and once capable of making a decision between
good and evil—or rather, to be more accurate, between good
and better—she saw clearly in what true love of God consists.
His love had called forth her love in return, and from her

[1] C.L. pp. 214-5.

earliest years she gave her heart and will entirely to God. All
her subsequent development was the growth of the seed thus
planted, making the love of God the supreme purpose and sole
orientation of her life. Because she reduced herself to nothingness and believed in the power of love, Thérèse released a
power which opened the Heart of God.

At the risk of being wearisome it must be repeated that this
is not a new way, but the gospel way expressed all over again
in a modern idiom. Long before Thérèse did so, our Lord
used the image of a little child to illustrate the humility and
confidence necessary for eternal life, i.e. sanctity. Becoming a
little child is, in His own words, an essential condition for
entry into His kingdom. And He did not address this direction to the crowd in general, or to the women and children,
but to those destined to be the pillars and foundation stones
of His Church. It was the apostles, adult men with wives and
children of their own who were bidden to be converted and
become as little children. One scripture commentator at least
considers that it was one of St. Peter's children whom
our Lord chose to illustrate the humility, childlike trust
and affection that He expected in the members of His
kingdom.

Thérèse's first reference to the little way appears in a letter
to Céline of July 1893, where she explains the value of little
sacrifices; and a few days later she wrote again: "A LITTLE
child all alone at sea, in a boat lost amid the stormy waters—
could it know whether it was close to port or far off? . . . the
further away the shore becomes the vaster the ocean looks . . .
Then the child's *knowledge* is reduced to nothing, it no longer
knows where its boat is going. It does not know how to handle
the helm; so the only thing it can do is let itself be borne along,
let its sail go with the wind . . . How *touched* I am
to see that Jesus had inspired in you the idea of small
sacrifices."[1]

However, from her autobiography, it is obvious that she had
clearly formulated her little way some months earlier than
this at the very least; for she was in full possession of it in

[1] C.L. pp. 170-1.

March 1893, when she was appointed assistant to Mother
Mary Gonzaga, who was then holding the office of novice
mistress. She recalls the occasion in the manuscript she wrote
to that prioress four years later. Seeing that the work given her
was beyond her powers, she "went to God in the spirit of a
child that throws itself into its father's arms", and confided
her inability to supply the nourishment His children required.
If each novice was to receive what she needed, He must put
it into her hand, and she would pass it on. "I'm not going to
leave your arms or turn my head to look at them, but simply
pass on what you give to me for each soul"; for she knew that
had she to depend upon her own resources she would soon be
bankrupt and unable to fulfil the task.

Three years later, in a letter to her sister Léonie, Thérèse
expounds the little way more fully: "I find perfection quite
easy to practise, because I have realized that all one has to do
is *take Jesus by the heart*. Consider a small child who has displeased his mother, by flying into a rage or perhaps disobeying
her; if he sulks in a corner and screams in fear of punishment,
his mother will certainly not forgive his fault; but if he comes
to her with his little arms outstretched, smiling and saying:
'Kiss me, *I won't do it again*', surely his mother will immediately press him tenderly to her heart, forgetting all that he
has done . . . Of course, she knows quite well that her dear
little boy *will do it again* at the first opportunity, but that does
not matter, if he takes her *by the heart*, he will never be
punished . . . *the smallest actions* done for love are the actions
which win His heart. Ah! if we had to do great things, how
much to be pitied we should be!"[1]

Almost exactly a year after this, and a few months before
her death, Thérèse, in explaining the little way to Abbé
Bellière, one of her missionary "brothers", uses practically the
identical figures of speech, except that the parent is now a
father and there are two sons, both guilty, but one terrified
of the merited punishment, the other fully confident of a
pardon because he knows his father's love and "takes him by
the heart". Of course the father is unable to resist such filial

[1] 12th July, 1896, C.L. pp. 241-2.

trust and forgives the second son much more readily than the first, although he is equally mischievous and disobedient.

In the year that had elapsed between the writing of these two letters, Thérèse had apparently used her "parable" on more than one occasion, possibly in letters not preserved; almost certainly verbally in talks with the novices. The whole letter to Abbé Bellière (a lengthy one) is an exposition of the text "Love has no room for fear; and indeed, love drives out fear when it is perfect love." (1 Jn. 4 : 18.) Many of the details of her parable have received more finish and polish, but as they were in fact simply her own characteristics as a confident and loving child, she was able to set forth the tableau with the ease of familiarity and with no need of any rehearsing.

Her little way is a reminder that sanctity is the universal and individual call of every member of the Church, for Christ became man in order to raise all to the Father in full and perfect adoption as sons and heirs. It is also a reminder that perfection is quite within the scope of all, and that if we do not achieve the goal it is nobody's fault but our own, as God never withholds the means. Her contribution to Christianity is not merely another and more simple method for individuals to follow in the pursuit of perfection; beyond that it is a definite means towards the reformation of human society as proposed by Pope Pius XI. The fortifications of the Church against the attacks of atheism and paganism can only be built up by the sanctity of the members that compose the Church, and it is St. Thérèse who has put within our grasp the means to attain that sanctity. "When a strong man, fully armed, mounts guard over his own palace, his goods are left in peace." (Luke 11 : 21.) So with the Mystical Body. As a guide to the interior life, St. Thérèse is unique.

(ii) Taking up the Cross

"Say and have it given out," Pope Pius XI told Mgr. Picaud, Bishop of Bayeux and Lisieux, "that they are making the spirituality of St. Thérèse much too insipid. How strong she is, and how virile—a 'great man' whose whole doctrine preaches renunciation."

Those who consider that the little way is an easy short-cut to heaven because it is the way of children, and therefore reserved for those who are too faint-hearted to make the grade by any other route, are very far from a real understanding of the little way. There is no easy road to heaven. If there were, our Lord would have told us of it, but He has assured us that the way is narrow and the gate small, through which few manage to find their way in.

Notice, however, that the road of physical penance, fraught as it is with risks of pride and permanent injury to the spirit, can often prove to be a "very long way round". For Thérèse corporal suffering was not the principal means of renunciation and redemption. She even considered that certain authors, in writing the lives of the saints, have erred in insisting so strongly on their extraordinary penances as the proof and almost indispensable characteristic of sanctity. This, she told Mother Agnes, was a source of trouble to souls who imagine that to please God they must undertake extreme forms of mortification, when it becomes easy for the devil to lead them astray into pride, self-absorption and all manner of deceptions. "It is necessary to have great moderation in such practices, lest there is in them much more of nature than grace." She quoted the example of Blessed Henry Suso, whose excessive penances had all but ruined his health, when in a vision an angel made him see the superiority of the spiritual conflict over the mortifications of the flesh, saying 'You are to fight no longer as a simple soldier; I now arm you as a knight'. This understanding God had granted Thérèse from the outset, arming her, as she said, as a knight, so that she had engaged in the war against self by abnegation and little hidden sacrifices, finding peace and humility in the unseen conflict where nature finds nothing for herself. There is no more meritorious mortification than the simple and conscientious accomplishment of daily tasks, and the patient acceptance of difficulties and annoyances that are inevitable in the life of everyone.

Many of Thérèse's mortifications were of the sternest stuff; mostly, however, they were things trivial in themselves, but which cost her a great deal, and with disarming humility she confesses the conflict she endured in winning some of her early small conquests of self: resisting the temptation to justify herself when her actions were misinterpreted, refusing to plead innocence if wrongly blamed for the small carelessness of another, refraining from airing her grievances at the negligence of a companion, struggling for self-control when the urge to argue her own case was almost overwhelming. And, she adds candidly, so far was she from finding this easy, that the only way she could repress her natural instinct to assertiveness was by reflecting that on the judgment day the truth would come out, when all would see that Thérèse had really been guiltless and know who was the actual culprit! The misdemeanour of which she was "unjustly accused" and of which she would be vindicated before the whole world was the accidental breakage of a small glass vase of no value whatever. On another occasion it was a penknife some sister had "borrowed", or paint-brushes left unwashed, or the affair of who should hand the prioress the sacristy keys. Thérèse's guileless confession of the intensity of her struggles over these petty "sacrifices" indicates the toughness and tenacity of her inborn will to power; it also gives us a glimpse of how far from effortless she found the practice of little virtues, and what she meant in claiming to have never done her own will on earth. She herself could smile later at the memory of these elementary skirmishes, but they were a real effort at the time, and the victories gained strengthened her for subsequent and more costly ones.

She accepted each trifle as coming from God, chosen especially for her by His omnipotent love, regardless of whether it was an all-embracing renunciation or the matter of an indifferent opinion. In fact, it would seem that her preference was for the latter, as she could be certain that the small, easily avoided inconvenience was a direct gift from God and none of her own contriving; whereas something on the grand scale, voluntarily undertaken, is very often all one's own idea.

This type of mortification constitutes the very fabric of the little way, and it runs like a single thread through the autobiography from beginning to end. However, the greatest emphasis is laid on mortification of the will, on continual fidelity in little things rather than spectacular and extraordinary acts of supererogation—and by fidelity Thérèse means that minute-by-minute response to the promptings of grace and obedience to rule and custom which, faithfully adhered to, does by the end of the day add up to a large amount of real self-discipline. As she says, she tried to do good on a small scale, having no opportunity for anything greater, and this found its outlet by taking the occasions of denying herself that circumstances provided. She realized that penances voluntarily undertaken would not afford any more scope for self-surrender and mortification of the will than the humble "flowers of little sacrifices" which are always crowding in on all of us, and of which she availed herself unstintingly. Her corporal austerities consisted of those prescribed by the Rule, no more. Her interior mortification was ceaseless. However, these small stiflings of one's ego, when repeated constantly throughout the day, constitute anything but the trifle they may appear; for little sacrifices are not necessarily cheap and easy victories. They can at times exact the maximum exertion of faith and will power. We may manage on the first and even on the second occasion, with great interior struggle, to control our features when displeased or disconcerted, but the third time our irritation will almost certainly overcome us, and the sharp or impatient retort will be out before we have realized it. Mortification of the will in faith is the most exacting of all penances, for which reason it is declared the most meritorious. St. Thérèse admired Mother Geneviève of St. Teresa, the saintly foundress of the Lisieux Carmel, because she was not the kind of saint who defies imitation. Her virtues were the hidden, unobtrusive sort, the outcome of a life lived completely under the domination of the Holy Spirit who acted in and through her. That, to Thérèse, was the best and most genuine kind of sanctity because there seemed no danger of illusion about it, and she set herself from the beginning of her religious life to attain it.

A person who regularly fasts and keeps vigils or sleeps on boards undoubtedly mortifies her flesh; but sometimes she can be an irritable and tiresome person to live with, and as

Thérèse constantly impressed on the novices, nothing is more difficult in community life than moods and unevenness of temper. It is not impossible that some of us have known the person given to penitential practices, who does not take much trouble in checking an impatient answer and is incapable of rendering the least service without considerable fuss. Generally she imposes far more mortification on her companions than on herself; while on the whole she feels rather pleased with herself for her serious and mortified life, she is rapidly becoming one of those persons whom Thérèse delightfully declared one would go a good long way round to avoid meeting.

"The man who prefers to approach the discipline of purification and sanctification by giving up now one satisfaction and now another may see more clearly what his commitments involve, but he is handing over only pieces of himself and not the whole. Such pieces may be dear to him, and it may cost him much to see them sacrificed. But as he sees them following one another to the place of holocaust, he has at least the satisfaction of noting the extent of his renunciation. The other man, without a list before him of items sacrificed, is hampered by no such distraction. He gives himself as completely as he can, and that is all there is about it. For him the problem is not what to give next, or even how to give more, but simply how to go on in the disposition of letting God take. There is no more generous giving than this, no sharper penance."[1]

One of the sisters, seeing St. Thérèse walking with great effort in the garden during her last illness, remonstrated with her for needlessly tiring herself. Thérèse replied that she was offering each step on behalf of some missionary wearied by his labours. This is often misrepresented as a voluntary and supererogatory act of penance and virtue. It was not. It was an act of absolute obedience. She did not undertake this painful pilgrimage for a missionary; she faithfully took a walk each day no matter what the cost to herself because the infirmarian had told her to do so, unaware that the effort fatigued rather than refreshed her. She would have been the first to realize its

[1] Dom Hubert van Zeller O.S.B. *Approach to Penance*, pp. 5-6.

worthlessness as a sacrifice had she elected to do so after having been ordered to rest.

Our Lord warned us against spiritual self-seeking, such as that of the Pharisees, which masks itself under exterior acts of virtue. Those who love to stand praying at the street corners, Jesus said, have their reward already; that is to say, they have their recompense in the form of human admiration, but have done nothing whatsoever towards meriting eternal life. Thérèse understood Him, and so successful was she in concealing her self-denial beneath the disguise of a cheerful smile, an eager willingness to volunteer for the difficult or unpleasant task, that nobody realized that what she was doing did not come perfectly easily and naturally to her. Generally her interior struggles were concealed and largely unsuspected. When her cause for beatification was first proposed an objection was made that she had done nothing extraordinary; there were in her life no works on an heroic scale. But perfection can be achieved through everyday events even more surely than by one or two spectacular deeds, and there is no doubt that the continued and multiplied stabs of pinpricks are even harder for nature to endure—thus forming a longer-drawn-out martyrdom—than one mercifully swift blow from an executioner. The most timorous of persons can, under the impetus of urgent necessity, rise to the occasion with an act of heroism deserving of a Victoria Cross, but the real test of mettle is the ability to endure day after day without complaint the irritating and the irksome, neither evading hardships nor taking the line of least resistance, yet always remaining cheerful and contented.

In the case of Thérèse, however, the salient point is that nobody around her even suspected the existence of the pinpricks. Most of the community believed that her charming manners were the outcome of merely natural virtue, and that a pleasant smile or an agreement with a divergent opinion came easily to her. One of the sisters summed this up by remarking that Thérèse, although a good little religious, had never known any real suffering, and her life was colourless and insignificant. Her arms were filled with roses, but each one bore its full quota of thorns. She knew that the price one pays for interior joys is denial of self in season and out, and her only consolations were those won through suffering—until she reached the point where the very suffering itself became a consolation because it united her more closely to Christ—but this was also the reason why she could claim that despite all trials there was always great peace in the depths of her soul.

Some weeks before her death when she was burning with fever and feeling parched with thirst, the infirmarian came one evening to put a hot-water bottle at her feet and anoint her chest with a tincture of iodine to ensure that the patient would be safe during Matins. Thérèse never dreamed of protesting, but reflected what a comfort it would have been if, instead of adding more heat and fire, they had given her even half a glass of water. The very thought of the water increased her thirst and discomfort. However, turning to our Lord she said: "I am very glad to have this opportunity of resembling you more closely."

During her retreat before taking the habit, when she was just sixteen years of age, Thérèse wrote to Mother Agnes: "Today more than yesterday, if that be possible, I have been without any consolation. I thank Jesus, since He sees that it is good for my soul; perhaps, if He gave me consolations, I should rest in their sweetness, but He wants *all* to be for Him! Good! Then all *shall* be for Him, all! Even when I feel nothing that can be offered to Him, I shall (as tonight) give Him that nothing! . . . If Jesus does not give me consolations, He gives me a peace so great that it does me more good!"[1]

On the same page is another letter written a day later: "Ask Jesus that I may be very generous during my retreat. He RIDDLES me with *pinpricks*, the poor *little ball* can take no more; all over it are tiny holes which cause it more suffering than if it had but one great gash . . . All the same I am VERY *happy*, happy at suffering what Jesus wants me to suffer. If He does not Himself pierce His *little ball*, it is He who guides the hand that pierces it " The essential point here is one that is

[1] C.L. pp. 70-1.

6

fundamental to the whole spirit of the little way: that suffer-ings—whether they are pinpricks or a great gaping hole that has torn the bottom out of our world—are not self-chosen or self-inflicted.

The little way is not primarily an expression of private devotion. It is first and foremost an apostolate. Its outward expression is through little sacrifices, but always they are to be offered in conjunction with the redemptive sacrifice of Christ, uniting and associating us with Him as co-redeemers. Loving acceptance of suffering imbues it with apostolic power, for the real value of our crosses is not the amount of suffering they inflict but how closely they are related to Christ's redemp-tive suffering. Thus the very suffering itself can be a means of drawing nearer to God and at the same time a pledge of that nearness, for it is His hand that places the cross on our shoul-ders.

The only true glory is the glory that is everlasting. And, St. Thérèse soon realized, to attain that brilliant exploits are not necessary. All one need do is live the hidden life faithfully and sincerely, performing one's duty conscientiously and doing good unostentatiously. This enlightenment she declared to be one of the greatest graces she ever received, and indeed it does largely characterize the whole spirituality of her way of per-fection. She did not attempt to emulate the heroic and awe-inspiring deeds of the great saints, but contented herself with ordinary things, the kind of things possible and even obligatory to all God's children, doing them with the utmost perfection and love.

Early in her religious life she adopted the practice of season-ing her food with wormwood, or contriving somehow to make it unpalatable; but later she dropped all such tactics and found that by accepting what was placed before her as it was pre-pared, she had ample material for mortification of a more meritorious kind. St. Jane de Chantal reproved her daughters for failure to comprehend this virtue when they sought per-mission to take extra disciplines and perform other penances, yet complained of the food they were served or the places allotted to them at recreation, for she considered that a cheerful acceptance of these inconveniences would have been a harder penance to nature and a more acceptable one to God.

This was something Thérèse had grasped with unusual clearsightedness from the very beginning. When God will have us suffer, she said, there can be no evading it, and if we try to do so we often bring upon ourselves not only a different and more painful, but perhaps a less meritorious suffering than the one He had prepared for us. When her eldest sister Marie was procuratrix and had the ordering of the meals, Thérèse said "she looked after me with a mother's tenderness." All thought Thérèse was pampered by this solicitude, yet she herself admits that the mortifications Marie imposed on her were "endless", because she catered for Thérèse according to her own taste, which was quite different. There are few who would have been able to resist the temptation at least to drop a hint that would have let Marie know about the misfiring of her good intentions.

At one time Thérèse took to wearing an iron cross, the points of which cut into her flesh and caused some indisposition. This she said would never have happened had God not wished to make her understand that such penances were not for her or for those who would tread the same way of spiritual childhood.

From then onwards Thérèse did not contrive penances to mortify her flesh, which is the standard entrance into the ascetic way. Instead she did nothing to mitigate those which nature provided so plentifully: the heat, the cold, the longing for human companionship, the unsympathetic neighbour, the fidgety companion, the food that disagreed with her. It is not uncommon to find a person seeking permission to use instruments of penance, and then stooping to remove a pebble that has worked into her sandal. St. Thérèse would have taken the opposite course. She would never have put the pebble in her sandal deliberately; but if it happened to get there, because she had done nothing to acquire this particularly painful form of penance, she would have left it there until it fell out again of its own accord and managed not to limp in the meantime.

Her shrewd commonsense, coupled with remarkable spiritual insight, put mortification as all else in its correct place in the scale of spiritual values, and she would not choose her own sufferings any more than her joys. She felt that thus and thus only was she on the safe and sure way, free from illusions or subtly disguised pride.

And so Thérèse, bent on missing no opportunity of giving God whatever He placed in her hand to give, found the small irritations of community life completely satisfactory links with which to forge her chain of heroic abnegation. Whether the incident was small or great she put her whole heart and the entire offering of herself into it. Every little sacrifice is like a grain of incense, which is nothing until placed on the fire, when it is transformed to fragrant perfume. When grace and love permeate our lives, we become a censer from which arise perfumes that rejoice the Heart of God; as St. Paul says, we are Christ's incense offered to the Father.

Those who are tempted to criticise the trifling nature of Thérèse's difficulties, and who consider such nothings scarcely merit the title "sacrifice", are unlikely to be meek or charitable in relation to their own neighbours. It is true that in themselves such things are but trifles; yet what faith and effort of will they demand even on one occasion, and what heroism is implied when they are repeated minute by minute, day after day, with monotonous regularity. St. John Berchmans, another hero of the little things, once confessed that his greatest mortification was community life.

Writing to her sister Léonie, Thérèse stated that in her opinion it was not difficult to become a saint; all that was necessary was to aim in all things at giving pleasure to Jesus. Perhaps this does not sound very heroic. We may feel that it is rather elementary; but it is very far removed from childishness, particularly when coupled with the desire to feel no pleasure oneself, to miss no single opportunity of making some sacrifice, be it only the deference to a contrary opinion, a kindly word in reply to a tart question, a smile when one is tempted to show annoyance, "always doing the smallest things right and doing it for love". This brings us to the plane where we must be living in a state of continual recollection, practising the presence of God, participating in what Père de Caussade termed "the sacrament of the present moment". If not, looks and words will frequently escape us which are not in keeping with a programme of relentless self-conquest. There were times when Thérèse herself was caught off guard, and let slip the chance of some small sacrifice, as when she showed her dismay and distress on being suddenly accosted with a request for assistance on a large and difficult assignment of work. The sister, seeing her discomposure and realizing that her demand had been inopportune, immediately apologized, and it was only then that Thérèse saw that she had departed from her own programme of minute-by-minute acceptance of the "flowers of little sacrifices". She did not lose heart, however, but simply resigned herself to the loss of a little interior peace, resolving to be more alert in future.

It may perhaps come as a surprise to learn that St. Thérèse's sacrifices were not always successful—she, the humble, faithful child who claimed that from the age of three she had never refused God any sacrifice He asked of her. But there is a world of difference between failing and refusing to try. Thérèse often felt a thing was beyond her capacity, but she never concluded that it was therefore not worth the attempt as it could only fail. This was the time when she put her confidence and trust to the test. She knew she had but to make the attempt and persevere in it, although of herself she could never succeed. By acting thus, she knew that she would compel God, as it were, to come to her aid and complete the task for her. Nevertheless in the early stages she frequently did not succeed, and God did not always come and pick up His child after each tumble. "What does it matter," she said, "if I fall at every instant . . . Thereby *you see* what I can do, and so you will be more moved to carry me in your arms . . . if you do not, it is because you wish to see me *on the ground* . . . so I am not going to be disquieted, but shall go on stretching out to you arms of supplication and love! I cannot believe you would abandon me."[1] The refusal to make the effort may mean that we

[1] C.L. p. 88.

are too self-reliant to surrender the results of our efforts to God. Thérèse wished never to lose sight of her weakness and helplessness to do any good, but determined to "keep lifting her foot" thus constraining God to assist her. It is difficult when experiencing our own weakness not to feel the bitterness of failure. But, said Thérèse wisely, "What does it matter if I fall at every instant, for thereby *I see* my weakness, which for me is great gain." It is better to arrive and fling oneself into the arms of God, hot and dusty from having run so hard, stained and scratched from having fallen so often on the way, than to stroll in cool and immaculate—but too late! Having by an act of faith and hope (which is within the power of us all) surrendered ourselves entirely to the providence of God, the dispositions of our hearts must be "audacious confidence" that He will from then onwards direct all our affairs: acting vigorously in every circumstance as though the outcome depended solely upon ourselves, while trusting in God as though grace did all and we nothing. Grace never fails where there is good will; it is our will that often fails to respond to grace. Our sole business is to see to it that we do not take back any of the offering we have made Him as a free gift.

A child can only express its love through the things of childhood. Our heavenly Father does not look at the greatness of our actions, nor even at how much they cost, but at the love with which we do them. And so, having only trivial things through which to demonstrate her love, Thérèse exploited them to the full for the love of God and the salvation of souls. A little thing is indeed a little thing, but *to be faithful in little things* is a great and glorious thing. Thérèse's patient acceptance of the splashes of dirty water from the communal laundry tub is just a case in point.

(iii) "I am thy reward exceeding great"
"Jesus has no need of our works," Thérèse rightly insisted, "but only of our love." This statement should not be misunderstood, particularly in view of her constant reiteration of the "unprofitable servant" theme, but in fact it is widely misquoted as "Jesus so much NEEDS our love."

God needs nothing from any of us. All through the history of His dealings with man, from the first chapters of the bible to the last, the emphasis is on this unique God who loves the people He has chosen, not for any good He perceives in them, or for any advantage He hopes to gain from them, but because He Himself is goodness and love, desiring to give Himself and draw mankind into the embrace of that love. Everything comes from His grace and bounty; no one has any claim on His favours or can merit any reward, for even the response to grace is His gratuitous gift. We have nothing that we have not received.

How thoroughly St. Thérèse understood this. "Jesus must himself pay all the expenses of the journey and the price of admission into heaven," she wrote to Léonie a year before her death, realizing clearly the pride that lies at the root of insistence on working one's passage, demanding the right to merit heaven, or refusing to come empty-handed before Jesus and admit one's complete indigence and dependence. Her simile of the child standing at the foot of the staircase, unable to mount the first step, yet never growing discouraged by its continual failures, perfectly illustrates her own attitude here. For the whole of our earthly life consists in the earnest, whole-hearted attempt to gain heaven, while all the time acknowledging that if we are to receive it at all, it must be as a free gift, being beyond our powers to win through our own endeavours. Then, Thérèse asserts confidently, touched by your fruitless efforts, He will come down to you like a good father and carry you up in His arms. But—also like a good father—He will leave you there as long as you sit and sulk or refuse to make any effort. The holy Innocents, the good thief, those who so to speak "stole" heaven, always appealed greatly to her.

At the end of her life Thérèse was not merely resigned to her poverty, she actually derived real pleasure from it, for the realization that she had nothing at all meant that she must rely absolutely on God's love and mercy. He does indeed *need* our love in order that He may accomplish His work in our souls, but not in the sense that without our homage or service He would lack anything or be deprived of any glory because we had withheld our meed of service. The soul who gives herself to God without reserve does truly give Him something—an empty vessel to be filled. This is the only sense in which we give to God, and even here our role is principally that of receiver.

It is the love which inspires and directs our actions that gives them their value in the sight of God. This cannot be too often emphasized, as it is a basic principle of the little way. Not only by our love, but by every act of virtue, we ourselves gain immeasurably. It is we who are constantly being enriched. God, being infinite in all perfections, can gain nothing at all. It is not in our power to add to Him or take from Him; but it is true that we can *offer* Him things that He would not otherwise have, for example our willing service and love. We are, of course, bound to do this, and we are the gainers, for our efforts united to Christ acquire a power far beyond their natural efficacy.

Thérèse has recorded that even if by an impossibility God Himself could not see her good actions, she would still do them because of her desire to give Him pleasure by her love without obliging Him to make any recompense. She also admitted the reluctance she felt at Sext when she came to the verse of Psalm 118: "I have inclined my heart to do thy justifications for ever, because of the reward." She always added in her heart: "My Jesus, you know I do not serve you for the sake of a reward, but solely from love and a desire to win souls for you."

This statement has been a prolific source of misunderstandings. We may often delude ourselves into thinking that despising a reward is a sign of pure and selfless love, that it lowers our motive if we work for a recompense.

But the fact is that God wants every one of us in heaven, and our Lord constantly spoke of a "reward" (cf. Matt. 6: 18, 11: 42, 16: 27, 19: 29, 24: 47, 25: 34, and many others). It is of faith that of ourselves we are incapable of so much as a good thought without God. Apart from Him we can do nothing, we are nothing; nevertheless He has said that the labourer is worthy of his hire. We are bound to seek our eternal reward, and as that reward is God Himself, obviously we may not despise it. This St. Thérèse certainly did not do. She was vitally aware that Christ's death did not dispense her from suffering, but conformed her to Him and made her sufferings meritorious through being united with the Passion; so that when He acted in and through her, the spiritual treasures she amassed were not ultimately her own, but belonged to the whole Mystical Body. And in this way we do "give" to God, for without our free consent His hands are tied as it were, He is unable to act through us because we have blocked the outlet.

Thus there is a sense in which He needs our love, although we cannot give it first. It is true that we have nothing that was not given us, but once He makes the gift it is our own, and by our free-will we can offer it back, a love-gift He is pleased to accept for souls and for the Church. St. Thérèse realized the infinite value of the small sacrifice because it could win the conversion of a sinner; and this she desired because she saw that nothing could be more pleasing to God. In short, the rejection of a trifling pleasure, the repression of a momentary curiosity, was a sacrifice made out of pure love, and the reward was valued only because it could be offered back to God, not for the purpose of amassing treasures—even spiritual ones—for herself.

God wants nothing from us except what He gives us, and there is in fact nothing else we can offer Him. It is a typically pagan, Stoic tenet that to practise virtue in order to win heaven is selfish, mercenary, or imperfect, lacking in purity of intention. How St. Paul revelled in the fact that "each of us will receive his due reward from God" (I Cor. 4 : 5), and looked forward to his recompense, "the prize that is waiting for me, the prize I have earned". (II Tim. 4 : 8.) The idea of a reward can only be undignified if we have a faulty conception of God and what His love means. It is His divine power that enables us to love him; as it is from Him that we must receive gratuitously both the love that enables us to serve Him and the due reward for that service. When we see this, we can glimpse the vast difference between the pride that wants to practise virtue solely for its own intrinsic goodness, and the spirit that prompted Thérèse's desire to work for the sole reward of winning souls and extending God's kingdom. When love is really pure, it develops beyond all motive of recompense, not because one's arrogance refuses to be beholden even to God, but because the soul now loves Him simply because He is God and "power and Godhead, wisdom and strength, honour and glory and blessing are His by right". (Apoc. 5: 12.)

Just a little over a month before her death, Thérèse confessed to Mother Agnes her conviction that were she to indulge in complacency about her ability to practise a certain virtue, she would be relying on her own strength which would assuredly not support her. "Were I to say 'My God, I love you too much to listen to a single thought against the faith', my temptations would become so violent that I should most certainly succumb." Thérèse's goal was never static, a fixed mark which was to be the aim and end of her striving, but the moving target of minute-by-minute fidelity that is docile to the graces and inspirations of the present moment, and which, when it falls, far from being discouraged, rises and begins all over again. Self-denial was more important to her than consolations, and with shrewd, good-humoured commonsense, she regarded her infidelities as so many inevitable stumbles of a child learning how to walk. "After all, what else can one expect of the poor, helpless thing?"

And so she was content to go to meet God, empty-handed but confident of her welcome. She never pictured herself weighed down with heavy-eared, sun-ripened sheaves. All she would bring to Jesus was the ability to say truthfully: "I have never ceased trying". Had she the certainty that she had prayed easily and without distractions, always practised the most perfect charity and humility, never given way to impatience or weariness, then indeed she might have feared the complacent sense of having, in the strength of her own virtue, achieved the victory. But no! "I feel exactly like a child waiting at the railway station for his father to put him on the train. But the train departs, and he does not come. Still, there will be others, and I shall not miss them all."

When Mother Agnes made a pointed remark that the

thought of having nothing to give God at the hour of death saddened her, Thérèse rose at once to the hint and replied: "You are not like me; but yet I am in the same state. All the same, if I should have accomplished all the works of St. Paul, I should still consider myself an *unprofitable servant*. I should find that I had empty hands; but it is just that which gives me joy, for having nothing, I shall receive everything from God."[1]

Having nothing, yet possessing all things . . . To practise constant self-denial in small things and great, to return humbly but trustingly to God after each infidelity, and to cling stead-fastly to His grace; to ask no other reward but that of doing His will, and to recognize everything as coming from His hand and humbly thank Him for it: this is the "self-sufficiency" Thérèse would seek and teach first to her novices, and then to all who would following in her footsteps.

(iv) "We shall never have finished with charity"

It is not within the scope of this sketch to go into the practice of the various virtues by St. Thérèse in detail. That has already been done by other commentators better qualified to make judgments than I am, but it is interesting to note that one rarely reads any spiritual book right through without finding some reference to St. Thérèse of the Child Jesus as typifying the author's particular subject—another demonstration of her universality, or one might almost say ubiquity, in the life of the spirit.

Reiterating the statements of his predecessors, Pope Pius XII wrote to the Carmel of Lisieux in September 1947: "This way of childhood ranks high in the spiritual life, and yet it is a way suited to every child of God, even those of advancing years. St. Thérèse of Lisieux was struck by the similarity of ordinary childhood and spiritual childhood; but she was also quick to note the difference between them. The resemblance is clear. A child is generally simple, without guile, lacking complications. He realizes his own weakness because he must turn to his parents in every need. Consequently he believes all that his mother tells him, he gives her his implicit trust

[1] N.V. 23rd June.

and all his love. The child of a mother who frequently speaks to him of God learns early in life to practise the three theological virtues: he will believe in God, will hope in Him and love Him long before he learns to say his acts of faith, hope and charity.

"But spiritual childhood is marked by a difference: by a maturity of judgment supernaturally inspired by the inner voice of the Master: 'Brethren, do not become children in sense, but in malice be children'. (I Cor. 14: 20.) Furthermore, St. Thérèse of the Child Jesus emphasizes that in the natural order, as a child grows, he must learn to be self-sufficing; whereas in the supernatural order a child of God in growing comes to realize more and more that by himself he can accomplish nothing, that he must live in a dependence guided by prudence and dominating his personal activities, a dependence which will finally bring him into the bosom of the Father for all eternity.

"And so this way of childhood, rightly understood, recalls us to that outstanding simplicity of soul which goes straight to God with an utterly pure intention. It stresses once again the importance of the humility which leads us to ask God's grace, since without it we can do nothing in the order of salvation. Thus by following this way, one's faith becomes more fervent, more deep, more understanding, for it pleases God to enlighten those who listen to His voice. Hope becomes increasingly confident and tends with certainty towards salvation. We are saved from discouragement by the thought that our Lord, because of our very weakness, watches carefully over us and delights to help those who implore His aid. In this way charity leads us more quickly to love God with our whole heart, to love Him not only for our own betterment, but solely for Himself and in order that He may reign in souls and draw them to Himself. Finally, the child of God who is simple in his attitude to God and to the saints will be inspired by the gift of counsel to exercise extreme prudence towards those whom he cannot trust. And realizing his own weakness, he will be strengthened by the gift of fortitude to persevere in the face of overwhelming difficulties. He will remember the words of St. Paul: 'When I am weak, then I am powerful', (II Cor. 12:10), for it is in God alone that he puts his trust.

"This message according to our Lord's own words, is first of all 'revealed to little ones' (Luke 10:21) who are thereby called to sanctify themselves by responding to the graces of the present moment in the most ordinary things of life and who, by accepting each daily sacrifice as it comes, may attain to constant union with God. And when they have learned to put this message into practice, these 'little ones' must pass it on to others, to all those who need to hear it, to those who, ignorant of their own poverty, would receive life abundantly if they would but open their hearts. The way of spiritual childhood protects us from the danger of that excessive and too natural activity which hinders interior reflection and prevents prayer, and which cannot produce supernatural fruits of sanctification and salvation. Those who realize this have found the pearl of great price spoken of in the gospels; they see that the true Christian life is the beginning of eternal life, and that God is working in them to establish His reign more deeply in their hearts and minds."

From these penetrating words of the Pope, the following lines stand out forcefully: *When they have learned to put this message into practice, these little ones must pass it on to others.* The example of St. Thérèse in this matter of loving encouragement to her neighbours, like her teaching on fraternal charity as given in Chapters XXXIV and XXXV of *Autobiography of a Saint*, is unsurpassed in the history of the saints. For her daily life provided heaven-sent opportunities of proving her love for her sisters. It meant the positive performance of innumerable acts of kindness and considerateness, always giving her neighbour the preference, going out of her way to undertake some irksome and often unappreciated service; and this included as well the hidden virtues of forbearance and patience with others, self-control and even a willingness to be misunderstood and if necessary neglected. "Do not feel sad if you are misunderstood, misjudged, overlooked," she counselled the lay-novice, Sister Marthe of Jesus who was suffering because of some real or imagined slight, "but forget all that is not Jesus, forget even *yourself* for His love."

We love God in our neighbour and our neighbour for God, not for any lovableness or lack of it which we perceive in the exterior she presents to us, but because God loves her and therefore she has a claim on our love. As St. John of the Cross points out, the soul most beloved by God is the one most worthy of our love, and we have no means of knowing who it is that God loves most. As a father He wishes that all His children should be united with Him and with each other in peace and love. So we must love our fellow-men as God loves them. "Well," says St. Thérèse, "how did Jesus love His disciples? And why did He love His disciples? You may be quite sure that their natural qualities did nothing to attract Him ... To love your neighbour as yourself—that was the rule God laid down before the Incarnation; He knew what a power-ful motive self-love is, and He could find no higher standard by which to measure the love of one's neighbour. But this wasn't the 'new commandment' Jesus gave to His apostles ... I am not just to love my neighbour as myself; I am to love them as Jesus loves them, and will love them till the end of time."[1]

St. Thérèse, however, has no illusions about her inadequacy for this task, so she continues: "Dear Lord, you never tell us to do what is impossible, and yet you can see more clearly than I do how weak and imperfect I am; if then, you tell me to love my sisters as you love them, that must mean that you yourself go on loving them in and through me—you know it wouldn't be possible in any other way. There would have been no new commandment if you hadn't meant to give me the grace to keep it; how I welcome it, then, as proof that your will is to love, in and through me, all the people you tell me to love! Always, when I act as charity bids, I have this feeling that it is Jesus who is acting in me; the closer my union with Him, the greater my love for all the sisters without distinction."

In that short passage the very essence of Christianity may be discerned, and there is no theologian either living or dead who could have expressed it more perfectly. "Yes, indeed," she says,

[1] A.S. pp. 265-6.

"Jesus' teachings do *indeed conflict* with the intincts of nature. Without His grace we would not merely be unable to carry them out; *we would be incapable even of understanding them.*"

CHAPTER SIX

FATHER AND DAUGHTER

*"Since Father John of the Cross left us I have not found
another like him in the whole of Castile, nor anyone else who
inspires souls with such fervour to journey to heaven. Consider what a great treasure you have in that saint, and see that
all the sisters in your house talk to him and tell him about
their souls. They will see what good it does them and will find
themselves in every way greatly advanced in spirituality and
perfection, for our Lord has given him special grace for that
purpose . . . for, small in stature though he is, I believe he is
great in the sight of God . . . I believe our Lord has called him
to this work . . . he is indeed the father of my soul."*

(From the letters of St. Teresa of Avila)

(i) The Life of Faith

It has been suggested by various commentators that the
writings of St. John of the Cross come within the category of
"spiritual treatises in which perfection is shown with a thousand
obstacles in the way". Of these, St. Thérèse confessed that her
mind soon wearied, and, closing the learned book which left
her head muddled and her heart parched, she turned to holy
Scripture. But she was too truly a daughter of her spiritual
father, too much of a kindred soul, to be anything but stirred
and spurred on by the burning words of St. John of the Cross.
At the unusually early age of seventeen to eighteen she *fed* on
his writings. He wrote, as he himself said, for those who wished
to make the ascent of the Mount of Perfection by the direct
path which leads straight up to the summit, in order to give
them the necessary guidance how to go about it. "When we
study his treatises," said the late Father Silverio of St. Teresa,
O.C.D., "principally that great composite work known as the
Ascent of Mount Carmel and the *Dark Night*, we have the

impression of a master-mind that has scaled the heights of mystical science and from their summit looks down upon and dominates the plain below and the paths leading upward."

On 24th August, 1926, the second centenary of the canonization of St. John of the Cross, Pope Pius XI proclaimed him a doctor of the universal church, and in his allocution stated: "St. John of the Cross, as if divinely illumined, points out to souls the way of perfection, and supplies *lucid explanations* of the gifts that are bestowed from above. The *Ascent of Mount Carmel,* the *Dark Night,* the *Living Flame of Love,* and some other of his treatises and letters, although they treat of things difficult and obscure, nevertheless so abound in spiritual doctrine, and *are so adapted to the reader's understanding* that they may deservedly be looked on as *a norm and tutor for any well-disposed souls* desirous of attaining to a more perfect life." (Italics mine.)

"With what desire and with what consolation," said Thérèse, "I have repeated to myself from the commencement of my religious life those words of St. John of the Cross: 'It is of the highest importance that the soul exercise herself much in love, so that her course may be quickly finished, and that but little delayed down here, she may swiftly come to see God face to face.' "[1]

The writings of St. John of the Cross, like those of St. Thérèse of the Child Jesus, are autobiographical. Both these Carmelites have set down their own experiences and difficulties on this rugged ascent, in order to point out to others who wished to assay it, what they had found by experience to be the sure and safe path. The only difference is that St. John of the Cross writes in the language of a trained theologian, and never once speaks in the first person; yet despite this, he cannot but betray the fact that he is speaking and directing from his own mystical experience, nor can he conceal the sublime heights of that experience.

The essence of holiness for St. John of the Cross is that the creature, having realized his nothingness apart from God,

[1] N.V. 27th July.

must offer himself gladly to the divine All, in order that this
All may become the inspiration of his whole being. Her Carmelite father helped St. Thérèse greatly, by teaching her to
base her whole spirituality on the conscious awareness of her
natural insufficiency and on the simplicity of love. When they
made their total self-immolation to God, both St. John of the
Cross and St. Thérèse requested the identical grace. Celebrat-
ing his first Mass, John asked that he be permitted to preserve
his baptismal innocence, and he was given to understand before leaving the altar that his prayer had been granted. On the
day of her profession, Thérèse's request was the same: "Take
me from this life rather than allow me to stain the robe of my
second baptism." (See Note 9.)

There is no doubt that the doctrine of spiritual childhood
can best be comprehended in the light of St. John of the Cross'
teaching on faith and poverty of spirit, as St. Thérèse's "little
doctrine" is based upon that of her father, and although it is
only in the façade of the edifice that hers differs, here the diver-
gence is certainly very great.

St. Thérèse saw spiritual poverty as a dependence on God
as a child upon its father. To expect that God will "fill the
hungry with good things" to the point of making them self-
reliant and independent of Him would be a contradiction in
terms. Always God's method of enriching us is to make us
more dependent, more willing to find our completion in Him
alone. The higher the soul rises in the spiritual life, the more
clearly can she see that her advance has been solely the work of
God's grace, and that her own contribution has been no more
than accepting and co-operating with this grace. Therefore
she must become ever more aware of her natural limitations,
also of her obligation to return to God all the glory for whatever good is in her, whether natural or supernatural. To be
able to do this is to receive increasing light on one's own weakness; and this St. Thérèse said did her more good than particular lights on faith, for this interior illumination showed her the
utter folly of self-complacency. Candidly she admitted that
she did not rely on her own merits, simply because she realized
that she had none; instead she placed all her confidence in

Him who is virtue and holiness itself. "My feeble efforts are all He asks. He can raise me up to Him, clothing me with His own infinite merits, and so make a saint of me." It was because Thérèse never took her eyes off her model and goal that her own efforts appeared feeble. She never visualized herself as anything but a weak and helpless child; and she expected no miracle which would transform her overnight into an Amazon. She realized her way to sanctity was that of remaining little, of bearing patiently her own limitations, and placing all her reliance in God's power and mercy, which would bring her to the perfection she desired, since our Lord does not demand great achievement, but only self-surrender and gratitude.

It is not my intention to imply that St. Thérèse's message can be understood only in the light of the treatises of St. John of the Cross. Were that so, the real necessity of the little way to this modern age would be greatly reduced. Certainly those who are familiar with both works know and penetrate more surely the profound depths of her teaching; but there are many who do not know or do not wish to know the teaching of St. John of the Cross, whereas they are perfectly eligible and willing to follow the lead of St. Thérèse. For that purpose indeed she has been given to us. Her message, essentially the same, is expressed in terms familiar to our understanding as compared with the weightier doctrine of the official teacher.

"Since this instruction relates to the dark night through which the soul must go to God," says St. John of the Cross in the prologue to the *Ascent of Mount Carmel*, "let not the reader marvel if it seems to him somewhat dark also . . ." However, this need be no hindrance to us in following St. Thérèse along her little way, for she has assimilated and made her own the profound wisdom and lofty ideals of St. John of the Cross, and now gives it back to us in a manner which we can all understand, provided that God grants us the necessary light. For us, then, the autobiography is a safe guide for this ascent. It is guaranteed by the Church as a sure and profitable method of arriving at perfection through the solemn pronouncements of the sovereign pontiffs, Benedict XV and Pius XI.

St. John of the Cross is a mystical theologian of austere and meticulous phraseology, carefully classifying and elucidating spiritual experiences with impersonal exactitude, although we sense all the time that he is speaking of his own personal odyssey. St. Thérèse on the other hand, the favoured child of God, writes her memoirs using the language of childhood; and in doing so, she expounds a doctrine no less lofty, showing us how sanctity of the highest order can be achieved within the simple framework of an ordinary life, even illustrating it with the small daily incidents out of which she made material for such high perfection and union with God. Thérèse does not possess the ability of her father as an exegete, or his skill in careful analysis and vindication of the principles he proposes. Beside his expositions some of her metaphors, such as that of the Blessed Trinity seen through the image of a child's toy kaleidoscope, may appear petty and trivial; but they are in reality no less profound.

Take, for example, her thoughts about perfection in its varying degrees. She tells us how she had always wondered why God had his preferences rather than bestowing an equal degree of grace on every soul, and how she found the solution by contemplating nature, where all the flowers are beautiful and no two are alike. "The rose in its glory, the lily in its whiteness, do not rob the tiny violet of its sweet perfume or the daisy of its charming simplicity." What if all these humbler blooms demanded to be roses? Surely it would be a loss rather than gain were there no "little flowers" to gladden the eye in spring and to star the fields and hedges with their simple and casual grace? The universe of the spirit, she saw, was subject to the same principle. "Perfection consists simply in doing God's will and being just what He wants us to be."

Everything spoke to her of God's loving mercy. Quite unaffectedly she declared her gratitude for the opportunity of recording the unmerited favours He had showered upon her, acknowledging that there was nothing in her that could have attracted Him, for any good she possessed was solely the effect and gift of His mercy. This is only another way of expressing the truths taught by the apostles that "God has first loved us" (I Jn. 4: 19), or as St. Paul puts it: "What hast thou that thou did not receive as a gift? And if they be a gift, why dost thou boast of them?" (I Cor. 4 : 7.)

In describing the months of fervour, the "little ecstasies" she and Céline shared during her last year at *Les Buissonnets*, Thérèse draws on the *Spiritual Canticle* of St. John of the Cross, paraphrasing Stanza XVI as follows: "Light of foot we followed our Lord's footsteps; the sparks of love which He spread so generously in our souls, the strong, satisfying wine which He gave us to drink, made transitory things vanish from our sight; our lips breathed tender aspirations which He, no other, had communicated to us . . . How everything conspired to turn our thoughts towards heaven! How beautiful it must be if this, the obverse side of it, was so calm and clear! . . . How light and transparent it seemed, this veil which hid Him from our sight! How could there be room for doubt, how could there be any need of faith or hope? It was love that taught us to find, here on earth, the Bridegroom we searched for."[1]

Referring to Stanzas III and IV of the poem *On a Dark Night*, Thérèse remarks: "For me, the place where our Lord waited was Carmel."

The lights and loving aspirations in Thérèse's soul became clearer and grew in strength once she was within the walls of Carmel, despite the bewildering aridity which descended upon her ardent spirit almost immediately. Patiently she endured this trial, supported by the encouragement she drew from St. John of the Cross, assured by his reiterations that she was on the right road in this dark and arid night of contemplation in which she must remain as long as God so willed it, trusting herself to Him, leaving her direction in His hands. The strength, ardour and delicacy of St. John of the Cross could not do other than call forth a response from the depths of her being, joyfully confirming her own inner conviction that Jesus was leading her by a way she knew not. "In order to arrive at that which thou knowest not," counsels St. John of the Cross, "thou must go by a way thou knowest not." The doctrine of her Carmelite father, which was already hers by intuition, she

[1] A.S. pp. 134-5.

henceforth made her own, building upon it, as on a foundation of rock, her own spiritual life, and eventually her doctrine.

(ii) Family Likenesses

The effect of St. John of the Cross on the spiritual development of St. Thérèse can scarcely be exaggerated; no other writer ever exercised an influence over her comparable with his. Throughout the autobiography and letters of Thérèse, quite apart from the numerous quotations and direct references to his writings, traces and echoes of the teaching of St. John of the Cross are everywhere and very evidently visible, while the manner and independence with which they are incorporated into her own synthesis is sufficient evidence of her familiarity and complete harmony with them. The affinity between the two is too deep and fundamental for it not to become apparent. It would be possible to go through her writings, and set against almost every one of Thérèse's propositions a corresponding directive from St. John of the Cross; and as a matter of interest, I give a few of the more outstanding examples of this which spring to mind.

St. Thérèse	St. John of the Cross
1. If, by an impossibility, God Himself did not perceive my good acts, I should not be troubled. I love Him so much that I would give Him pleasure by my love and my little sacrifices without His perceiving that they come from me. Seeing and knowing, He is, so to speak, obliged to make me a recompense . . . and I would not put Him to that trouble. (N.V. 15th May.)	1. He that with pure love works for God not only cares not whether or not men know it, but he does not even do these things that God Himself may know it. Such a one, even though it should never be known, would not cease to perform these same services and with the same gladness and love. (Maxims for Mother Magdalen of the Holy Spirit. No. 1.)
2. We can never have too much confidence in our God who is so mighty and so merciful. As we hope in Him, so shall we receive. (M. & D. p. 232.)	2. God is so pleased with the confidence of a soul who relies on Him and looks to nothing else, that it may be truthfully said of her, she receives as much as she hopes for. (Maxims.)

St. Thérèse

3. I understood the true object of human ambition; our Lord hadn't wanted any kingdom in this world, and He showed me that "if you want to learn an art worth knowing, you must set out to be unknown, and to count for nothing"; you must find your satisfaction in self-contempt . . . to suffer and to remain unnoticed, that was all I longed for. (A.S. p. 188.)

4. The smallest act of self-denial is worth more than the writing of pious books or of beautiful poems . . . You have just done something more glorious than if, through clever diplomacy, you had procured the good will of the government for all religious communities and had been proclaimed throughout France as a second Judith. (C. & R. pp. 302, 306.)

5. That others should find you imperfect is quite right; *therein lies your gain,* for you can then practise the humility which consists in not only thinking and saying that you are full of faults, but in being happy that others, too, should think and say the same. (*The Spirit of St. Thérèse,* p. 124.)

6. All we have to do is humble ourselves, to bear with meekness our imperfections. Herein

St. John of the Cross

3. Strive always to choose not that which is easiest, but that which is most difficult . . . not that which gives most pleasure, but that which gives no pleasure . . . not that which gives consolation, but that which gives no consolation; not that which is greatest, but that which is least; not that which is loftiest and most precious, but that which is lowest and most despised . . . and to have detachment and emptiness and poverty with respect to that which is in the world for Jesus Christ's sake. (Maxims for Mother Magdalen, No. 4.)

4. More precious in God's sight is one work or act of the will performed in charity than are all the visions and communications that they may receive from heaven, since these imply neither merit nor demerit . . . many souls who have known nothing of such things have made incomparably greater progress than others who have received many of them. (*Asc.*, Book II, Ch. XXII, paragraph 19.)

5. First, let the soul strive to work in its own despite, and desire all to do so. Secondly, let it strive to speak in its own despite, and desire all to do so. Third, let it strive to think humbly of itself, in its own despite, and desire all to do so. (*Asc.*, Bk. 1, Ch. XIII, para. 9.)

6. Meek is he that knows how to suffer his neighbour and to suffer his own self. (Other

St. Thérèse

lies—for us—true holiness. (C. & R. p. 303). Perfect love means putting up with other people's shortcomings, feeling no surprise at their weaknesses, finding encouragement even in the slightest evidence of good qualities in them. (A.S. p. 265.)

7. Often He "*treads the winepress alone. He seeks for those who may give Him aid and finds none*". Many serve Jesus when He consoles them, but *few* are willing to keep company with *Jesus sleeping* on the waves or suffering in the garden of agony! . . . Who then will be willing to serve Jesus for Himself? Ah! it must be you and I. (C.L. p. 201.)

8. There are some faults which do not *offend* God, but serve to make love stronger. (C.L. p. 119.) If I am humble, I may fall into little follies till death. (N.V. 7th August.)

St. John of the Cross

Maxims, No. 6.)

7. Christ is known very little by those who consider themselves His friends; we see them seeking their own pleasure and consolations in Him because of their great love for themselves, but not loving His bitter trials and His death because of their great love for Him. I am speaking now of those who consider themselves His friends; for such as live far away, withdrawn from Him . . . and are eager about their ambitions and their prelacies, may be said not to know Christ; . . . for to seek oneself in God is to seek the favours and refreshments of God; but to seek God in oneself is not only to desire to be without both of these for God's sake, but to incline oneself to choose, for Christ's sake, all that is most distasteful, whether as to God or as to the world; and this is love of God. (*Asc*, Bk. II, Ch. VII, par. 12,5.)

8. For the soul to come to unite itself perfectly with God through love and will, it must first be free from all desire of the will, howsoever small. That is, that it must not intentionally and knowingly consent with the will to imperfections, and it must have power and liberty to be able not so to consent inten-

St. Thérèse

St. John of the Cross

tionally. I say knowingly, because, unintentionally and unknowingly, or without having the power to do otherwise, it may well fall into imperfections and venial sins . . . for of such sins as these which are not voluntary and surreptitious it is written that the just man shall fall seven times in the day and shall rise up again. (*Asc.* Bk. I, Ch. XI, para. 3.)

9. Since Thou hast loved me so much as to give me Thy only-begotten Son to be my Saviour and my Spouse, the infinite treasures of His merits are mine . . . I offer them gladly to Thee . . . I offer Thee all the merits of the saints in heaven and on earth, together with their acts of love, and those of the holy angels. I offer Thee the love and the merits of the Blessed Virgin, my dearest Mother. (Act of Oblation).

9. Mine are the heavens and mine is the earth; mine are the people, the righteous are mine and mine are the sinners; the angels are mine and the Mother of God, and all things are mine; and God himself is mine and for me, For Christ is mine and all for me. (Prayer of an Enamoured Soul.)

10. To love Thee as Thou lovest me, I must borrow Thy own love—thus only can my desire be satisfied. (A. p. 192.)

10. The soul (in the state of union) loves God with the will of God, which is also her own will; and thus she will love Him even as much as she is loved by God, since she loves Him with the will of God Himself, in the same love wherewith He loves her. (*S.C.* Expos. St. XXXVII Red. 1.)

11. Perfection consists simply in doing His will, and being just what He wants us to be. (A.S. p. 34.)

11. What profit is it that thou give one thing to God if He asks of thee another? Consider that which will please God and do it. (Spiritual Sentences and Maxims No. 70.)

Similar examples could be multiplied almost endlessly, but while they would no doubt serve to illustrate clearly the com-

mon heritage of the two, they would at the same time and even
more strikingly manifest Thérèse's individuality and original-
ity; for she never merely repeats or even adapts his words to
her own purposes. Still less can she be said to be nothing more
than an echo of St. John of the Cross. She has integrated his
doctrine, but always she remains herself. The hidden bond
between them was none other than the Holy Spirit who, says
Abbot Vonier, "awakens the sentiments and the affective
powers of Christians differently at different times", creating
in them with wonderful variety "a Christ entirely in conformity with that truth which is His very essense". St. John of
the Cross, on the one hand, was a trained theologian of the
Salamancan school, an experienced director of souls sure of
his ground, and his treatises cover every aspect of the essential
union in Jesus Christ between the soul and God. St. Thérèse,
on the other hand, was little more than a child, neither very
well educated nor widely read; and in venturing to delve
deeply into the mysteries of the Heart of Jesus she had to rely
solely upon her spiritual instinct or attraction towards what is
highest and most practical, seeing by the light of faith within
her rather than by anything she had learned naturally. Yet she
has come back to us laden with her riches; and we need have
no fear in availing ourselves of them, for in canonizing St.
Thérèse the Church has also canonized her doctrine. Such
diversity in unity or unity in diversity is a unique characteristic
of the Catholic Church and one of her most outstanding
glories. With St. Augustine, for example, it is a favourite theme.
Abbot Vonier, however, has perhaps done most to explain the
phenomenon for the benefit of ordinary Catholics, and his
writings on the great dogmatic mysteries are in every way
complementary to the works of the Carmelite mystical theologians. "The total Christ is in heaven, not only in the totality
of His twofold nature, but also in the totality of His character," he says in *The Spirit and the Bride*. "No one here on earth
can embrace such a totality. So the Spirit breaks up that glory,
as the prism breaks up the white light; and infinite varieties
of the Christ-Person are received by the saints as their own
share in the boundless mystery of the Son of God."

(iii) Christ, the Way

The teaching of St. John of the Cross was the support of
Thérèse even more in the dark night of her temptations against
faith and hope than in the days when the veil of faith had
seemed so light and transparent. Although Thérèse knew intuitively that the path she was travelling was of God and led
to God, and that she was in no way a victim of self-delusion,
still she always sought the approval of those who were in a
position to give it, the priests with whom she came into contact
as confessors to the Carmelites or as retreat masters. For three
years she had sought in vain for encouragement in her belief
that, despite her faults and failings, she could abandon herself
with unlimited confidence to the mercy of God. "It seems to
me," she wrote to Mother Agnes in August 1890, "that Jesus
could easily give me the grace never to offend Him again, that
is to commit only faults which do not *offend* Him, but serve
to humble one and make love stronger." Thérèse was seventeen at this time, making her retreat prior to profession, and
drawing her spiritual nourishment almost exclusively from
St. John of the Cross. However, despite her certainty that
Jesus, her "only director", was leading her along this path,
she still felt the need for confirmation from an authoritative
source, and up to this time had received only chilly rebuffs
and warnings against presumption.

"It is a difficult and troublesome thing at such seasons for a
soul not to understand itself or to find none who understands
it," says St. John of the Cross. "For it will come to pass that
God will lead the soul by a most lofty path of dark contemplation and aridity, wherein it seems to be lost, and, being thus
full of darkness and trials, afflictions and temptations, will
meet one who will speak to it like Job's comforters, and say
that it is suffering from melancholy or low spirits or morbidity
of temperament . . . Let such guides of the soul as these take
heed and remember that the principal agent and guide and
mover of souls in this matter is not the director but the Holy
Spirit, who never loses His care for them."[1]

It is incorrect to conclude, as many have done, that because

[1] *Asc.*, Prologue, para. 4; *L.F.*, Stanza III, para. 46 (red. 2).

no director was able to give her the help she sought, Thérèse obstinately refused all direction, insisting on going her own self-willed way. She constantly sought help, but mostly met with misunderstanding, if not total incomprehension. St. John of the Cross says that God is "desirous that the government and direction of every man should be undertaken by another man like himself. Whenever He says or reveals something to a soul, He gives this same soul to whom He says it a kind of inclination to tell it to the person to whom it is fitting that it should be told. Until this has been done, it gives not entire satisfaction."[1] This not only adequately describes, but also fully explains Thérèse's attitude and position with regard to direction: the work God intended and planned for her did not include direction, but through lack of it she was forced, so to speak, to discover her own way and formulate it for others.

It was not until the retreat of 1891 that Thérèse was granted her spiritual liberation. She tells how, after hearing that the reputation of this year's preacher, Père Alexis Prou, was for converting sinners rather than directing religious, and being convinced that he was unlikely to understand her, she did not feel inclined to confide her intimate doubts to him, because she was not even sure that she could express them properly. "I'd been going through a bad time spiritually in every way, even to the point of asking myself whether heaven really existed . . ." She approached the confessional, and to her astonishment found that her soul was an open book to this priest, a complete stranger to her, in which he could read better than she herself could. He assured her that her faults were not such as to merit God's displeasure, and launched her in full sail on that ocean of love and confidence on which she had not dared to venture, although it attracted her so strongly. Later she asserted this advice unhesitatingly: "So long as I remain humble," she told Mother Agnes, "my little follies do not offend God."

Such an authoritative assurance, confirming her own attraction, was the only impetus Thérèse needed; from then onwards this path of trust and love was the one by which she travelled,

[1] *Asc.*, Bk. II, Ch. XXII, para. 9.

penetrating ever deeper into the mystery of the boundless love and mercy of God. When she was finally plunged into darkness and apparent unbelief, she had reached spiritual maturity, and was able to draw on her resources to sustain herself in it.

What St. John of the Cross asks of us is to make the ascent to the summit of the Mount, which is divine union in transforming love, and he sets out to show us the attitude necessary for one who would go generously and wholeheartedly the entire way. Setting aside the complex divisions which many of the mystics use when speaking of union with God, in the *Ascent of Mount Carmel* he begins by treating of that which is our own immediate concern, the active union which, with the aid of grace, we can acquire by our own efforts. Later, in the *Dark Night of the Soul*, which is in reality the second part of this great composite-treatise, he deals with the action of God on the soul. But although the *Ascent* places the emphasis on the work of the soul, while the *Dark Night* stresses the initiative taken by God, these two divisions are by no means mutually exclusive. (See Note 10.) This union, or loving transformation of the soul in God, is the end and goal of all St. John of the Cross' writings, and those who label him "Doctor of the Dark Night" or "Doctor of Nothingness' denigrate or fail to comprehend his teaching. The dark night and the nothingness are the ways through which the soul must *pass* if it is to arrive at the goal of transforming union; it is not a way in which we linger for its own sake or look to take our ease. As has often been pointed out, a road is a good thing to travel over in order to reach our appointed destination, but it is not the place on which we expect to take up a permanent abode.

By union, St. John of the Cross means "a linking and conjoining of two things which, though united, are still different, each keeping its own nature, for otherwise there would not be union, but identity. Union of the soul with God, therefore, will be a linking and conjoining of the soul with God and of God with the soul, for the one cannot be united with the other if the other be not united with the one, so that the soul is still the soul and God still God. But just as, when two things are united, the one which has the most power, virtue and activity communicates its properties to the other, just so, since God has greater strength, virtue and activity than the soul, He communicates His properties to it and makes it, as it were, deific, and leaves it, as it were, divinized, to a greater or lesser degree, corresponding to the greater or lesser degree of union between the two."[1] This union by means of the theological virtues, is within the reach of all who are prepared to do their own part to attain it, and St. John of the Cross says that the reason why so few reach it is not because God wills that their number be limited, but because there are few who are prepared to undergo the purgations and trials which are necessary preparation for it.

We are all called to divine union, either in this world or in the next. It is not the prerogative of canonized saints but of all Christians, and those who fail to reach the goal here below will find themselves detained in purgatory. The sufferings there are not only beyond our present powers of comprehension (by reason of their spiritual intensity), but are also without merit; whereas here on earth we have the opportunity to do all that is required of us, at relatively small cost, and at the same time to be meriting untold graces both for ourselves and others. Neither St. John of the Cross nor St. Teresa had any illusions on this point; nor did their daughter of Lisieux.

It is true that God is present substantially in every soul, even that of the greatest sinner; but the purpose of this kind of presence or exercise of the divine power is simply to maintain the gift of existence which He Himself has bestowed on each one of us. Without the presence of sanctifying grace in the soul there can be no indwelling of the Blessed Trinity, still less any union of transformation; for this last is wrought only when there exists that perfect likeness which comes from love and the elevating effects of the theological virtues on our natural powers.

This is the loftiness of the ideal, the height of the goal, and St. John of the Cross never allows his gaze to drop below it. He knew perfectly well that his teaching would not be acceptable to all, but he knew also that those who really wished to

1 *Asc.*, Bk. II, Ch. V (note 3).

make this ascent would not find his teaching too rigid or his
guidance obscure; for he had first accomplished in his own
soul that which he now set out to communicate to others, and
although we may not be sent the searching trials of his own
particular dark night, nevertheless if we take the first steps
which he counsels in order to enter into it, God will not be
backward in doing His part, and the requisite grace is never
likely to fail us. Even before she entered Carmel, Thérèse was
putting into practice his teaching on interior mortification,
which she found to be the most fruitful of all forms of self conquest, and the most meritorious. At the age of fifteen she set
herself a programme of resisting all the impulses of self-will—
repressing those retorts which spring unbidden to the tip of
one's tongue, doing small acts of kindness without any fuss or
attention, sitting upright instead of leaning back in her chair,
performing little services for others unnoticed. All these small
stiflings of self-love had a wonderfully strengthening and
liberating effect, she soon found, and each little victory made
the next one proportionately easier.

"Upon this road," says St. John of the Cross, "we must ever
journey in order to attain our goal; which means that we must
ever be mortifying our desires and not indulging them . . .
Strive always to choose not that which is greatest, but that
which is least; not that which is loftiest and most precious, but
that which is lowest and most despised."[1]

Thérèse, his apt pupil, acted literally upon these words,
and sought even in her penances and mortifications not the
grand and sweeping renunciations which are still capable of
providing natural satisfaction and at times even consolations,
but the unknown and hidden sacrifices that were seen by none
but God and herself; which fact alone is sufficient to constitute
"a mortification". She relates for instance, that one evening
after Compline (the only free time in a Carmelite's day) she
was anxious to begin a particular piece of work, but one of the
sisters had, through mistake, taken her cell lamp, so that she
was left in the dark. As it was the Great Silence, she could not
go and ask for another; nor did she merely sit feeling sorry for

[1] *Asc.*, Bk. I, Ch. XI, para. 6; Maxims.

herself or nursing a grievance. Instead she began to reflect on the meaning of her vow of poverty, realizing that it entails more than simply renouncing personal property or forgoing luxuries. To be really poor means also to be deprived of necessities, and that in times of greatest need. Sitting in her cell in the dark, making of the unexpected deprivation a joyous gift to God, she was granted "fresh infusion of interior light". After this incident she became more than ever aware of the value of such minor renunciations, prizing them so highly that she actually developed a preference for clumsy or inconvenient articles; and she felt delighted rather than annoyed when an attractive little jug, which had hitherto given her much pleasure, was removed from her cell and replaced by a large, badly chipped one.

And so, with the help of grace acting on her own spiritual insights, Thérèse had reached a solution which modern psychology approves as the ideal "tranquillizer" in resolving mental and emotional conflict, and which those expert psychologists St. Teresa and John of the Cross had counselled centuries earlier. It was simply to recognize and accept the frustration as it was, whether caused by circumstances, the weather, the carelessness of another, and facing the fact that she could do nothing to remove it; then, instead of allowing it to depress her or turn her attention inwards on herself and her own deprivation, offering the frustration itself to God. Thus did Thérèse learn to find the fruit of interior peace and even joy in the sacrifice of her own satisfaction.

When we can effect this, no "sacrifice" is too small to be used as a "straw to feed the fire of love".

(iv) "All things are mine"

St. John of the Cross, before St. Thérèse, drew his inspiration from holy Scripture. His knowledge of it was deeper than hers, for not only did he know the New Testament by heart, but, according to the deposition of one of his novices, he could also recite from memory many books of the Old Testament, and when writing he rarely looked up or verified a quotation. When one considers the number and variety of quotations from the Old Testament in all of his treatises, one can realize the fullness of his familiarity with the bible, which enabled him to draw out his masterly exegeses. To it he turned for his authority for the laws he stated as governing the dealings of the Holy Spirit with souls, humbly confident in the guidance of the same Spirit, and submitting himself to the judgment of the Church, for in all things St. John of the Cross was completely orthodox.

But the Word of God is essentially Christ. "One Word spake the Father, which Word was His Son"; and therefore the gospels above all contain God's word. "I have spoken all things to thee in My Word, which is My Son . . . set thine eyes on Him alone, for in Him I have spoken and revealed to thee all things, and in Him thou shalt find yet more than that which thou askest and desirest . . . For progress comes not save through the imitation of Christ, who is the Way, the Truth and the Life, and no man comes to the Father but by Him."[1]

These passages should be compared with the following from St. Thérèse: "To keep Jesus' *word*—that is the sole condition of our happiness, the proof of our love for Him. But what *is* this word? It seems to me that Jesus' *word* is *Himself, Jesus, the Word, the Word of God!* . . . He says so further on, in the same Gospel of St. John. Praying to His Father for His disciples, He expresses Himself thus: 'Sanctify them by thy *word*, thy word is *truth*'. In another place Jesus tells us that He is the *Way* and the *Truth* and the *Life*. We know then what the *Word* is that we must keep, we do not, like Pilate, ask Jesus: 'What is truth?' We possess *Truth*, we *keep* Jesus in our *hearts*."[2]

Nobody has ever spoken of renunciation as St. John of the Cross has done. His powerful words ring across the years, making suffering and affliction appear to be the one desirable good on this earth, and never for a moment does he allow us to lose sight of the shining summit towards which he is leading us, while he encourages us over the rough way by which he must perforce lead us. This road, however, is not meant for our unaided human nature; and if we attempt it through sheer

[1] *Asc.*, Bk. II, Ch. XXII, para. 5; Ch. VII, para. 8.
[2] C.L. pp. 200-1.

7

will-power, it will lead only to mental or nervous breakdown. In order to journey in safety and be assured of arrival at our destination, our strength must at all times be drawn from the Heart of Christ, even as St. John of the Cross says: "Set thine eyes on Christ alone, and thou shalt find the most secret mysteries, and the wisdom and wondrous things of God which are hidden in Him." To St. John of the Cross as to St. Paul, Jesus Christ is at the same time "the origin and the crown of all faith" (Heb. 12:2), and Thérèse too never doubted for an instant that her Father's possessions were there for her to use. Referring to St. Luke 15:31, she commented: "God is my Father, I am His daughter, therefore everything that He possesses is mine also!" In the matter of love especially she adds: "To love you as you love me, I must borrow your own love—thus alone can my desire be satisfied." On another occasion she expressed the longing for God so to possess her faculties that her acts would no longer be her own, or even human acts, but divine: inspired and directed by the Spirit of Love. And on her deathbed she made the well-known remark: "I have no works, therefore God will reward me according to His own works."

These are not merely sentimental euphemisms. Thérèse was vitally aware that the satisfactions of Christ were as truly hers as if she herself had undergone the Passion. It was this awareness of the doctrine of the Mystical Body, upon which she comments so forcibly in her manuscript letter to Marie, that is the basis of her daring familiarity. Through the recent encyclicals of Pope Pius XII we are more familiar with these truths, but Thérèse was alive to their practical value considerably in advance of any of her contemporaries' real and effective application of them. Knowing that all the merits and riches of Christ were hers, she confidently approached the Father, conscious of her great possessions and assured of being treated as one with Jesus. Her words in the act of oblation: "Since you have so loved me as to give me your only Son to be my Saviour, the infinite riches of His merits are mine", are very reminiscent of St. John of the Cross' prayer: "All things are mine and for me, since Christ is mine and all for me."

St. John of the Cross has been declared a doctor of the universal Church. "Mystical Doctor" is the title which assures all contemplative souls that in him they are guaranteed an experienced guide for their journey. It is true that his teaching can be misconstrued by those who have failed to acquaint themselves thoroughly with the mind of the Church in other respects, but it can never delude those who remain one with Jesus Christ through faith, hope and charity. Delusion is most often a divine punishment for spiritual and intellectual pride. Many people, too, are attracted to St. John of the Cross far more on account of his poetic and philosophic gifts than through genuine appreciation of his doctrine; and because they are blind to the real meaning of his words, so likewise the heavenly wisdom of St. Thérèse is too simple for them to see. "If you would make rapid progress on the path of divine love," she says, "you must remain *small*. That is what I have done, and now I can sing with our holy father, St. John of the Cross:

> But, as I sank and sank so low,
> Higher and higher did I go,
> And in the end I reach'd my prey."

For Thérèse the "consciousness of her own littleness" and "confidence to the point of audacity" are not merely predominant virtues, or even those virtues which in her stand high above all others as characteristic traits. They are habitual dispositions of heart and soul, dominating all her actions and permeating everything that touched her life. Her way like that of St. John of the Cross is a way of love; for he was no gloomy ascetic, incapable of enjoying the natural gifts with which God has endowed us. He revelled in the beauties of nature and never counselled their rejection unless they hindered the soul in its quest of God by holding it back in sensible pleasures; as a means of drawing the soul nearer to God (once freed from its inordinate affections), he considered them to be superlative.

Joy comes to us from creatures, and we are not forbidden to enjoy them for it is from God that they originally proceed, and it is He who has attached the joy to their use. However, it is sometimes necessary to sacrifice them in order to draw nearer to God, lest we stop short at the pleasure He has allowed them to give us. They must lead back to God, so that we love nothing outside Him, but love all creatures as He loves them. In short, these creature joys are only secondary.

Thérèse's desire to remain poor and lowly in the sight of God, combined with her daring confidence in His merciful love is only another way of expressing St. John of the Cross' unbounded hope which "attains as much as it hopes for".

It was by recognizing then humbly accepting her own littleness and powerlessness that Thérèse was able to receive the great graces God showered upon her, possessing them in utter poverty of spirit. We too can possess our souls in like poverty because faith and hope—according as they purify our understanding and memory in the Dark Night—bind us ever more firmly to God, the giver of all these good things. The way of spiritual childhood unfailingly leads through peace and joy to the heights of union described by St. John of the Cross. No matter how obscure our spiritual state or how slow our progress may appear, as long as we have goodwill and sincerity, we will find the writings of St. John of the Cross a storehouse of practical help and comfort when, in the enveloping darkness of the Night, our soul is being purified in the crucible of suffering.

On the pretext of imitating Thérèse's liberty of spirit, however, let us not make the mistake of throwing overboard all spiritual reading or set methods of meditation unless we have something higher and better with which to replace these good things. Thérèse was able to dispense with books and methods because she had quickly grasped and assimilated the principles to which, ultimately they can all be reduced; and this she did under the sure and safe guidance of St. John of the Cross, who showed her how to apply the gospel truths on which she meditated to her daily life. For those of us who follow her on her "little way" she can be for us all that St. John of the

Cross was for her, and we have the confident assurance of the Church, our wise and holy Mother, that her way is not only safe, but *the* way, *par excellence,* for the average and the many.

CHAPTER SEVEN

THE GIFT OF SELF

*"To be a victim with Jesus does not necessarily mean to be
subject to great afflictions or to bear extraordinary sufferings.
No, it is to be ever ready to receive from His hand the sweet
or the bitter, things pleasant or disagreeable, health or sickness, consolation or interior trials. O victim soul, your life in
its simplicity is sublime. You are wholly at the service of Jesus.
Without suffering more than others, you are unceasingly
immolated by love. You celebrate without interruption with
the eternal priest the sacrifice of Calvary. Your life is a continual Mass, and your death will be the last stroke which will
immolate the victim."*

(Fr. Joseph Schryvers, C.SS.R)

(*i*) *"Thérèse, living victim, united to the victim perpetually
offered."* (Pope Pius XII)

During recreation one evening in the winter of 1894-5, Sister
Thérèse of the Child Jesus recounted some of her childhood
recollections, and Sister Mary of the Sacred Heart (her eldest
sister Marie) thinking it a pity that they should not be preserved, asked permission of the prioress, Mother Agnes of Jesus
(Pauline), for Thérèse to write them down. Mother Agnes
turned to Thérèse and gave her an order to do so, although
apparently she felt the same anxiety as Thérèse lest this un-
precedented and seemingly irrelevant task should prove a
source of distraction to her.

This was to be the last year of Mother Agnes' first term as
prioress, and Thérèse after begging our Lady to guide her pen
so that nothing she might write would be displeasing to her,
set to work and finished the task given her under obedience in
time to present it to Mother Agnes for her patronal feast (St.
Agnes, Virgin and Martyr) on 21st January, 1896. These

memoirs now comprise the first eight chapters of the *Auto-biography* and Book I of *The Autobiography of a Saint*.

The year 1895 was an important one in the history of St. Thérèse, for as well as writing most of the autobiography (See Note 11), she was also to attain to that degree of interior love which inspired her famous act of oblation to the Blessed Trinity. In odd moments of free time after Compline, Thérèse began to write of "the mercies of the Lord". She used for this purpose a cheap school notebook, and in the interests of holy poverty she wondered ought she not to interline her writing in order to save paper! She felt that the merciful love of God had penetrated and surrounded her all her life. It explained why she, a frail and weak creature, had been chosen as the recipient of His great favours. God indeed has His preferences, and some of the flowers in His garden are brought to full bloom by the sun of love "in the twinkling of an eye". Why, she asked Céline, was she of that number? What reason had Jesus for showing such partiality towards her?

The love of God goes out to that which most resembles Himself; His mercy to that which is furthest removed: the weak and the frail and the sinful. And so merciful love had stooped to the weakness of Thérèse and raised her up to transform her into Himself, making of her nothingness fuel for the flame of love, since He reaches out to us "the very moment He sees that we are fully convinced of our own nothingness".

Humility such as this cannot be acquired directly, but it is in fact bestowed upon the soul by our Lord as a result of her intense confidence in His power to help her on all occasions. This faith-inspired confidence is what St. John of the Cross calls "the light burning in his heart", and so he declares:

This light guided me, more surely than the light of noonday
To a place where He (well I knew who!) was awaiting me . .
A place where none appeared. (*On a Dark Night, Stanza* 4.)

From that point on there is no degree to which we may not be raised in union with Jesus, as and when He wills; but He does not force His creatures. The soul must open the door to Him of her own volition, and always hold it open if she wishes

to be invaded by merciful love; also she must desire nothing
except the fulfilment of His will in her regard. Faults and
imperfections arising from human frailty do not hinder this
union; in fact nothing does at this stage of advancement except
lack of faith and hope, or the deliberate turning aside to follow
our own will. This knowledge was an immense comfort to
Thérèse. She realized that on the way of love, although one
may stumble at times or fail to correspond with grace, yet
always love knows how to turn everything to advantage, so
that whatever may offend God is burnt away in its fire, leaving
nothing but a humble, abiding peace, in the depths of one's
heart.

Because Thérèse was already in full possession of this knowledge and living in this disposition of heart and mind at the
time when she wrote the first pages of her autobiography, the
early chapters of her manuscript are of more importance than
is usually given to them. They are not the first elementary
attempts, feeling her way, gradually climbing towards perfection along the path from which she never deviated, and
reaching their due climax and denouement in the finished
saint. These stages were all vividly described by one looking
back on her past life from the heights of near-perfection. Some
of the pages where she recalls the divine generosity in bestowing so many spiritual privileges without merit on our part, in
giving each soul its own individual endowment, and in going
out to meet the least as well as the greatest with the same all-
embracing love, are often dismissed as childish prattle. But her
opening pages run on parallel lines with her closing ones, in
which she describes the making of and the effect on her of the
oblation to the merciful love of God; the only difference being
that in the former, speaking of her childhood, she uses exclusively the metaphors of childhood and poesy to convey the
deep secrets God had revealed to her.

Thérèse found (as so many of us do) that the simplest form
of spirituality was intimacy with Jesus, who in turn led her to
the Father. She had always tried to give pleasure to Jesus. All
her sacrifices and joys and tears had been for that sole purpose;
now she tells us that on Trinity Sunday of this year,

which fell on 9th June, she received the grace to understand more clearly than ever that "love is what our Lord really wants".

"What returns shall I make to the Lord for all He hath rendered unto me?" cries the psalmist. It was in answer to this question that, during her thanksgiving after holy Communion, Thérèse received the interior call to offer herself as a victim to the merciful love of God.

She was thinking about the souls who offered themselves as victims to the divine justice with the idea of diverting the punishment due to sinners and accepting it themselves instead. She fully appreciated the generosity and courage demanded by such self-immolation, but she did not herself feel drawn to make it. Her attraction was no less generous, but quite different: Why should only the justice of God claim victims? should there not also be victims to His merciful love? Everywhere that love is misunderstood and rejected when human hearts turn from God to created pleasures, seeking their happiness in the fleeting joys of the moment. Divine love stands at the door knocking and waiting, but few turn to Him and accept His gift of infinite love. Must this rejected love then remain shut up in His own Heart?

"The spirit breathes where He will" and He leads us all to God in varying ways and through different and seemingly arbitrary means. We may centre our devotion around His omnipotence, beauty, mercy, truth, justice; but it is the same God we adore in spirit and in truth, and we cannot grow in the knowledge of one divine attribute without a similar increase in that of others. As St. Thérèse found, it is impossible to contemplate God's justice without also knowing His mercy. Each soul is a unique universe, and as no two are alike, so in finding our different attractions, we honour all God's perfections severally and individually. The attribute that dominated Thérèse's devotional life was infinite mercy. In contemplating all His other perfections against the background of mercy, all assumed a radiant glow of love. In particular, divine justice, illumined by love, captivated her soul, and in this light she rejoiced to think that God really *is* just, that He makes due allowance for human frailty as well as weighing our offences, for He knows our natural weaknesses and limitations. Rather than instilling dread, such a perspective of justice became the basis of all her daring hope, for she realized that if God pardons the prodigal so graciously, He will be equally just and merciful in His treatment of her, the child who—like the elder brother of the parable—was always at His side.

St. Thérèse's comprehension of divine justice was, therefore, permeated with the tenderness of her experimental knowledge of His mercy. She did not visualize a stern and unbending judge who counts and weighs as in a scale every infidelity, but the infinitely just and loving Father who reads His children's hearts and gauges their desires and intentions as well as their miserably inadequate works. "Fear," she said, "brings us only to *strict justice* as it is shown to sinners. But that is not the justice Jesus will have for those who love Him." God's justice, which terrifies so many souls, was actually the foundation of her joy and confidence, for she realized that it implies not only the exercise of severity in punishing guilt, but also of magnanimity in assessing intentions and rewarding virtue. As Shakespeare says "earthly power doth then show likest God's when mercy seasons justice". She hoped as much from divine justice as from merciful love, because as the psalmist says, "He knows our frame and remembers we are but dust." The recollection of her faults humiliated her, to be sure, and taught her never to rely on her own strength (or weakness); but even more it demonstrated God's mercy and love.

Thérèse never lost the consciousness of the predominantly merciful character of divine love at work in her soul. Infinite love cannot be fully satisfied, she says, until He has stooped down even to nothingness and transformed that nothingness into His own fire. The growth of sanctity is the action of the merciful love of God transforming the nothingness of His creature into the All of himself. To achieve this He uses diverse instruments and circumstances, but usually those that are close at hand, waiting ready for the purpose, so to speak: those who are about us, the trivial events that fill our days, the most worthless instruments; and thus by accomplishing His marvellous work, shows clearly that it is His hand that guides everything and that He alone is the master worker.

It all seemed quite obvious to her. The smallest happenings of our life are directed by God, who moves us to desire, then grants our desires. And so she felt that if only He found souls willing to offer themselves as victims to be wholly consumed in the furnace of love, He would immediately satisfy their desire, finding thus an outlet for the pent-up force of His infinite tenderness. If justice, which finds its scope on earth, must take its inevitable course, surely love, whose impetus is stronger, could not fail to take possession of souls prepared to surrender themselves to it. "Jesus, grant me the happiness of being such a victim, wholly burnt up in the fire of your divine love!"

Thérèse's offering of herself as a victim to love was made spontaneously during her thanksgiving after holy Communion on Trinity Sunday of 1895. But she knew that in order to give it the official character she desired such an oblation must receive the sanction of her superiors. A religious is not free to make an offering of her life, which it is no longer within her power to dispose of. In effect, by her profession, she has already given over all autonomy, even her life, which now belongs to the Church and to her community. This no doubt was what Mother Geneviève, the saintly foundress of the Lisieux Carmel, had meant in saying that she did not understand how a Carmelite could offer herself to God as a victim, since she was already a victim by her religious profession. Thus St. Thérèse sought and obtained from her prioress and sister, Mother Agnes, permission to make this offering, but to ensure that there was nothing in its wording contrary to the teaching of the Church, she drew up a formal document which she submitted to her confessor for approval. This obtained she, together with Sister Geneviève of the Holy Face (Céline)—and a little later Sister Mary of the Sacred Heart (Marie)—officially and explicitly offered themselves as victims to God's merciful love, with the desire and intention of releasing the oceans of infinite tenderness which the neglect and callousness of mankind had caused to remain pent-up, unwanted and

unappreciated, in the Heart of the God who waited only for
their desires to pour forth these floods of mercy and grace
upon them.

Thérèse's act of oblation is rather long. Characteristically it
begins: "O my God, most Blessed Trinity, I desire to love
you and to make you loved." The actual form of offering comes
at the end after a prayer of thanksgiving and petition. "In
order that my life may be one act of perfect love, I offer myself
as a holocaust to Thy merciful love, imploring Thee to consume me unceasingly, and to allow the floods of infinite tenderness gathered up in Thee to overflow into my soul, so that
I may become a martyr to Thy love, O my God! May this
martyrdom one day release me from my earthly prison after
having prepared me to appear before Thee, and may my soul
take its flight without delay into the eternal embrace of Thy
merciful love." This act she wrote out and carried in the little
copy of the gospels which she always wore near her heart. The
act is well known and has many times been dissected and commented upon by theologians. It contains both and unsurpassed
comprehensiveness of vision of God's loving mercy, and the
depths of humble trust. Surely it is a daring ambition to set
free, for herself and for other souls, the floods of infinite tenderness which the sinful neglect of humanity has, so to say,
imprisoned and cast back upon God. As Abbé Combes asks,
who else had ever conceived such a notion? We merely take it
for granted because we are so familiar now with the idea.

To become a victim of merciful love is to surrender oneself
not so much to suffering, and certainly not only to suffering,
as to the transformation of self which that love requires, leaving God free to act in the soul as and how He wills. By the gift
of free will, God has in a manner of speaking put His love—
the Holy Spirit—in our hands, making Him subject to our
own powers of acceptance or rejection. Infinite power allows
Himself to stoop to the finite heart; merciful love leaves Himself open to repulse, and by the same gift He puts within the
hand of the creature the means and power to bring consolation
to the Infinite; as it were to comfort the Heart of God against
the evil that wounds His love.

"Just as I sacrificed myself as a victim of love, so I want you to be a victim," said our Lord to Sister Josefa Menéndez. "Love never refuses anything." These words illustrate very aptly the truth that by the term "victim" is to be understood one completely surrendered in faith and hope to God's will and pleasure, perfectly subject to all His designs and sensitive to his lightest touch. It is incorrect to think that a "victim of love" is dedicated exclusively to suffering, although suffering does play an important role and holds a dominant place in the life of love. Our Lord has said repeatedly through many visionaries, that He seeks for victims who will lead the world back to love, and it is within the power of each one of us, by our everyday lives and without extraordinary sufferings, to become such victims, provided we are ever docile to His will and ready to embrace the cross when He offers it to us, "suffering all we have to suffer, and enjoying all our consolations, in the spirit of love".

"The essential point of the problem is not concerned with offering to the avenging anger of a God of Justice a point upon which it may fully concentrate, but with appeasing that thirst for love of the crucified who shed His own blood for the salvation of all souls. The intrinsic nature of the method concerns itself not with a herd of voluntary victims who spontaneously offer themselves to the blows of punishing Justice, but with the souls of sinners who must be drawn closer to the streams of redeeming Blood which alone can really save them."[1] Thérèse thinks of God as infinite love, longing to give Himself to the capricious hearts He has brought into existence, and meeting only indifference.

But it must be reiterated that it is a mistake to think that being a victim with Jesus means volunteering for extraordinary and unrelieved sufferings. The essential part of the contract is the unreserved gift of self. Thérèse explained her offering to Sister Mary of the Trinity as the surrender of herself entirely to God's good pleasure, with the expectation of sharing the humiliations and bitter chalice of Jesus. It did not mean that she would suffer *more*, but that because of her self-immolation

[1] Abbé André Combes, *St. Thérèse and Her Mission*, p. 126.

she would suffer in order to love God more purely and strongly, for those who neither love Him nor desire to do so. "If one were surrendering to justice," she told this fearful novice whose spiritual life at this time was dominated largely by dread of retributive justice, "there might be cause for fear. But merciful love is compassionate, He knows our weakness and treats us with gentleness and mercy."

(ii) "Thy measure shall be My measure"

"When one casts one's faults into the furnace of love," asked St. Thérèse, "how could they fail to be consumed past all return?"

The soul of Thérèse was now close to its final degree of maturity. Her aim in making the oblation is clearly expressed in the act itself and in her description of what led her to make it, as given in the autobiography, namely the desire to love God and make Him loved, to compensate for the refusal of mankind to return love for love, and at the same time to save souls and thus make Love loved.

This is her aim, and in order to reach it she employs the act of oblation, so that she may console the Heart of God by the complete surrender of herself to His love, and by so doing become a perfect instrument for winning souls who in their turn will love Him.

Her act is wonderful in its simplicity and comprehensiveness, summing up as it does the whole of her little way, her humble yet confident hope, strengthened by unwavering faith in the merciful love of God. Thérèse did not offer her love to God, but she offered herself to His created love as manifested in Jesus Christ, presenting herself to Him as a dedicated instrument which she desired Him to transform, begging that He stoop to her wretchedness and raise her to Himself.

"To represent the Thérèsian oblation to merciful love as the culminating point of a cantification exclusively personal is to be almost completely mistaken," says Abbé Combes. "If Thérèse offers herself 'to the end that she may live in an act of perfect love', it is certainly not in the hope of so putting the last touch to an egoistic saintliness. 'O my God, Blessed

Trinity, I wish to *love* you and make you *loved*, to work for the glorification of holy Church by saving souls on earth and delivering those who are suffering in purgatory'."[1]

The Spirit of Love produced within St. Thérèse—in spite of her habitual state of dryness and aridity—an ardent desire to love God, to suffer for Him, to save souls, to embrace all sorts of incompatible vocations at one and the same time, and most of all to die of love. These longings, verging on the infinite, became a veritable martyrdom and they may not be dismissed as mere day-dreams of wishful thinking. They were to be assuaged by the offering of herself to the merciful love of God, the opening of her soul to the floods of that love. The act in which she clothed her offering is not merely a pretty figure of speech. She was in deadly earnest when she referred to herself as a holocaust, that is to say a victim which is to be consumed by fire entirely. The vow of victim as she understood it lays one open to every kind of suffering. To hand oneself over to justice is not the same thing; strict justice can go so far and no further, but love knows no limit. To ask God to accept her as a victim was to surrender herself absolutely, to desire to live only for love and to live in even closer union with God, to compel Him to live in her, and at last to die of love.

Thérèse penetrated deep into the mystery of God's merciful love and, surrendered utterly to His action in her soul, she became in a short time possessed and impregnated by love as a log of wood which, when set upon the fire, is transformed into the same element, and so united and identified with it that it becomes a single glowing coal. Speaking of the "oceans of grace" which had inundated her soul since making the oblation, she told Mother Agnes that she was continually aware of the presence and reality of divine love, constantly renewing and purifying her soul from every trace of sin, so that all fear of purgatory was swallowed up in the consciousness of God's mercy.

Of the soul transformed by love St. John of the Cross writes: "The soul (is) so far transformed and perfected interiorly in the fire of love that not only is it united with this fire but it

---

[1] *St. Thérèse and Her Mission*, p. 127.

has now become one living flame within it. Such the soul feels itself to be . . . God permits the soul in this state to see His beauty and entrusts it with the gifts and virtues that He has given it, and all this turns into love and praise, without a trace of presumption or vanity, since there is no leaven of imperfection to corrupt the mass."[1]

Thérèse had applied herself with diligence to follow the teaching of St. John of the Cross, that is exercising herself in love, and now the flame burned bright in her, the flame that was to blaze and glow for all eternity. The latter part of the first section of her autobiography was written on the crest of the "floods of grace" that poured into her soul after the offering of herself, before the onslaught of her trial of doubts and temptations against faith.

The first eight chapters of the manuscript written for Mother Agnes were completed in just over twelve months, and even in the early pages it is obvious that Thérèse was fully penetrated with the merciful love of God which cannot rest content until He has stooped to the nothingness of a created heart and transformed it into a furnace of love. By the time the final pages were written (which was some time prior to 21st January, 1896), her soul was in the condition or attitude of a perpetual offering of herself to the action of God's love.

Not many days after Thérèse had thus offered herself unreservedly, she received the confirmation of God's acceptance of her gift by the special grace to which she referred as the "wound of love". She had commenced the stations of the cross in choir, when she suddenly felt herself "wounded" by a dart of fire so intense and ardent that she thought she would die. When she tried to explain it, she could not find adequate words, and said "it was as if an invisible hand had plunged her wholly into fire"—but a fire that was as unbearably sweet as it was cauterizing. "I was burning with love, and I thought one minute, even one second more, and I should not be able to support such ardour without dying." So she described the experience two years later to Mother Agnes, adding that she understood then what the saints have said about such states

[1] *L.F.* (Rcd. 2) Prologue, para. 4; Exposition of Stanza I, para. 31.

which they experienced frequently. For Thérèse, however, it was one isolated incident, a momentary ecstasy after which she relapsed again into her habitual state of dryness.

St. Thérèse's act of oblation is generally considered to have been made under the influence of the "transforming love" associated with spiritual betrothal. St. Teresa of Avila, in the *Interior Castle*, describes this stage as the sixth mansion "in which the soul has been wounded for love of the spouse and seeks more opportunity of being alone, trying, so far as is possible to one in its state, to renounce everything which can disturb it in this its solitude"; and St. John of the Cross sings of:

My Beloved, the mountains, the solitary wooded valleys,
The strange islands, the sonorous rivers, the whisper of the
    amorous breezes,
The tranquil night at the time of the rising of the dawn,
The silent music, the sounding solitude, the supper that
    recreates and enkindles love . . .

The joys of spiritual betrothal, however, have not the same permanent quality as those of the ultimate marriage, for which reason St. Teresa of Avila, speaking of the great trials which the soul must suffer, both interiorly and exteriorly, before entering the seventh mansion, declares that if we realized their intensity beforehand "it would be most difficult for us, naturally weak as we are, to muster determination enough to enable us to suffer them". During this period of intense purgation, the soul is held close, as it were, in the arms of Jesus—the prisoner of His love—yet "blind" and "dumb" like St. Paul on the road to Damascus; so there is nothing that need surprise us about the last eighteen months of Thérèse's life on earth. Jesus was still her only guide, apparent darkness of soul her daily portion, and thus were the virtues of the little way brought to their consummate perfection. "My God," she exclaimed, "you know that the one goal I've ever sought is to love you." She never coveted any other glory but that. In childhood His love went before her: as she grew, it increased also, until it had become an abyss whose depths she could not sound.

As has been seen, St. Thérèse prayed for a legion of "little

victims", the souls who were to follow her along the little way.
It is within the reach of these souls to follow her also in her
oblation; but being little is in itself a martyrdom, for it
demands real and constant abnegation, perseverance and
trust, and the essential part of holocaust is that the victim must
be consumed by fire, which is not a pleasant operation. We can
achieve it as St. Thérèse did only by casting ourselves with all
our weaknesses and imperfections headlong into the furnace
of divine love to be consumed. "I know of no other means
to arrive at perfection," she told Marie Guérin, "save only
love."

We are tempted to stop here, conscious of our radical unworthiness and inability to follow her to these heights; but
Thérèse has anticipated our timidity. "To love Jesus, *to be
His victim of love*, the weaker one is, without desires or virtues,
the more apt one is for the operations of that consuming and
transforming love. The *desire* to be a victim is enough of itself,
but one must consent to stay always poor and without strength,
and that's the difficulty, for where are we to find a man truly
poor in spirit? . . . What pleases God in my soul is not all that
(her "boundless desires"). What does please Him is *to see* me
*love my littleness and poverty, the blind hope I have in His
mercy*. That is my sole treasure."[1]

This act of oblation has been approved by the Church, and
it can be made by all who are of good will—preferably with
the knowledge and consent of their confessors—but we cannot expect it to have on our own lives the same transforming
effect that it had for Thérèse unless we bring to it the same
spirit of virtue and denial of self that she did. Words do not
suffice. The mere recitation of an external formula of offering
accomplishes nothing unless it is accompanied by the interior
immolation of self. To be a victim of love one must surrender
herself entirely, for "love will consume us *only* in the measure
of our self-surrender". At the close of the manuscript which
she wrote for her sister Marie, Thérèse prayed that our Lord
would choose for Himself "a whole legion of victims, so little
as to be worthy of your love." Pope Pius XI made this prayer

[1] C.L. p. 253.

his own in his sermon at the Mass of Canonization, and the Church, always extremely cautious in the matter of private vows and acts of oblation, has indulged this offering for the benefit of all to whom our Lord proposed the ideal of being perfect as our heavenly Father is perfect. We should bear these words in mind whenever we feel tempted to regard Thérèse's standard of perfection too exalted for us.

The invasion or take-over of merciful love in relation to "self" followed swiftly on Thérèse's act of oblation, and so it will for all who follow her wholeheartedly, provided that we exercise ourselves in the same spirit of faith, hope and fraternal charity. "I wish to renew this oblation with every heartbeat an infinite number of times . . . until death" is how Thérèse ends her formula, and it is beyond doubt that this perpetual offering became her habitual disposition. There can be no taking a week off to please ourselves without reference to Jesus, then expecting to be able to carry on as before; nor are we to suppose that this way of loves relieves the soul of all effort, requiring merely an attitude of passive surrender. That would be quietism. No, we must always be ready to sacrifice and deny ourselves, accepting the opportunities and the graces as given to us by Jesus, and then acting upon them. It is not a negative passivity, but a positive docility to God's will that is needed here. Given that, the Holy Spirit will not be backward in His share of the work of our sanctification. Thérèse gives her testimony. Although she never heard the sound of His voice whispering directions, she knew with certainty that He dwelt within her, guiding and inspiring her in what she did or said. "A light, of which I'd caught no glimmer before, comes to me at the very moment it's needed."

Such is the evidence of St. Thérèse herself; but she is no less careful to insist that love will consume us *only* in the measure of our self-surrender. God does not compel us, not even to be happy.

(iii) Salt and Fire

Thérèse, perhaps more than any other saint, has demonstrated that God's love for us is predominantly merciful. Yet to live a life entirely preoccupied with the interests of God requires the most absolute trust in Him; for, without this, we would undoubtedly fall back on ourselves during those periods of trial when we feel ourselves to have been rejected by Him. Our confidence, then, has to be all-embracing. We must, in the words of St. Augustine, "trust the past to the mercy of God, the present to His love, and the future to His providence".

Now Jesus told His followers that fire and salt were the proper seasoning for every victim (Mark, 9:48); therefore Thérèse gave herself up to whatever preparatory action God thought fit to subject her to, knowing that this as all else came from His hand. And what happened next? Suddenly she found herself in a world which previously she had not really believed to exist. Her faith was so transparent and vivid that the thought of heaven comprised the sum of all her happiness, and she could not concede that there actually were people who had no belief in God or immortality. Surely nobody could deny the existence of anything so obvious as heaven without doing violence to his own inner convictions? But, she realized, there *are* souls without faith, and during the Eastertide of 1896 her own soul became overshadowed by an impenetrable fog which made the thought of heaven, where God Himself would be her eternal reward, a subject of conflict and torment. "And this trial," she said, "was not to be a matter of a few days or weeks. It was to last until the moment when God should see fit to deliver me from it." And at the time of writing, June 1897, she admitted that that moment had not arrived. From this environment, in fact, Thérèse was to be released only by death. For the last eighteen months of her life, she was permitted to enter and participate more intimately than ever into the sufferings of Christ who, being without sin, took upon Himself the burden of our sins.

Faith in the world today is at so low an ebb that we are reminded of our Lord's own words: "God will give redress to His elect . . . with all speed. But, ah, when the Son of Man comes, will He find faith left on the earth?" (Luke 18:7-8.) To us brought up in this century of rational and atheistic doubt, the history of the saints and of the Church in the Middle Ages reads almost like the Golden Legend. In those days, however much men rebelled against God and openly sinned, they never doubted His existence or His power to punish them. Hell was still a reality, and so was the devil. Unbelief in the hearts of men and women, sheer soul-chilling indifference, is much more difficult for the Church to combat than the open enmity of persecution or militant atheism. It is true to say that a large number of church-going Christians do not seem to have much practical belief in the possibility of eternal damnation; nor do they appear to conduct their lives in a manner that might be expected of those intent on winning their everlasting glory and happiness. The fact that "created nature has been condemned to frustration, not for some deliberate fault of its own, but for the sake of Him who so condemned it" (Rom. 8: 20) means nothing to them.

From Easter, 1896, then, it seemed to Thérèse as though her very spirit had been walled in by unbelief; yet never once did she give up the struggle, never once in a year and a half of appalling mental and physical suffering did she say "What's the use?" Even as she saw her life ebb away in the midst of this crushing trial, never did she regret that she had placed her trust in Jesus alone. Instead she said, "Here am I, Lord, one of your own children, to whom your divine light has manifested itself," affirming her willingness to remain "eating at the table of sinners", offering her own sufferings and the sacrifice of all consolation that "those who have no light of faith may at least glimpse its rays". As for herself, her sole request was that she be preserved from sin while, by her own love and self-sacrifice, "the table they have defiled might be cleansed".

For Thérèse herself, this period of trial was not so much a test of her faith as the purification of her memory in hope, corresponding with the Dark Night of the Spirit as described by St. John of the Cross. The suggestion that she was mentally ill so obviously stems from a complete misapprehension of Thérèse's experience and the common teaching of mystical theology on the subject of passive purifications of the soul, that

it is scarcely worth mentioning; although certainly it frequently happens that souls undergoing this purification are
afraid of losing their reason. Such fear is mainly due to the
distressing forgetfulness associated with the trial, the impair-
ment of concentration, and the recurring fear of self-deception
as described by St. Teresa of Avila in the first chapter of her
sixth mansion in the *Interior Castle.* The general feeling of
"distress" experienced at this time is clearly described by St.
Teresa in Chapter XX of her *Life.* Mental illness can do nothing to enrich the personality or the spirituality of the soul thus
afflicted, whereas this is most definitely and visibly the effect
of the passive purifications of the Dark Night.

Again it has been suggested that this whole period of darkness was a figment of Thérèse's imagination. This is what she
herself has to say about it: "I get tired of the darkness all
around me, and try to refresh my jaded spirits with the thought
of that bright country where my hope lies; and what happens?
It is worse torment than ever; the darkness itself seems to borrow, from the sinners who live in it, the gift of speech. I hear
its mocking accents: 'It's all a dream, this talk of a heavenly
country, bathed in light, scented with delicious perfumes, and
of a God who made it all, who is to be your possession in
eternity! You really believe, do you, that the mist which hangs
about you will clear away later on? All right, all right, go on
longing for death! But death will make nonsense of your
hopes; it will only mean a night darker than ever, the night of
mere non-existence'."[1]

Then she confided to Mother Mary Gonzaga something of
her fears, admitting that the picture sketched above was as far
from an accurate description of her darkness as an artist's draft
is in comparison with his finished work. But she feared to talk
about it lest she should blaspheme, and asked forgiveness
should she have unwittingly offended God who, she was aware,
knew well enough that she did try to live the faith, although
she derived no satisfaction from it. And at about this same
time she told Mother Agnes that during the previous night
she had been overcome by a frightful sense of oppression and

[1] A.S. pp. 255-6.

anguish, feeling lost in a void from which came a diabolic voice: "Are you certain God loves you? Has He come to tell you of it Himself? If not, how can you be certain? The opinion of a few creatures will not justify you in His sight."

No one who is familiar with St. Thérèse and her writings and recorded conversations will make the mistake of belittling her suffering of body and soul, but the temptations she endured against hope, which were the culmination of her soul's martyrdom and the direct outcome of her total surrender to God, were the greatest trial of her whole life. She herself certainly considered them to be so. All other sufferings she could welcome with a smile, knowing that they came from God and brought her closer to Him and to that heaven which had always appeared as her real home, into which she, like an exile, was only awaiting re-admittance. This suffering excluded that consolation, as it removed the certainty of heaven from her. This was crucifixion, she was suspended in the middle of nowhere, lost in the void between heaven and earth, and God was absent. She had suffered intensely during her father's mental breakdown, for him and with him. Then she had said: "I no longer say that I can suffer more." But at the same time she could take this trial to her heart, call it "our great treasure", knowing that it was a cross laid upon them all by the loving hand of God, seeing it as a purifying action both for their father and themselves, and she knew it would one day win for them a higher degree of glory in heaven. She never called the trial of doubts a treasure, for although with the highest part of her soul she still clung to God, yet the very thing that had made all other sufferings precious—the thought of eternal beatitude which had been as a plank under her feet —had been removed. And yet, paradoxically, she welcomed this trial as all others, declaring "*All* that thou doest fills me with joy." How can we ever grasp and pin down the multitudinous facets of her holiness? When her suffering seemed at its height, she sent a message to Céline: "How good God is to His little victim! Even now when bodily suffering is added to my soul's anguish, I do not feel that 'the sorrows of death encompass me', but that 'I have gone down into the valley of the shadow of death, yet will I fear no evil, for you, Lord, are with me'." Always in the depths of her soul there was peace, the peace that can reside only where there is absolute conformity with the will of God. This humble and childlike submission to His holy will, tempered and perfected by suffering, produces a special quality of peace—although Jesus alone can bestow it—which is one of the most characteristic graces of St. Thérèse and the way of spiritual childhood.

Thérèse was one with the Church in regarding her sufferings as having a redemptive value. She tells us how, at the age of fourteen, the sight of a picture of the crucifixion pierced her to the heart, and our Lord's dying words *I thirst* kindled in her soul a zeal she had never previously experienced: the realization that she could allay His thirst for souls only by sharing it. To save souls from eternal damnation she offered her own sufferings to God, united to the infinite merits of the Passion of Christ. She never doubted that she had gained the soul of the criminal Pranzini, and to the end of her life she continued to pray for this "first child" of hers who, she realized, would need much assistance in paying off the interest on his debt, which was likely to be considerable.

She was equally aware of the redemptive value of the sufferings she endured from this new trial, the agony of doubt and fear of self-deception; and on one occasion she confided to Mother Agnes that she offered her interior trial especially for a family connection of theirs who had lost the faith and given up his religious practices. When the struggle was at its fiercest she wrote: "Every time the conflict is renewed, at each challenge from the enemy, I give a good account of myself—by meeting him face to face? Oh no; only a coward accepts the challenge to a duel. No, I turn my back in contempt, and take refuge in Jesus, telling Him that I'm ready to defend the doctrine of heaven with the last drop of my blood. What does it matter that I catch no glimpse of its beauties here on earth, if that will help poor sinners to see them in eternity?"[1] It was at this period of her life that she copied the creed, signed in her blood, into the small volume of the gospels she carried on her

[1] A.S. p. 256.

heart, and a few weeks before her death she expressed her conviction of suffering not for herself but for some other soul. "I can think of no explanation for the intensity of my sufferings other than the ardent desire I have to save souls."

She seemed to be in a state of spiritual conflict—to all intents and purposes God and heaven were to her as though they did not exist; and yet with her whole soul she clung to God as firmly as ever she had done when buoyed up by the certitude of His love and the anticipated bliss of the home awaiting her. But there is nothing contradictory here. It was merely that while the joy in the love of God and the hope of heaven had gone, her will was united with God and never withdrew itself for an instant from that warm focus. Cardinal Merry del Val has compared our will with a rock in the sea. "The waves may wash around it and even submerge it, but there it remains immovable; and when the sea dies down after the storm, it is left intact. So our will may remain firm despite all our feelings." Thérèse had entered into the realm where hope as she had hitherto known it—supporting her in the love of God and the expectation of the fruition of that love in eternity—had been eclipsed, so that she was left with a sense of being abandoned and blindfolded. As St. John of the Cross explains: "The nearer the soul approaches God, the blacker is the darkness which it feels and the deeper is the obscurity which comes through its weakness; just as, the nearer a man approaches the sun, the greater are the darkness and the affliction caused him through the great splendour of the sun and through the weakness and impurity of his eyes." He adds, however, that despite this darkness and affliction, "the soul immediately perceives in itself a true determination and an effective desire to do naught which it understands to be an offence to God, and to omit to do naught that seems to be for His service. For that dark love cleaves to the soul, causing it a most watchful care and an inward solicitude concerning that which it must do, or must not do, for His sake, in order to please Him."[1]

[1] *D.N.*, Book II, Ch. XVI, paras. 11 and 14.

St. Thérèse says, quite simply: "The only thing I want badly now is to go on loving until I die of love."

(iv) The Travail

As has been seen, the first reaction of St. Thérèse when plunged into the overwhelming trial of her hope was not one of panic, but a calm and trustful reiteration of her faith in the truths which seemed to have slipped from her grasp. "Here am I, Lord, a child of yours who has known your divine light." The temptation to doubt she put firmly from her as she would any other temptation, refusing to argue with it, but instead turning for refuge in God, unseen and unfelt. She knew well that such doubts were powerless to harm her unless she accepted their challenge, for it is we ourselves who give them their potency very often, by entertaining and trying to wrestle with them. So in order to vanquish them, she turned her back upon them and made a dry act of faith, for to will to believe is to believe.

Not only would Thérèse do battle with temptation in what seemed to her the most valiant manner, but she accepted its continuance for the remainder of her life if so God willed— as in fact He did. She never looked upon this or any other cross as something to be unburdened of as quickly as possible. Most of all it did not occur to her that she was really abandoned by God, that He no longer cared for her, even although He had withdrawn from her all sense of love and joy. She knew He loved her as tenderly as He had ever done, and so although the ordeal robbed her of all enjoyment in life, she could still reiterate that everything He sent her was a joy and delight. And this, while it sounds paradoxical or exaggerated, was the simple truth, because after all what greater joy can one experience than in accepting the gift and token of divine love, whether it comes in the form of consolation or suffering?

Yes, Thérèse knew that God does not abandon us, and in spite of the enveloping darkness she remained fully confident that He whose love is "full sweet and full gracious, full tender and full merciful" was only putting her good will to the test. She was sure that although she could neither see nor feel Him,

He was there as He always had been hidden now behind the clouds. Abandonment like this requires great trust and immense courage. It sounds easy enough on paper to surrender oneself unconditionally to the operations of God. We may enthuse in advance about these trials as the means of attaining our greatest good and ultimate happiness; but when one is actually put to the test, nothing is so difficult, so seemingly impossible, as to elicit the act of confidence required of us. That Thérèse had no illusions about this sort of trial is clear from the notes which she wrote for Mother Mary Gonzaga, in which she acknowledged that had the ordeal come to her earlier she might not have had the strength to bear it, but have given way under it and fallen into discouragement. "I don't think I've ever quite realized before how gracious and merciful God is," she exclaimed, for He who tempers the wind to the shorn lamb had matched her with this hour, and now the trial only served to purge away all natural satisfaction in her longing for heaven.

St. John of the Cross teaches that the period and intensity of suffering will vary in each individual soul, but he also adds that those who have the disposition and greater strength to suffer, God purifies with greater intensity and more quickly. Thérèse's doubts, had they been rooted in temperamental or nervous disorder, would have produced nothing but sterile self-pity and paralysing scruples. On the contrary, she not merely endured but welcomed this trial as all others, eager to suffer for and with Jesus while there was breath left in her body. "The angels are less happy than I am," she said three days before her death, "for they cannot suffer."

The failure on the part of most of us to realize and act upon the knowledge of the transience of this life, our tendency to ignore the fact that "we have an everlasting city, but not here" (Heb. 13:14), and our almost exclusive preoccupation with the futile attempt to provide ourselves with one, is well expressed in Alice duer Miller's poem *The White Cliffs*:

> If some immortal stranger walked our land
> And heard of death, how could he understand

That we, doomed mortals, draw our meted breath
Lightheartedly, all unconcerned with death?

At the age of fifteen Thérèse had been able to see things in their correct perspective. She knew that the kind of life which at any moment may be cut short by death cannot be true life. On Ash Wednesday of 1888, M. Martin made her an Easter gift of a new-born lamb. Thérèse was enchanted with it, but alas it died the same afternoon, and the death of the pretty little creature gave her much food for reflection. "Here on earth," she concluded, "we should be attached to nothing, even the most innocent things; for they all fail us just when we least expect it. Only eternal things can satisfy us." And a month later she observed to Pauline that life passes so swiftly, with both its sorrows and its joys, that it is obviously better to earn a splendid crown at the cost of a little suffering, than to have no suffering and only an ordinary crown. And after she had entered Carmel she pointed out to Céline that while life was undoubtedly full of sacrifices, it is but "a night spent in a bad inn"; and therefore it seemed preferable to spend it in an inn that was thoroughly inconvenient than in one that was only *half* bad. In other words, since suffering is unavoidable in this life, it is clearly a wise speculation to exploit it so as to merit increased grace and glory, particularly as the alternative is merely to endure it without any gain of supernatural interest whatsoever.

As to the obscuring of her faith, Thérèse says, "I wish I could put down what I feel about it, but unfortunately that isn't possible. To appreciate the darkness of this tunnel, you have to have been through it." She resorted once more to a "parable", picturing herself as having been born in a land which was fog-bound, so that she had never seen the beauty of a serene, sun-drenched landscape under a blue, cloudless sky. But since her childhood she had been told that such a country existed, where nature was smiling and gracious—a country that was her native land, from which she was exiled, and which was the object of all her hopes and dreams. What if this promise of lush meadows basking in warmth and light,

bright with flowers and gay with birds' songs, was merely a
figment of the imagination—the wishful thinking of the dis-
contented dwellers of the mist? "Oh, no," she said, "the fact
is quite certain, for the king of that fair country came to live
in the mist and darkness for thirty-three years."

From this we are enabled to see, in its perfection, the absolute faithfulness of Thérèse. What she had hitherto believed
with all joy and certainty, she could now only will to believe.
As the truths of faith betook themselves to a region where they
could no longer be followed or comprehended by the senses
or imagination, she clasped them more firmly than ever with
her indomitable will. Now, although she was habitually without any feeling of it, she truly lived by faith. And although she
constantly feared that she might in this state unwittingly
offend God, she was well aware that her consciously willed
efforts to live the faith were no less meritorious merely because
she derived no satisfaction from it as hitherto. "Faith is no
longer even a veil," she declared, "it is a great wall reaching
up to heaven and blotting out the very stars."

Once more Thérèse turned what appeared to be a complete
catastrophe right about, and, accepting the suffocating darkness of her soul so that through it unbelievers might receive
the light of faith, made of the very misfortune itself the fabric
of her virtues of faith and hope. She is one of them now, the
unbelievers are her brothers, and with them she will remain,
content to eat the bitter herbs of suffering and tears until it is
God's will to call her to the banquet of heaven.

It was the knowledge that the good Jesus works most lovingly
for His children and arranges what is best for them just when
things look darkest and most hopeless that enabled Thérèse
to cling with her will to the truths she had lost from her heart,
and to share in the redemption of souls who were really without the faith.

During her last months she admitted to having made more
acts of faith than during the whole of her life. These acts of
faith were not made in defiance, hurled as it were in the teeth
of the tempter, but in humble confidence in God, whose
paternal hand was guiding His child through the surrounding

darkness. Far from discouraging or weakening her faith, "ever since He began to let me have temptations against the virtue of faith, He has established the spirit of faith more firmly than ever in my heart". (See Note 12.)

Thérèse felt that God had granted her prayer, and that her desire to die of love was to be fulfilled. "All my smallest desires have been realized," she said. All had been completed; without doubt God would now do His part. Two months previously, Sister Mary of the Sacred Heart had remarked on the happiness of a death of love. Thérèse replied simply that one could only enjoy that happiness if in life one had practised fraternal charity. For her the life of love was no mere abstraction. The virtues, the positive acts of charity and self-abnegation that daily life impose, must be the warp and woof of its fabric. She had lived as she had asked to be permitted to do, in an act of perfect love, and now she was ready to die of love. She had read and nourished her soul on the writings of St. John of the Cross, and was well aware of what he understood by the death of love, which has been expounded fully in his poem *The Living Flame of Love* and its prose commentary. In particular she had meditated on the lines:

> Perfect me now if it be Thy will,
> Break the web of this sweet encounter;

and she had asked God to effect these things in her own soul. "It is unbelievable how all my hopes have been realized! When formerly I read St. John of the Cross, I asked God to operate in me that which I found described there—that is to say, in a few years to sanctify me as if I had lived a long life, so that I might be rapidly consummated in love . . . and I have been heard!" And two months before her death she quoted the above lines from St. John of the Cross saying: "I have always applied these words to the death of love which I desire. Love will not wear out the web of my life, but will break it suddenly."[1]

On 2nd September she came back to the same thought.

[1] N.V., 31st August, 27th July.

"Oh, indeed I desire heaven! 'Break the web for this sweet encounter', my God!"

By the last months of her life St. Thérèse had reached a very high degree of love and union, which she had endeavoured to express in words in her letter to Sister Mary of the Sacred Heart, written in September 1896, which now forms the second part of her manuscript autobiography. If the mere *desire* to love God could yield such happiness amid the sufferings and uncertainties of life what, she asked, would it be to possess and enjoy that love with no fear of separation in the fullness of face-to-face vision?

As the life of love can be lived without the accompaniment of miraculous graces and favours, similarly the death of love can be effected without the transports that have so often been associated with it. Although St. Thérèse is often mistakenly regarded as an incurable sentimentalist, in this as in all essentials, she was in fact a stern realist and wasted no time on pious fancies. Just as in life she had never desired anything that went beyond the common round, so in death Thérèse sought nothing that "little souls" could not aspire to. Here on earth her sole consolation had been "to have none on this side of the grave". And so, all those sufferings that every human being can expect when dying slowly—pain, oppression, mental exhaustion, difficulty in breathing—were present in full measure in the case of Thérèse, even though spiritually hers was a death of love, crowning a life of love and total self-surrender. She herself did not expect her last days to be without great suffering. She specifically warned her sisters not to grieve if they saw no signs of happiness at the moment of her death, reminding them of Calvary; for although our Lord died a victim of love, and His was the most sublime death of love ever known, yet His agony and dereliction were also the most intense. "To die of love does not necessarily mean dying in rapture, and candidly I do not expect any such consolation." It is is interesting to compare Thérèse's views on this subject with the teaching of St. John of the Cross in Chapter VII, Book II of the *Ascent of Mount Carmel*, and see how closely her ideas coincide with his here as in all else.

On the Feast of the Assumption, Mother Agnes mentioned the prose commentary of St. John of the Cross on the stanza of the *Living Flame of Love* already quoted, where he says that the death of such souls is sweet and gentle, amid delectable encounters and sublime impulses of love. Thérèse immediately replied that any transports she enjoyed were only in the very depths of her soul. And she added that this should be made clear, for souls would not be encouraged in their own travail were they to believe that she had not suffered greatly. During her last days the darkness of soul and agony of body grew in intensity until she cried: "I would never have believed it possible to suffer so much. I cannot breathe, I cannot die . . ." adding, however, "I am very willing to suffer more."

The last agony of Thérèse was dreadful to behold. "Oh, mother, I assure you the chalice is full to overflowing. Yet God will not abandon me; He has never abandoned me. Yes, my God, do all you will, *but have mercy on me!*" Earlier she had said that the words of Job, "Even though He should slay me, yet will I trust Him" had ravished her from childhood, but it was a long time before she herself had become established in such a degree of *abandon.* "Now I am! The good God has taken me in His arms and placed me there." And now, in the midst of her intense sufferings she did not desire death as a release from pain. She asked neither to live nor to die, and would have been happy and content to go on living and suffering still more had God so willed. She rejoiced at her approaching death only because it was the expression of His will for her.

The description of Thérèse's last moments have been recorded by Mother Agnes:

"The sisters came and knelt around the bed and were witnesses of that last ecstasy. The face of our saint assumed again the lily-like tint it had possessed in full health; her eyes remained fixed on high, irradiated and expressing such happiness as surpassed all her desires. She made certain movements with her head, as if at intervals she was divinely wounded by shafts of love. After that ecstasy, which lasted for the space of a *Credo,* she closed her eyes and breathed her last sigh."

Commenting on this, the late Fr. Gabriel of St. Mary Magdalen, O.C.D., has said: "We may all aspire to this direct meeting with God when leaving this life, for not even visible ecstasy is an essential part of the death of love. Only one thing is required as being indispensable to a death of love—a life of love which has attained to full maturity. We know what is necessary in order that we may reach this. St. Thérèse has declared to us her programme and ours, a simple and clear programme made up of generous faith and loving trust. When we have done our part it is impossible that merciful love should not do His. God will perfect the work which we by ourselves cannot do—He will make us saints."

CHAPTER EIGHT

UNTIL TIME IS NO MORE

We must get before we can give, and the higher angels transfer to the lower ones only the light of which they have received the fullness. The Creator has established this order with regard to things divine: he who has the mission to distribute them must share in them first and fill himself first of all abundantly with the graces that God wishes to grant to souls through his agency. Then, and only then, will he be allowed to share with others.

("Denis the Areopagite")

(i) *Da mihi animas*

St. Thérèse, as has been seen, was little more than a child when the burning zeal for the salvation of souls took possession of her. Henceforward this was to be an integral part of her interior make-up, the basis of her special call by God to a definite apostolate.

She describes the experience in her manuscript addressed to Mother Agnes. One Sunday a picture of the crucifixion slipped sideways out of her missal, and suddenly the sight of the blood flowing from Christ's pierced hand struck her in a way she had never before known. To her it seemed that the precious blood was being allowed to fall, unnoticed and unregarded, to the ground; and in that instant she resolved to remain in spirit at the foot of the cross to gather it up in order to apply it to the needs of souls, not to hoard it as a personal treasure. This was a spontaneous impulse, but it did not fade from her memory or consciousness as is the usual way when such sudden impacts lose their sharp outlines with the passage of time. That determination remained with her for the rest of her life, and she translated the resolution into practical and consistent action.

Her letters to Céline on this subject are overflowing with a sense of urgency, of time running out with work still unaccomplished, as the longing to save souls for Christ grew ever stronger in her heart. Life is short and passes rapidly; eternity has no end. The single day of our mortal life is all the time that is given to any of us, and it is folly to waste a second of it. "There is but one sole thing to do: love Jesus with all our strength, and to save souls for Him that He may be loved." Never for a moment did Thérèse leave off working for this one sole thing. As a postulant she had written to her aunt, Mme. Guérin, paraphrasing the text of John 9:4: "I mean to work hard while the daylight of this life lasts, for after that comes the darkness, when I shall be unable to do anything." And when, nine years later, she lay dying in the infirmary, Mother Agnes made a note of a small act of mortification Thérèse had mentioned. "Perhaps," she said doubtfully, "the merit will be lost now that I have told you of it and you are writing it down."

"So, you want to acquire merits, then?" asked Mother Agnes.

"Oh yes; but not for myself. For souls, for all the needs of the Church, to scatter roses on the whole world, the just and the sinners."

By nature Thérèse may not have been unselfish and generous. Perfected by grace she gave all—her spiritual alms never ceased while she had breath left to earn them. Her merits, her prayers, all were for others. She appropriated nothing for herself since she felt the zeal of a Carmelite ought to embrace the whole world. Had she lived to be eighty she would still remain poor, for no sooner had she acquired any spiritual treasure than she thought of souls in danger of hell, and immediately made out in their favour a blank cheque for whatever merit she had gained, keeping in her hands nothing of which she could say "This is all my own". On another occasion during her last illness, she told Mother Agnes of the great pleasure she derived from the realization that someone was praying for her. "Then I told God that I wished Him to apply it to sinners."

"Do you not wish even that for your own consolation?"

"No."

St. Thérèse chose the silent and austere life of the Carmelite in preference to that of a missionary, to which she felt so strongly attracted that once, during their pilgrimage to Rome, she begged her sister Céline not to show her a missionary magazine. This she considered a temptation to a way of life which would have gratified her nature but to which she did not believe herself to be called by God. She felt with all her soul that the life of contemplation and abnegation was, all other things being equal, more useful to the Church. In other words, she had a decided and strong contemplative vocation.

"I will not read them," she said when Céline offered her the magazines, "for I have too keen a desire to consecrate myself to works of zeal, and I wish to be hidden in the cloister so as to give myself more completely to the good God." By this, Céline commented, she meant to sacrifice all the consolations and satisfactions of an active apostolate, thus finding "how to ease her heart by a greater sacrifice of herself".

Céline (Sister Geneviève of the Holy Face) related this incident in detail during the beatification process of her sister. It was, she said, the hope of saving more souls by mortification and self-abnegation that determined her to seek admission to Carmel. "She confided to me her reason, which was in order to suffer more and thereby win souls for our Lord. In her opinion it was harder for nature to work without ever seeing the fruit of one's labours, with no encouragement or diversion, and that the hardest work of all was that undertaken in order to gain the mastery over self. In short, when she entered Carmel her special aim was to pray for priests and to immolate herself for the needs of the Church. She referred to this kind of apostolate as 'trading wholesale', because through the head she reached the members. She declared her personal intention at the canonical examination preceding her profession stating: 'I have come to save souls, and especially to pray for priests'. This answer is uniquely her own, as each answers this question according to her own inclinations."

Thérèse felt certain that in embracing the Carmelite life she would, in her contemplative vocation, reap the maximum apostolic harvest and vivify the missionary activity of the world. The higher the perfection she attained as her spiritual life progressed and developed, the more vital grew its apostolic character. A "dying life" she called it, precious above all others for the salvation of souls, where through her own death to self she could bring souls to the life of grace and give them the joys of heaven.

Her parents had prayed for a son who might be a priest and a missionary, but this was not possible as both their sons died in infancy. It was no mere pious fancy on Thérèse's part when she felt the urge to assume this unrealized vocation. "I was," she says, "still being tormented by the question of unfulfilled longings which was becoming a distraction to my prayer." But she could not be a priest, and Thérèse was not the person to waste time in useless regrets over irremediable circumstances. It was within her power to become the universal missionary, she realized, but only by curtailing her activities. Not in this place or that, but in all places and at all times would she, a Carmelite, be a missionary. It was not a *mission* she would evangelize, but *all missions.*

Like St. Paul, every successful preacher or missionary is conscious of what he owes to the prayers of those who thus assist him in his work. "The man who plants, the man who waters, counts for nothing; God is everything, since it is He who gives the increase." (I Cor. 3 : 7).

Thérèse took her painful steps under obedience for some missionary. Who can tell the impetus given to other missionaries by other Thérèses—monks and nuns in the obscurity of their cloisters—faithfully performing some minute, tedious, or even seemingly unreasonable prescription of rule or custom. This is how Thérèse saw her life, a victim to the merciful love of God, which was to open the Heart of Jesus and allow His love and graces to pour themselves out unchecked upon sinners.

The life of love, for Thérèse, seems to be crystallized in the gospel scene where Mary's reckless love breaks the box of spikenard to anoint the feet of Jesus, so that "the whole house was scented with the ointment". (Jn. 12 : 3.) In the poem *Vivre d'Amour*, she points out that in the eyes of the world her sacrifice was needless, the waste of a life that had years of service ahead of it; but for Him alone, and to give Him pleasure, is the pure spikenard of her life poured out, and the world may remonstrate as much as it pleases, she has succeeded in her attempt and knows that "to give all for love is a most sweet bargain".

"The apostles murmured against Magdalen," she wrote to comfort Céline who was meeting opposition in her desire to follow her three sisters into Carmel after their father's death. "It is very much the same with us, the most fervent *Christians*, the *priests*, consider that we are *too extreme*, that we ought to *serve* with Martha instead of consecrating to Jesus the *vessels* of our *lives* with the perfumes contained in them . . . but after all, what matter that our *vessels* are broken, since Jesus is *consoled*, and since, in spite of itself, the world is forced to *awareness* of the perfumes they breathe forth, perfumes which serve to purify the poisoned air the world is ever breathing."[1]

As already indicated, one does not enter religion to save one's own soul. It is, after all, to be hoped that most of us would have managed to achieve that minimum had we remained in the world; and indeed it has been claimed that one who enters religion solely in order to save her own soul will not even accomplish that. Zeal for the salvation of others must be a large factor in the spiritual life. We do not go either to heaven or to hell alone, and no-one can gain eternal life unless, according as she is able and called, she does her share in this universal work of charity. Contemplatives are not exempted from the general obligation devolving on all Christians, any more than the practice of the evangelical counsels dispenses one from observing the precepts laid down in the ten commandments. If they evade this responsibility, they are not fulfilling their role, and in that case would deserve the charge of being a drain on the resources of the Church; for they who are expected to contribute more generously than others would then not only be giving nothing, but drawing on the general fund. In withdrawing themselves from their own immediate family circles, they do not cease to belong to the great family of the Church, and as members of contemplative orders, they

---

[1] C.L. p. 210.

belong more than ever to this body—more to it than to themselves. The vows that free them from worldly affairs do so in order that they may without hindrance give themselves entirely to the service of the Church.

Truly the contemplative, consecrated in a particular way to God finds in God an increased contact with her neighbour. This is necessarily so for "the man who loves God must be the one who loves his brother as well". (I Jn. 4: 21.) "Do you think that such persons will love and delight in none save God?" asks St. Teresa of Avila. "No; they will love others much more than they did, with a more genuine love, with greater passion and with a love which brings more profit; that, in a word, is what love really is."

The very real and fundamental bond of union which links the life of the enclosed contemplative with that of the active missioner and secular priest is not always fully realized, and the missioner himself does not generally advert to it; but in the mind of the Church, as expressed by Pope Pius XI in the Apostolic Constitution *Umbratilem*, the missionary's activity is dependent for its fruitfulness upon the contemplative life and the spiritual support which he is entitled to expect from the cloister. Not that the latter will do the work without his efforts; both are necessary elements, and a mutual understanding of that will help both to appreciate and co-operate fully with each other.

"In order to accomplish His works Jesus needs no-one," Thérèse wrote to Père Roulland, "and if He accepted me for the missions it would be sheer kindness." Let us not make the mistake of thinking that we are indispensable instruments for the smooth working of God's designs; that without us He would be left in a quandary as to how to bring His plans to fruition. He has bidden us "pray the Lord of the harvest that He should send labourers". God is the principle of every fruitful action achieved in this world in the supernatural order; actions, that is to say, whereby the life of grace is planted and nourished in souls, thus ensuring that the reign of Christ is extended continually in the world of men. *Without me, you can do nothing.* The realization of this truth must penetrate all our works if we wish them to be fruitful in the sight of God. Truly, when we have done all that had been commanded of us, we are forced to admit that we are unprofitable servants, nothing more.

(ii) "Infinite Desires"

Thérèse's manuscript for Sister Mary of the Sacred Heart, which is a practical treatise on the Mystical Body of Christ, sets forth the details of her mission and forms the last chapter of the autobiography. Not content merely with being a daughter of Carmel, or by her union with our Lord, being the mother of souls, she desires to embrace every vocation and to extend her mission to every soul, to be a fighter, a priest, an apostle, a doctor of the Church, a martyr; in order to satisfy the needs of her nature she must perform, for Christ's sake, every kind or heroic action simultaneously. Most of all, however, she desired to travel all over the world, extending His kingdom and bringing His name and salvation to the heathen. But even this fell short of her soul's "infinite desires", for she felt that one mission in a particular locality could never content her, however distant or needy. She longed to encompass all places and times, to have been a missionary since the beginning of the world and go on being one until the end of time.

These desires and aspirations grew in strength through meditation on our Lord's life as related in the gospels. She realized that His death on the cross poured out infinite benefits on all men, but that He invites us to share His work, to be co-operators in distributing the fruits of His redemptive sacrifice.

But how was she to satisfy her desires and longings, let alone reconcile all these conflicting vocations? Again she turned to scripture and studied the doctrine of the Mystical Body as outlined by St. Paul, but was unable to identify herself among the interdependent, interrelated members of that compact and complex body, mainly because she longed to recognize herself in them all. It was charity that gave her the key to the combination, for if the Church was a body composed of different members, it could not lack the noblest of all; it must have a heart, warm and pulsing with love. And logically, this love is the true impulse and principle of life by which all the other members act. When the heart ceases to function, all the other members fail, and without the stimulus of love, there would be no apostles, martyrs or confessors. Thus truly love is the vocation that includes all others, a vast, supernatural force, embracing all times and places because it is eternal.

And so, having discovered her place in the bosom of the Church, she, a little child, would remain close to the throne of her royal father, while her elder brothers engaged in battle, and carry on with the work of loving on behalf of all those under fire in the front line.

Thérèse was always practical. Love, she saw, must be proved by deeds, and her programme of sending others out to do the fighting and working while she stayed safely at home and assumed the duty of loving, was no shirking of labour or the lazy rule of least effort. No, even though a helpless child, she could scatter flowers and sing the great canticle of love. That would be her life—to miss no opportunity of making some small sacrifice by a smiling greeting or a word of comfort, suffering life's inevitable setbacks and enjoying its consolations in a spirit of love; that sometimes would cost as much effort and will-power as facing enemy fire. Always the least and most trivial action would be performed thoroughly, and in giving consistently of her best under every circumstance, she would do all for love. Nothing, however trifling, that came her way, would be wasted; all should yield their petals to strew before the Lord, and while scattering these flowers of little sacrifices, she would sing.

Prayer and suffering are the two great means Thérèse proposes to use in expressing her love. Love and suffering are inseparable, and the smallest suffering was used by her as material for the salvation of souls. It was by prayer and suffering, bound into a fragrant bouquet by the golden thread of love that Thérèse won so many souls for Christ while still on earth, and in heaven continues to draw them into His loving embrace.

Thérèse did not work in spurts—a burst of fervour followed

by a slackening of effort, however slight. By means of faith and hope, her actual union with Jesus Christ was maintained without the slightest interruption. From the beginning of her religious life until her death she could claim: "I have never yet found the moment in which I could say: 'Now I am going to work for myself'." This ever-absorbing zeal for the apostolate drew her not merely to the foot of the cross but nailed her to it, hand and foot, until, breathing only in painful gasps, she still reiterated that all she had written about her desire for suffering was quite true, and that experience of its reality did not make her retract a single word. "I have no regrets that I have delivered myself up to Love."

However she did not desire suffering for its own sake, but recognized it as the price of the souls she so ardently longed to save, and therefore she counted it as her greatest treasure here below. One of the graces she acknowledged was the enlightenment she received in her early teens, when our Lord made her understand that if she wished to win souls for Him it must be through the cross; and after that realization of its purchasing power, suffering not only attracted her, but she set about making it a joy. It was not necessary for her own salvation that she should tread, step by step, the road to Calvary in the bloodstained footprints of her Master, but Thérèse had no intention of winning eternal life merely for herself. She wished to draw with her the whole world, to empty purgatory, to bring every sinner into the arms of her loving Saviour, and for this ambitious programme she would not only have been prepared but actually longed to endure in her own body all the torments of all the martyrs. Her desires, she says, were boundless, and the further she travelled on this road the greater became her desire to give.

Every beat of her heart has caused ripples that will spread to the limits of the world and the end of time, widening the frontiers of the kingdom of God and carrying the gospel further and further afield. Thus, without ever leaving her cloister, she succeeded in her ambition of becoming a most efficacious missionary.

Her life in religion was but the preparation for her real

apostolic mission, however, and at her entry into heaven her vocation burst at last into full flower. She had entered Carmel solely that she might work there more singlemindedly for the salvation of souls, and in heaven her ability to do so can know no limits. She herself was quite confident that she would not remain "inactive" in heaven, for her desire was to go on working for the Church and for souls, and two months before her death she confessed: "If I am leaving the battlefield prematurely, it is with no selfish desire to rest." The idea of eternal beatitude scarcely stirred a vibration in her heart. Her continual prayer was that she be permitted to continue "doing good upon earth", and she felt certain that it had been granted.

(iii) Universal Apostle

One of the accomplishments of St. Thérèse which has caused most astonishment is that she, an enclosed religious who had left the world at an age when most girls are still at school, and for less than ten years afterwards lived in the complete concealment and obscurity of Carmel, should have merited the honour of being proclaimed patroness of the missions on an equal footing with the intrepid apostle St. Frances Xavier. Yet to this dignity she was raised by the great Pope of the Missions, Pius XI.

"I may give away all that I have, to feed the poor; I may give myself up to be burnt at the stake; if I lack charity, it goes for nothing." (I Cor. 13:3.) The least act of faith and hope, however, if informed by charity, can work miracles in the order of grace. This great and salutary lesson has been underlined by the Church in naming her hidden and humble child universal patroness of all missions. For she indeed understood and put into practice the principle that in order to become effectively a missionary one must first be apostolic in soul. She herself possessed a zeal for the apostolate in the highest degree, and this she recognized as a precious grace. Such missionary ardour as was hers, embracing the whole world and every age, drew her not to a foreign mission society but to the cloister, where she effected the immolation of herself—a holocaust all the more complete because of its utter hiddenness

and silence, and the absence of any of the consolations afforded
by the contemplation of a job completed and well done. All
true Christians must be in some sense apostles, although only
a comparatively small proportion will be called upon to carry
the gospel to distant lands. But Thérèse demonstrates to us
all how to make of daily life and the ordinary and rather dull
incidents that make it up, an apostolic offering highly pleasing
to God and extremely efficacious for souls.

In 1923 the newly beatified Thérèse of the Child Jesus was
proclaimed patroness of the Carmelite Missions. After her
canonization in 1925 Pope Pius XI named her the special
patroness of the Association for the Education of Native
Seminarians. The missionary apostolate was under way, she
was gradually moving towards her triumphant nomination as
the official custodian of all missions. Two hundred and thirty-
two ordinaries of the missionary world, archbishops, bishops,
vicars and prefects apostolic, both of the Western and Eastern
churches, joined in petitioning the Holy Father to declare St.
Thérèse special patroness of all the missions of the world. The
Pope himself supported the cause when it was presented to
the Sacred Congregation, but despite this weighty advocacy
the petition was not favourably received. It was not considered
fitting that a woman, a nun who had never set foot on mission
soil, should be proclaimed patroness of the missions in preference to the great missionary saints who had laboured,
preached, and laid down their lives in witness of the faith they
toiled to propagate. Not for nothing was Pope Pius XI the
pontiff who had been entrusted with her cause. He overrode
the decision of the Sacred Congregation, and on his own
authority declared St. Thérèse of the Child Jesus "Special
Patroness of all Missionaries, men and women, and of Missions
existing in the whole world, on an equality with St. Francis
Xavier". And time has fully vindicated the decision and his
confidence in the "dear little saint".

In a pastoral letter on "The Missions of our Order", the
late General, Fr. Silverio of St. Teresa, O.C.D., wrote: "It
seemed strange to many persons that a saint whose life was
consecrated to contemplation in the cloister of Carmel should

have been the one to be proclaimed the principal patroness of missions alongside St. Francis Xavier. Yet it was not incongruous to thoughtful souls well acquainted with the doctrines of the Church, who know and appreciate thoroughly the mutual help which the interior life and apostolate for souls render each other not only in regard to the missions, but in every other religious activity. Such persons fully understood and looked forward to this proclamation as a very logical one in the Catholic world. For the apostolate, no matter how active and brilliant it might be, would be condemned to sterility if the breath of prayer did not circulate through its lungs. Long ago the first and foremost missionary of Catholicism, the great convert of Damascus, said 'Neither the planter nor the sower is worth anything, but He who gives the increase, God.' (I Cor. 3 : 7.) A typical example (of the ideals of monastic life proposed by St. Teresa of Avila and St. John of the Cross) resplendent with everything a Carmelite should be . . . is St. Thérèse of the Child Jesus, who did not have to leave her beloved cloister of Lisieux for even five minutes in order to become at the proper time the greatest contemplative and the greatest missionary of modern times.

"St. Thérèse and St. Francis Xavier are august representatives of the two modes of the gospel precept. A sagacious pope saw that the commandment (love of God and love of neighbour) gracefully divided into two parts, and should have two outstanding protectors who would jointly guard both parts of the commandment: the perfect Catholic missionary personified in St. Francis and the perfect contemplative in St. Thérèse. It is clear that the two parts are inseparable according to sound dogmatic, ascetic and mystical theology. St. Francis Xavier would not have been a good missionary without a deep interior life, nor would St. Thérèse of the Child Jesus have been a perfect contemplative unless her torrential flood of love of God were watering the huge fields of evangelization throughout the world which still await the preaching of the gospel, thus bringing fertility to those deserts of faith and Catholic spirituality."

The secret of her power in the missions is to be found in

her own words: "Undoubtedly prayers and sacrifices are the best assistance one can give to missionaries"; for through our acts of charity and courtesy, our self-control and forbearance, practised as it were "in the dark", we gain alms of grace which purchase conversions and assist the missions. In the poem to Blessed Théophane Vénard she wrote: "My actions, my small sufferings of today, can make Jesus loved beyond the seas."

One of Thérèse's great pleasures had been her appointment as "sister" to two young seminarians preparing for ordination; the Abbé Bellière who was to join the White Fathers in Africa, and Père Roulland of the Foreign Missions, who left for China almost immediately after his ordination. It was, Thérèse felt, an indulgence on the part of her heavenly father thus to gratify her desire. On her profession day she had prayed that she might be entrusted with an apostolic soul; since she could not be a priest she wanted to be linked with one who would receive in her stead the Lord's graces, and be fired by the same aspirations and desires as herself. She had thought then that it would only be in heaven that she would meet the apostle who was the "brother of her soul". But to her joy she had the consolation of knowing while still on earth two priests whose auxiliary she became in their work for the salvation of souls.

"It was such a strange fulfilment of my wish! I can only describe it as a childish joy; I had to go back to my childhood to recover the memory of joys like that, so keen that the soul isn't big enough to contain them. Not for years had I experienced happiness of this kind; I felt as if my soul had taken fresh roots, as if chords of music, long forgotten, had stirred within me."[1]

However, despite the vivid sense of personal pleasure she derived from her intimate association with these two missionaries, Thérèse knew that her correspondence with them was not the assistance they were most in need of. And so she set about praying for them and offering her sacrifices for them with redoubled energy and fervour. Before her death she warned Mother Agnes of the real risk of dissipation of spiritual energy that could lie in such pen-friendships unless they were

[1] A.S. p. 302.

kept on a purely supernatural level. She foresaw that in years to come, on hearing that she had been given as spiritual sister to missionaries, many young priests would request a similar favour. But for certain souls, those of the religious especially, this would be a real danger, and rather than acting as a spur to their zeal, would lead to preoccupation with non-essentials, and even vanity in the exchange of empty compliments, rather than the mutual assistance of prayer and self-denial. "It is by prayer and sacrifice *alone* that we can be of use to the Church."

The apostolic value of prayer and sacrifice is personified in St. Thérèse whom Almighty God has raised up to illustrate to us the irresistible power which such a life can be for the Church, whether it be spent in the world or within the restricted limits of a cloister.

The offering of herself to the missions did not, with Thérèse, find its expression in a missionary vocation to teach or labour, but in the life of solitude and austerity, which she knew to be the greatest apostolate and the farthest-reaching. Because her mission was to be universal she was given a contemplative vocation. It was not in the mind of God to entrust her with a message such as the appeal of divine love which He revealed to Sister Josefa Menéndez. Thérèse's mission was to draw souls to God, to reach every corner of the earth, every age and condition of man, whether within the fold of the Church or not. To fulfil this universal mission it was not only unnecessary but even undesirable that she be bounded on any side by a predominant spirit such as would hall-mark her as belonging to one particular sphere rather than another. For all, her example and teaching are practical and imitable with the help of grace, although it is true that a Carmelite is possibly able to appreciate and understand St. Thérèse more fully than anyone else, and find in her a unique model and exemplar for her own interior and exterior life. I say this because the Carmelite life is undoubtedly the perfect framework in which to live a life of spiritual childhood. But Thérèse's vocation, lived out within the confines of a Carmelite cloister, nevertheless embraced the whole Church on earth, and this has been recognized by the Holy See in giving her the patronage not only of her own country, France, but also of all missions of the world and of Russia. It was to a recluse's cell that God called her in order to assist most effectively in the work being carried out by others on the mission field. For the decade of her religious life, she spent herself without respite for the salvation of souls, and her zeal only increased with the passing years, burning into her own soul as surely and rapidly as disease consumed her body. This devotion was no passing emotion of a young and sentimental religious, fed on complimentary letters from two immature seminarians; it obsessed her, became a "veritable torment". But, as with everything else in Thérèse's spiritual life, it has its foundations in one of the richest and most satisfying doctrines of the Church, that of the Mystical Body: the realization that the Church, composed of different members, must have a heart, within which she would be love. "It's love I ask for, love is all the skill I have. Sensational acts of piety are not for me; not for me to preach the gospel, or to shed my blood as a martyr, but I see now that all that doesn't matter; my elder brothers will do the work for me while I, as the baby of the family, stay close to the King's throne, the Queen's throne, and go on loving on behalf of my brothers out on the battlefield."[1]

(iv) The Flood will bear me far

"Draw me after Thee where thou wilt; see, we hasten after Thee, by the very fragrance of those perfumes allured." (Cant. 1 : 3.) Commenting on these words, Thérèse has written: "As I understand you, Lord, there is a fragrance about the thought of you, and when I allow that fragrance to cast its spell over me, I don't hasten after you in the first person singular—all those whom I love come running at my heels. This happens without effort or constraint; it is the automatic consequence of that attraction which you exercise over me. Just so, the swirling river rushing down to the sea bears along with it everything it has met in its course. Your love, Jesus, is an ocean with no shore to bound it; and if I plunge into it, I carry with me all the possessions I have. You know, Lord, what those

[1] A.S. p. 237.

possessions are—the souls you have seen fit to link with mine; nothing else."[1]

The setting in order of charity has a twofold effect: God and our neighbour. Divine love stoops to embrace us, reaches out to our neighbour, and then leads back to God. The further advanced we are in fraternal charity, the greater the love we will have for God—and the movement is reciprocal.

The soul must strengthen the bonds of her union with God and then, incorporated into Christ, her spiritual life takes a new orientation. Zeal for souls is no longer an "overflow" from one's personal fullness, the passing on merely of one's superfluity to others. It is a deep and fundamental movement arising from the hidden source from within, and as Thérèse says, it carries along on its flood not only her own soul, but also those committed to her care. And thus she finds her own perfection and the salvation of others in the complete gift of self, with no reservations, to Christ for souls and for the Church.

The apostolate is accordingly a necessary complement to holiness. Since the glory of God is the goal of religious life, the salvation of souls must hold a predominant place in that life, so that sanctity will issue in an effective desire to save souls. Indeed, St. Teresa of Avila roundly declares that any other sanctity is spurious.

Yet it is all too true that there are many religious who are by no means "eaten up" with zeal for the salvation of souls. Their vocation is genuine, and they embraced religious life because of a sincere and even generous desire to love God, to serve Him, and to grow in virtue. But their fervour was, so to speak, turned inwards; their primary motive was to seek God and achieve perfection for their own sakes, and not a consuming desire to give themselves to Him for others. They have come not so much to save other souls as to safeguard their own. This is the explanation of the sometimes frightening mediocrity to be found amongst those dedicated to God's service, who, even though well advanced in the ways of prayer and the practice of virtue, are able to dissipate their energies on

[1] A.S. pp. 305-6.

trivialities, even when there is a world crying out for redemption and sanctification. As Pope Paul VI recently said of
Christians in general, it is not sufficient that we regard our
purpose on earth as being solely (in terms of the catechism
answer) "to know, love and serve God here on earth, and to be
happy with Him forever in heaven". This must be amplified
into the obligation to know God and make His name known;
to love Him and make Him loved; to serve Him in our neighbour and thus draw all men into His service; so that we will
enjoy His presence throughout eternity because we have
wholeheartedly done our share in the work of redemption, and
the number of the elect is complete.

Consistent minute-by-minute perseverance in little sacrifices in the same surroundings within the restricted confines
of her enclosure as practised by Thérèse, is beyond merely
human strength. It is easier to rise to the occasion and perform
a great and heroic deed under the impetus of an urgent necessity, than to carry out consistently and wholeheartedly the
humdrum duties that are usually unnoticed and seldom
appreciated by one's fellows. St. Thérèse, however, was not
viewing her actions against the backdrop of her immediate
surroundings, the limited space or restricted social intercourse
or confining circumstances that were the exterior adjuncts of
her life in Carmel. Her vision swept the world and embraced
all places and times. Of what value were her trifling sacrifices?
What pleasure could the omnipotent God take in these flowers
of little worth, "the fragrant shower of petals" as she thought
of them?

But can anything be worthless when it is done for the love
of God? He Himself has given us the answer: "When you did
it to one of the least of my brethren here, you did it to me . . .
(and) when you refused it to one of the least of my brethren
here, you refused it to me." (Matt. 25: 40,45.) Thus Thérèse
knew that He would take pleasure in her childish game of
scattering blossoms. "And because they give you pleasure, the
Church triumphant in heaven will smile upon them too."
Thus the whole Church would participate in her childish
game by scattering her flowers, now hallowed by Jesus' accept-

ance of them. They would serve to relieve the sufferings of the souls in purgatory, and to strengthen for fresh conquests the members of the pilgrim Church on earth.

Is this just artificially pretty and sentimental imagery? Surely no-one can fail to recognize beneath these "flounces" the heroic ideal, the valiant soldier who chose always to try to conceal behind a gay smile or a façade of perfumed rose-petals the price of the favours thus secured.

Every act was an act of love, and for Thérèse it was a heart-beat of the great Mystical Body, pumping life-blood through not only the Church on earth—Thérèse was nothing if not broad in her vision—but the whole communion of saints. It was the consciousness that she, of herself a nothing, a grain of sand, had the power to send this pulsing life coursing through the great arteries of the Church that sustained her in her heroic life of dying minute-by-minute to self. This certainty can divinize the daily round, even if the work itself is sheer drudgery or just monotonous, day-by-day grind.

It was by unremitting sacrifices that Thérèse carried on her great apostolate. She did not aim at unusual mortifications, but at a faithful observance of the smallest prescription of rule and custom, however great the inconvenience or however trivial or indifferent the regulation, in never seeking alleviations or dispensations from things that were difficult or disagreeable. In the thousand and one little sufferings and annoyances which come into everyone's life—whether it be lived in or out of the cloister—she found ample opportunity for sacrifice, abandonment, submission of will, not by going out of her way to seek them, but merely by accepting joyfully and never avoiding those presented to her by circumstances. "To pick up a pin through love could convert a soul," she told Léonie. But only Jesus can give such value to our acts, and on the other hand she added that she would not pick up a straw to avoid purgatory. All she had done had been solely to give God pleasure and to save souls. Truly, in the words of the *Imitation*, "love bears a burden without being burdened; and it makes all that which is bitter, sweet and savoury." (Bk. III, v.iii.)

Such is the power of prayer and the contemplative life in the work of evangelization. Our materialistic civilization has reversed the scale of values for many minds, reducing or even nullifying the sense of the supernatural. Even many Catholics consider the contemplative life meaningless, and the lives of enclosed religious either useless or egoistical. To them the worker in school and hospital is a more useful member of society than a Carmelite nun or a Carthusian monk, mainly because they can see the outward good that results from the labours of the former. Whether or not those labours would be fruitful without the supernatural aid of the contemplative is something that cannot be assessed by the reckoning of this world's statistics; therefore it is not taken into consideration. A Cistercian may arise from his bed in the middle of the night to chant the praises of God in the divine office, but what is the connection between that and the material relief needed for the sick and the destitute? In what way does it help to build schools or to give instruction to the ignorant? How can it possibly affect life on the mission-field? In themselves these questions are perfectly reasonable and should not cause surprise when put to us by those outside the Church; but Catholics at least should know that the teaching of the Church is there to guide them, bringing the necessary light to their minds in matters beyond the immediate comprehension of human logic. The tragedy is that so many today will not make this effort to develop and sanctify their intellectual faculties in the spirit of faith in hope; instead they try to scale down the vision and authority of the Church to correspond with their own fixed ideas, and remain uncomprehending or even scornful of those who live in the true spirit of supernatural conviction.

In declaring St. Thérèse of the Child Jesus patroness of the missions the supreme pontiff has given the answer of the Church to all who challenge the age-old ideals of faith and poverty of spirit. He tells us of the importance of prayer and the hidden life, and its effect on the apostolate. The hidden and unknown contemplative may, if she is faithful to her vocation, do more for the Church and win a far greater number of souls—although it will never be a tangible result that can be demonstrated in this life—that a missionary who is so engrossed and overworked as to have little time for the needs of the spiritual life. She is the unseen, silent dynamo that supplies the power for his lamp, and without its quota of fuel, no lamp, however excellent, will burn brightly or for long. Human talent or learning, powers of organization or eloquence, can never touch the hearts of men or lead them to the love of God unless He first bestows the grace; and this is obtained almost exclusively by prayer and penance. The greatest help each and every one of us can give to our missionaries is the support of our prayers and sacrifices, the joyfully accepted trials of our daily lives, and the little acts of charity that are prompted by love.

Pope Pius XI set in motion immense missionary activity, and great forces of prayer. He knew that the most skilfully organized activity would remain sterile unless there was abundant prayer to vivify it. "Contemplatives contribute a great part to the progress of the Church and to the salvation of the human race," he said in the constitution *Umbratilem*, *"far more than those who work in the harvest of the Lord.* For if the former did not call down from heaven an abundant rain of divine graces to make this harvest fertile, the workers of the gospel would reap less fruit." (Italics mine.)

Even in the ordinary round of parochial work action is of little use unless it is supported and animated by prayer, as the same Pope points out in his encyclical *Rerum Ecclesiae*: "Although the heralds of the gospel take pains and toil, and even shed their blood to bring the heathen to the Catholic religion; though they employ every effort and skill and every kind of human means, still it will be of no avail and all will be in vain, if God does not touch the hearts of the heathen, and, softened by His grace, draw them to Himself." The decree proclaiming St. Thérèse principal patroness of all missionaries and missions points directly and with the full authority of the Church to the fundamental connection between the contemplative life and missionary activity.

On Calvary our Lord paid once for all the full price of our redemption, and merited to have always at the disposal of the

Church the necessary labourers and the requisite graces, but they will be given only in proportion as the members that comprise the Mystical Body—and that is you and me, all of us, each and every one of the "faithful of whatever age, sex or state of life"—draw them down by prayer, work and sacrifice. Christ merited, but He wills that we participate in the work of salvation, sharing in His sacrifice by earning the graces that He has purchased; and love can give a missionary value to everything. St. Thérèse well understood the necessity of practising the contemplative work faithfully before activity could be remunerative, and she put it into effect in her own life. It was for souls and their sanctification that she became a Carmelite, as she told Père Roulland, for being unable to become a missionary in action, she wanted to be one by love and penance like her holy mother St. Teresa.

Pope Pius XI and St. Thérèse, "the star of his pontificate", worked hand in hand for the missions. That energetic and intrepid pontiff created two hundred and twenty new mission districts; he consecrated the first Chinese bishops; during his pontificate the number of missionaries was more than doubled, as was also the number of native clergy, and the number of children in mission schools trebled.

That Thérèse, the humble Carmelite, should have care of all the world's missions is only another revelation of those two great paradoxes of Christianity: the power of prayer and the hidden life in the battle for souls, and that in the kingdom of heaven it is the least who is the greatest while the master must be the servant of all. Our Lord did not bid the disciples to go out reaping the fields which were crying out for harvesting, but to "ask the Lord to whom the harvest belongs to send labourers". (Matt. 9: 38.) Even as a child Thérèse had felt the call of the missions. She described in her autobiography the grace of awakening zeal for the salvation of souls which was gradually to consume her. This vehement desire to share in Christ's redemptive work by co-operating in His Passion was, says Abbé Combes, "an obviously supernatural call to the apostolate, epoch-making for her spiritual life and consequently for the universal Church". And from that day forward an ardent zeal for the apostolate was an integral part of her personal spiritual life and also of her religious vocation.

God had indeed destined her to be a missionary and an apostle, but not merely in one small and restricted area with a handful of souls in her care. Her zeal was to give birth to an apostolate which would be world-wide in extent, overreaching the limitations of space and time. She was given a vocation that was not for time, but for eternity. Thus her impassioned cry was realized: "I would want to be a missionary everywhere from the beginning of creation, and go on being one until the world came to an end."

In her letter to Marie, speaking of her seemingly contradictory longing to embrace all vocations and suffer every form of martyrdom, she says: "It has pleased Jesus to grant my least and most childish desires, so now He will also realize those others, vaster than the universe." And a year later as she lay dying she said: "My smallest desire has been realized. God will not fail to fulfil my greatest ones." Here she was referring specifically to her desire to die of love, but the words can also embrace this other consuming desire which was about to be fulfilled after she had thrown off the "envelope" which held her imprisoned in space and time.

And so from her narrow cell to the limitless mansions of eternity, and during her journey from the one to the other, Thérèse became the universal missionary, through prayer, suffering, and the unremitting pursuit of perfection. By sanctifying herself she became an apostle of the apostles, reaching out to the very ends of the earth. Her greatest desire was to make for herself disciples of such priests as would spread her apostolate. She would pray for and lead along her own way to sanctification priests who would labour on the mission fields of the world, at home and abroad, and thus through them she would reach everywhere and encompass all places and times.

From the day when she received this grace of zeal for souls, born at the foot of the cross, she determined to remain there in spirit, never ceasing to work for souls, gathering up the precious blood falling from the wounds of Christ and applying it to their needs. This explains her insatiable desire for suffering, which would seem morbid but for the activating motive. Pope Pius XII made this matter quite clear when he said that growth in the love of God and abandonment to His will do not come from the sufferings themselves, "but from the intention in the will supported by grace".

"Just because my heart suffers so easily," Thérèse declared, "I mean to offer Jesus all the suffering it is capable of." As the Abbé Combes put it, hers was a vocation to the cross. She now understood experientially the essential identification of the love of God, which had been the basis of her whole life, with the love of her neighbour, which was its orientation and the foundation of her apostolic zeal and contemplative vocation; and so was realized the necessary union of contemplation and the apostolate.

During her last illness, as has been mentioned, Thérèse took a walk in the garden each day in obedience to the infirmarian; and as this caused her much suffering, she offered each painful step for some missionary worn out by his labours. To lighten his fatigue she offered hers to God. The fruit of such prayers and sufferings will never be known on earth. It was not until after her death that God permitted, first her sisters, and finally the whole world, to realize the power and efficacy and fullness of this silent apostolate of love. Then, as she had foretold, her mission began: her mission to make God loved, an eternal mission which will reach its completion and conclusion only when nothing remains to be done, when the angel shall announce: "Time is no more", and, Thérèse's last sinner gathered into the merciful arms of God, the number of the elect is complete.

As her least desires were granted in a way that surpassed her own confident expectations, so were her immense ones fulfilled with a prodigal liberality that only God can achieve. She became, as she had so desired, in the heart of the Church the love without which its work would neither be fruitful nor possible.

"If you could start at the beginning and live your life all over again," she was asked shortly before her death, "what would you do?"

"It seems to me," Thérèse replied simply, "that I should do exactly as I have done."

Please God, in our own last hour, each one of us will be able to say as much.

NOTES

1. (p. 52) "Obsessive-compulsive" neurosis is characterized by a compelling force in the emotional life, so that the individual no longer conducts himself in a free and rational manner, but is forced into a certain way of acting because of his mental condition. If an emotion is repressed through fear, it then becomes the dominant manifestation, resulting most commonly in the well-known "fear neurosis" which is known to most priests in the form of scruples.

2. (p. 63) It may be as well to point out that by Carmelite nomenclature Thérèse always remained a "young sister", never having left the novitiate so to speak. After her profession she was not permitted to take her place in Chapter and would thus not enjoy the privileges of the "senior sisters".

3. (p. 89) The photograph of Thérèse at this age, with her hair piled in a rough bun on top of her head (as she "put it up for the first time" on her visit to the Bishop) is considered the best likeness ever recorded, although her sisters remarked that her hair appears much darker than it actually was. We see a sweet, sensitive mouth, a firm chin and bright alert intelligent eyes. It is the face of a child, wise and serene, on the threshold of young womanhood, while at the same time humour and deep reserves of understanding are clearly delineated.

4. (p. 90) A cause of misunderstanding in this connection is the failure of many critics to realize that the issue of the photographs is entirely distinct from that of the manuscript. In his book *The Search for St. Thérèse*, Father Peter-Thomas Rohrbach, O.C.D., points out that "Thérèse made no predictions whatsoever about the photographs, nor did she ever request their distribution. The judges at the trial did not ask to examine them, and of course they made no decision at all about them. Thérèse's manuscript was to be the means of spreading her message and person; thus she had no concern

beyond that, nor did the ecclesiastical judges. The photographs are a secondary and incidental question."

5. (p. 90) *Visage de Thérèse de Lisieux* is the title of the two-volume album of authentic photographs recently issued by the Central Office, Lisieux, of which the English translation, *The Photograph Album of St. Thérèse of Lisieux*, was released in Britain in 1962. It is an excellent work, containing many splendid enlargements, and showing Thérèse to have been a person of character, refinement and deep convictions. The French original was edited by Père François de Ste. Marie, O.C.D., who was also responsible for the earlier production of *Manuscrits Autobiographiques*. This was his last work before his accidental death in July 1960.

6. (p. 92) Thérèse's facility with these verses and the spirituality of her themes was so much admired that she was at times requested to write them for other specific occasions, and even as homilies on certain virtues. A nun of the Carmel of Avenue de Messine (Paris) asked her for a poem on detachment, which resulted in *La Rose effeuillée* (The Unpetalled Rose). Sister Mary of the Trinity says that the recipient was delighted, but wrote that a final verse was lacking, for at death God would gather up the fallen petals and re-fashion a beautiful rose to bloom throughout eternity. Thérèse replied: "Let the good mother compose the verses as she wishes. That is not my idea. I wish to remain forever unpetalled to give pleasure to God."

7. (p. 101) Speaking on the religious and moral aspects of pain prevention in medical practice in 1956, Pope Pius XII made this question quite clear: "It is possible that suffering may be preferable for a particular person in a definite situation; but in general the harm caused forces men to protect themselves against it . . . often the acceptance of unrelieved suffering involves no obligation and corresponds to no rule of perfection . . . to declare that the dying have a greater moral obligation than others (whether from natural law of from Christian teaching) to accept suffering or to refuse its alleviation, is in keeping neither with the nature of things nor with the sources of revelation." (*Catholic Documents*, No. XXIII.)

8. (p. 131) Apart from the apparently playful remark made to her sister Marie: "You know well you are nursing a *little saint.*" Here the words seems to have been used in the same sense as it is so often found in the letters of all French Carmelites, "little sister", "little mother"—an endearment rather than a diminutive.

9. (p. 178) This term refers to the teaching that the effect of grace in the soul is the same at religious profession as at baptism, i.e., the entire remission of all sin, leaving the soul of the professed as stainless and pure as that of one newly baptized.

10. (p. 189) e.g. in Book II of the *Ascent of Mount Carmel,* St. John of the Cross deals also with the things to be avoided at every stage of development (even after our Lord has begun to lead the soul by the passive ways), and some of his "positive teaching" towards the end of this book applies solely to the last three Mansions of St. Teresa (viz. Mans. V. *Full Union*; Mans. VI, *Spiritual Betrothal*; and Mans. VII, *Spiritual Marriage*—cf. *Ascent* Bk. II Ch. XXVI, paras. 5-10, and Ch. XXXI). The first fifteen chapters of Book III of *Ascent* apply exclusively to those whom our Lord is leading by the passive ways; and the remainder of Book III can only be interpreted fully in the light of what St. John of the Cross has taught previously concerning the sanctification in faith of the natural understanding.

11. (p. 199) Of the 179 pages which comprise St. Thérèse's autobiography in Mgr. Taylor's translation, the first MS. addressed to Mother Agnes occupies the largest portion of 120 pages, with 13 pages of the MS. for Sister Mary of the Sacred Heart, and 46 pages for Mother Mary Gonzaga. These three MSS. in Mgr. Knox' translation, *Autobiography of a Saint,* have respectively 190, 15 and 67 pages.

12. (p. 222) Thérèse made continual acts of faith during this period and often speaks of her trial in the same terms. Nevertheless the fact remains that the divine action was primarily concerned with the purification of her memory in hope. Just as our understanding and spiritual memory are not always regarded as separate powers, so is there the same closeness of relationship between faith and hope.

Lightning Source UK Ltd.
Milton Keynes UK
18 August 2009

142778UK00001B/20/P